The Young Co
Bilbury Tales

Vernon Coleman

Another collection of memories from the English village of Bilbury.

Note: As usual, names and details of individuals, animals and establishments have been altered to protect the innocent, the guilty and those who aren't quite sure where they stand.

The Author

Vernon Coleman is a *Sunday Times* bestselling author. He has written over 100 books which have been translated into 25 languages and sold in over 50 countries. His books have sold over two million copies in the UK alone though no one is sure whether two million people each bought one book or one person has a very large library. Vernon Coleman is also a qualified doctor. He and his wife (whose real name is Antoinette) live in Bilbury, Devon, England. He is an accomplished bar billiards player (three times runner up in the Duck and Puddle Christmas competition), a keen but surprisingly dangerous skittles player and an accomplished maker of paper aeroplanes. He claims to be one of the best stone skimmers in North Devon. (Nine bounces are by no means unheard of and he has a personal best of 12 bounces.) He is a long-term member of the Desperate Dan Pie-Eater's Club (vegetarian section) and although he can juggle three balls at once, he cannot knit. He has never jumped out of an aeroplane (with or without a parachute) but he has, on several occasions, lit bonfires in the rain and is particularly proud of the fact that he once managed to light one in a snowstorm. He has not yet availed himself of the extensive opportunities apparently offered by social media (he says he is waiting to see if the idea catches on) but details of his surgery opening hours can be seen pinned on the noticeboard outside Peter Marshall's shop in the village and he has had a website (www.vernoncoleman.com) since the day after King Alfred burnt the cakes. Entrance to the website is free of charge and there is ample parking space. Visitors to the site are requested to wash their hands before entering and to wipe their feet before leaving. There are no advertisements or refreshment facilities. The Author is Grade II listed and is also registered as an Ancient Monument.

The Young Country Doctor series

The author claims that this is the 13th book in the series and so, if he has done his sums right, there are probably around twelve other books about Bilbury. All the books in the series are available as e-books on Amazon. A few hardback editions of the first seven books were published but these are all now out of print. Film companies should know that my good friends Thumper Robinson and Patchy Fogg are both happy to play themselves if a movie is made. Frank and Gilly are prepared to make the Duck and Puddle available to filmmakers. Peter Marshall would like to talk money before making a decision about his participation.

Dedication

To Antoinette, the Princess of Bilbury: Who is My True
and Gentle Love

Foreword

Here is another collection of memories from the village of Bilbury.

As we age we all tend to see the past more clearly than we sometimes see the present and these memories from the 1970s are to me now as clear as day; and considerably clearer than many of the things which happened last week.

We are encouraged by some to think of nostalgia as some sort of sin. We are told that it is sad to cling to a past that can never return and that was probably never as joyful as we remember it. We are told that nostalgia is the antithesis of progress and that progress is all that matters.

But none of that is true.

I believe that our memories can heal us, bring us peace and allow us to escape from the rigours of modern life. I do not believe that all that happened in the past was inherently good or bad, any more than I believe that all progress is good or bad.

Incidentally, the word 'nostalgia' originated in the late 18th century and was devised to define an acute sense of homesickness. The word itself was created from two Greek words: 'nostos' which means 'return home' and 'algos' which means 'pain'.

Today, there seems no doubt that we can be nostalgic for a time as much as for a place.

My purpose in my books about Bilbury is to bring back the flavour, romance (and shortcomings) of a time before computers and mobile telephones. Life was very different then. I am not suggesting that it was all necessarily better (it clearly wasn't) but I strenuously oppose those who say that it was all necessarily worse. I do not share the view that all change is necessarily progress or the idea that everything new must be 'better'. I rather favour the view of Lord Melbourne, a 19th century British Prime Minister and a favourite of Queen Victoria, whose daily creed was said to be: 'Why not leave it alone?' Why not, indeed.

Back in the 1970s, I would not have believed anyone who had told me that the time would come when GPs would not be available their patients 24 hours a day and seven days a week. I would have been appalled if I had been told that GPs would regularly make diagnoses over the telephone or by using a computer. I wrote articles suggesting that computers would be useful for doctors as a source of up-to-date information and a way of sharing new information – particularly about drug side effects – but it never occurred to me that doctors would actively urge their patients to check their symptoms by consulting a computer website.

The fact is that life was simply different then. And in those very different times, a lot of things happened that could not possibly happen today.

If we ignore and suppress the past then we ignore and suppress much of that which we cherish in ourselves, our friends and our world.

I find that by revisiting things that happened half a century ago, I learn a good deal about human nature.

In *Bilbury Tales* I have tried to describe people and day-to-day occurrences, as well as illnesses, because I find people to be endlessly fascinating and their foibles and eccentricities to be forever enchanting and illuminating. As a doctor, I learned early on in my career that until you understand people a little you will have no chance of helping them get better.

And there are more than a few digressions.

In the real world, digressions are dismissed as 'wandering off the point'. But in literature, however lowly the form, digressions have form.

'Digressions, incontestably, are the sunshine; they are the life, the soul of reading,' wrote Laurence Sterne in *Tristram Shandy*. 'Take them out of this book for instance – you might as well take the book along with them.'

Who am I to disagree?

How accurate are my memories?

Well, that's a tricky one to answer since I have to rely on the collective memory of myself, my wife Patsy and my friends in Bilbury. As Frank Parsons said to me the other day: 'We are none of us as young as we were when we weren't as old as we are now'.

Since I am retired from general practice, I no longer have access to any medical records, of course, but I did keep fairly comprehensive diaries and those have been enormously helpful in triggering my memory. My friend Will, who retired some years ago and who now lives in France, has also been very helpful. As regular readers know, he was a frequent visitor to Bilbury and, although this may now sound unlikely and scarcely believable, the fact is that for many years he was the only other doctor I saw or spoke to regularly. Being a sole practitioner back in the 1970s could be a professionally isolated business. Patchy Fogg once reckoned that when you were in Bilbury, the nearest traffic lights were actually in Wales – across the Severn Estuary.

Readers sometimes express wonderment at the variety of characters and strange incidents in Bilbury. And, as a result, there are still some who question the existence of the village and the individuals about whom I write! (This, I confess, bewilders, confuses and even hurts my friends in equal measure.)

There are several explanations for the fact that my world in Bilbury seems to be full of incident.

First, in a small village, one tends to get to know far more about one's neighbours than is possible in a town or city. A GP working in a small village gets to know everyone who lives there.

Second, as a general practitioner, I was privileged to learn more about my fellow villagers than anyone else in the village. And, in addition to the villagers, there were many strangers who came to my surgery seeking treatment, advice or a disconnected, unprejudiced, unbiased hearing from someone whom they would probably never see again.

Third, the period in which the Bilbury stories are all set was the 1970s – and that's a decade worth of unusual events.

Some years ago, when I finally retired from general practice (largely because the strain of working 24 hours a day and 365 days a year was beginning to result in my body showing some signs of wear) Patsy and I moved away from Bilbury. We did this very reluctantly but we moved because it was nigh on impossible to stop the villagers knocking on our door or ringing for me on the telephone. And, of course, when I was called, I found it impossible not to answer.

Technically, a practice in Barnstaple had taken over my medical responsibilities. But that practice involved a number of doctors and they were at least half an hour away from the village. Moving away

e only way we could have some quiet and privacy. Naturally,
t in close touch with all our friends there.

~~~ we did something that, at the time, seemed to some people to be rather strange. We did not sell Bilbury Grange.

We didn't let it out either – although we had many offers and I have no doubt that we could have increased our income by letting the house to holiday-makers. In our hearts, Patsy and I both knew that we would be back in Bilbury before long. We lived in other parts of the English countryside and for quite a while, we had an apartment in the shadow of the Eiffel Tower in Paris. But when we decided that we wanted to return to Bilbury, we had no worries about finding somewhere to live.

We simply moved ourselves and our belongings back into Bilbury Grange.

And that is where I am writing this.

It is good to be back. Patsy (whose real name is Antoinette), and I love Bilbury for many reasons. We love the good friends we have there and we love the unique character of the countryside; even the harshness of the winters can be attractive.

But we love Bilbury most of all, I think, because it is a truly civilised community; in the old-fashioned sense of the word: polite, good-mannered and innately gentle. It is a community where, I think, everyone wants to make a difference.

As I get older, it seems to me that many of the standards upon which our civilisation was built have been brushed aside and forgotten. This seems to be particularly true of life in our large towns and cities. Maybe this is just a consequence of my age. But I think not.

Finally, I would like to thank you for allowing me to share more of my memories with you.

American bestselling author Dean Koontz once wrote that the joy of writing books is that the writer has a chance to leave his fingerprints on the reader's soul. 'It's not an invasion of privacy, but a small crime of kindness, a breaking and entering with the intention of giving rather than taking.'

And that is the spirit in which I write.

I love the village of Bilbury very much and it is a joy to share its history with you.

I very much hope you will enjoy this new batch of memories.

Vernon Coleman, Bilbury, Devon, England
2018

The Vet

'Got you a present!' said Patchy Fogg, handing me a large cardboard box.

Patchy, a good friend, is an antique dealer who lives in Bilbury.

'Thank you!' I said, accepting the gift and looking at the printing on the side of the box. 'However did you know I wanted 48 tins of baked beans? Are you coming in? The coffee is on.'

It was 8.30 in the morning. I was just finishing breakfast and we were standing on the doorstep.

'Open the box, you idiot,' said Patchy, grinning. 'I can't stop. I've got to get to a house clearance sale in Taunton.'

I put the box down on the hall table, opened the flaps on the top and looked inside. I still wasn't quite sure what I'd been given. I was, however, pretty sure that it wasn't 48 tins of baked beans. I reached into the box and pulled out something that looked like a wireless set.

'There are two of them,' said Patchy.

I looked back into the box. Patchy was right. There were two of them. I wasn't sure why I wanted one of whatever they were. At first glance, two of them seemed to be one too many.

'They're ex-army radio sets,' explained Patchy. 'Walkie talkies.' He plucked the other one out of the box and held it up to show me. 'They're two-way radios – the things that soldiers use when they're in the middle of a war. You know the sort of stuff. You've seen the films. 'This is General Headquarters calling Z Victor Pansy Quinsy. Put down mortar fire on SO 886040. Over and out.' And then Victor Pansy Quinsy puts down some heavy mortar fire on the old farm house and the hero rescues the girl, recaptures the missing code book and defeats the Germans single handed. You and Patsy can talk to each other when you're out visiting patients.'

'Why do I want…,' I began.

And then suddenly it dawned on me and I couldn't believe how slow I had been not to see what Patchy had seen so clearly.

When I had been out visiting a patient, I sometimes got back to Bilbury Grange only to discover that I had another visit to make only a short distance from where I'd just been.

If Patsy or Miss Johnson could reach me when I was out visiting a patient, they would be able to give me details of the new visit I needed to make. I would save the time consuming nonsense of driving back and forth unnecessarily and the patient would be seen more quickly.

The more I thought about it the more I realised that having two walkie talkie radios would revolutionise my life. There were still homes in Bilbury which did not have a telephone. If I were visiting a house with no telephone and I needed to organise an ambulance, I could simply call Patsy or Miss Johnson on the radio and ask them to arrange for an ambulance to be sent.

As things were then, I either had to return to Bilbury Grange to make the phone call or I had to drive round the village until I spotted a house which I knew to have a telephone.

'What a brilliant idea! Where did you get these? How much do I owe you?'

'You don't owe me anything,' said Patchy. 'I got them from an auction in South Molton. They were part of a pile of junk I didn't want but had to buy in order to get a 19th century commode chair I had my eye on.'

'Why on earth did you want a 19th century commode chair?' I asked. I turned a switch on one of the radios and produced a good deal of hissing and crackling.

'It's a convenience that was almost certainly used by Queen Victoria,' answered Patchy. 'The china pot, the business end of the chair, is missing but I've got a lovely one that will fit very nicely. It's got a wonderful, clear picture of Gladstone on the target area and Victoria hated Gladstone didn't she?'

I had to admit that I had no idea how Queen Victoria felt about Mr Gladstone. I knew that she had been fond of Lord Melbourne, her first Prime Minister, a wise man who flattered her endlessly, and also rather fond of Benjamin Disraeli who was clever enough to do the same, but I didn't have the foggiest idea whether or not she liked Gladstone.

'She hated him!' said Patchy. 'I looked it up in a book I've got about her. She absolutely hated him. She said he addressed her like a public meeting and she thought him arrogant, half-crazy and a fanatic. She'd have been absolutely delighted at the chance to take her revenge when using a commode.'

'But no one else at the auction realised that Queen Victoria had used that particular commode?'

I fiddled with a dial on the front of one of the wirelesses. The hissing went away and the crackling grew fainter.

'No provenance,' said Patchy. 'The seller didn't have any provenance. And no one else there had the china pot with Gladstone's mug grinning up at the royal behind!' said Patchy with a wink.

'But you've got the pot and you know where to find the provenance?'

'Absolutely,' said Patchy who always seems to know where to get hold of the essential piece of provenance that will turn a fairly ordinary piece of pretty worthless furniture into a rare and must-have rarity. He sells a good deal of the stuff he buys to Japanese collectors who already own every bed used by William Shakespeare and every desk and pen set belonging to Charles Dickens or Conan Doyle. (Patchy once managed to sell Sherlock Holmes' second best deerstalker hat to a Japanese banker.)

'And the radios came with the commode?'

'In with a pile of junk,' agreed Patchy. 'It was the end of the auction and the bloke with the gavel was getting tired, so he lumped the last four lots into one and I got them all for two quid: a 19th century commode, a complete set of encyclopaedias from 1910, a watering can with a hole in the bottom and two ex-army field radios in working condition.' He looked at his watch. 'Must go,' he said. 'You'll have to play around with the radios to see how they work.'

And with that he was back in his van.

Moments later, he had disappeared in a flurry of gravel and dust.

At the end of the morning surgery, and before I set off for the day's home visits, it took Patsy and me half an hour to find out how the radios worked. They were set on matching frequencies, which was handy, and the batteries for both of them had been charged by the seller or the auctioneer. To our astonishment and delight, they seemed to do exactly what they were supposed to do. Patsy worked out that we had to press the button marked with a 'T' if we wanted to say something and be heard by the person with the other radio.

When we were both satisfied that the two radio transmitters were working, I went down to the bottom of the garden.

I pressed the button marked T and spoke.

'Come in Bilbury Grange!' I said into the microphone area on the radio.

I have to confess that I felt rather embarrassed doing this.

I don't mind talking to the animals and I sometimes say encouraging words to struggling trees or bushes in the garden but talking into a radio transmitter felt suspiciously akin to talking to myself.

I waited to hear Patsy's reply.

And I waited.

And waited.

But there was no reply.

Feeling rather disappointed, I walked back up the garden to where Patsy was standing with the other transmitter.

'They don't work!' I complained.

'I could hear you,' said Patsy.

'I couldn't hear you at all.'

'Did you remember to press the R button?'

'No. What's the R button?'

'You have to press the R button when you want to hear what the other person is saying. I suppose it stands for 'receive'.'

Now feeling thoroughly embarrassed, I hurried back down the garden and tried again. I did my bit of broadcasting and then pressed the R button and waited. This time I could hear Patsy fairly clearly. There was some hissing and crackling but I could definitely hear her voice.

'This is Bilbury Grange calling the Flying Doctor!'

'Got you!' I said and waited.

Nothing.

And then I remembered the T for 'transmit' button.

I pressed the T button and repeated my response.

It was clearly going to take longer to master using these radios than I had anticipated. I was so accustomed to using a telephone, with which you can listen and talk at the same time, that I found it difficult to remember that I had to press a button to speak and another button to listen. Patsy, on the other hand, seemed to find the whole thing very easy to master.

Having tried them out, I was absolutely convinced that the two radio transmitters were going to revolutionise my working life. I left one of the field radios in the hall at Bilbury Grange, right next to the telephone, and put the other one into the 1920s Rolls Royce which I inherited from my predecessor, Dr Brownlow, and which was our only form of motorised transport.

As luck would have it, we didn't need to use the radios at all for four days.

And then, on the fifth day, Patsy and I had just finished dinner and were sitting down in front of the fire when the telephone went.

'Come at once, doctor!' said a panicky voice I vaguely recognised. 'It's urgent. My husband is going to die.'

'What's the problem?' I asked, trying to take the panic out of the caller by remaining calm. In a real emergency, there is no point in everyone starting to panic.

'My husband was putting our dog down,' said the caller. 'And he's injected himself by mistake.'

'What with?'

'I don't know. The usual stuff he uses when he's putting an animal to sleep, I suppose. His breathing has gone very strange.'

'Have you called an ambulance?'

'Yes, but they said they'll take at least half an hour to get to us from Barnstaple.'

I was pretty sure I had now worked out who was on the other end of the telephone. 'Is that Mrs Gaskin?'

'Yes.'

'You live on the Lynton road? Just before Blackmoor Gate? On the left?'

'Yes, yes. But my husband isn't at the house. Our dog is so big and heavy that Tom didn't think he'd be able to carry him down to the top of the hill so he took him up there to put him to sleep.'

'Which hill?'

'If you come to the house I can show you,' said Mrs Gaskin. 'I had to come back down to use the telephone.'

'You had to leave your husband on the hill?'

16

'Yes, I hated to leave him but I had to get to the telephone. And there's only the two of us here.'

'Of course,' I said. 'Do you have a big torch?'

'Yes.'

'Go back up the hill to where your husband is,' I told her. 'And take the torch with you. Keep the torch pointed down the hill towards your house so that I can see where you are.'

It was dark and getting darker.

I don't know why it is but I have noticed that tricky emergencies often seem to take place in the dark or the rain. Sometimes it is dark and raining.

'I understand.'

'I'll be there as soon as I can,' I promised, but I wasn't sure that she had heard me because the telephone had gone dead. Mrs Gaskin had clearly put the telephone receiver back onto the rest.

Thomas Gaskin was, I remembered, a veterinary surgeon who had a practice in South Molton.

I seemed to remember that he dealt mainly with large farm animals but also dealt with a few domestic animals – cats and dogs and so on.

I picked up my black bag, told Patsy where I was going and leapt into the Rolls. At the last moment, almost as an afterthought, I told Patsy to make sure that the other radio was turned on.

Less than five minutes later, I skidded into the Gaskin's farmyard. When I got there, the smell and the sounds reminded me that they kept horses. I could hear horses stamping and whinnying in the stable block. Animals always seem to know when there is something wrong. Hearing the animals, I remembered that Mrs Gaskin did some point to point racing and I also recalled that they had a daughter who was away at university but who had won several show jumping cups.

I climbed out of the car and looked around. I could see a bright light some distance away at the top of a hill. The front door of the house was open and all the lights were on but the house looked as empty as it undoubtedly was. How is it that it is possible to tell that a house is empty just by looking at it?

I picked up my medical bag, and one of the radios which Patchy had given me, and made my way up to the bottom of the hill where Mr Gaskin had taken his dog to die. There was, I thought, no little irony in the fact that he might die there himself. I assumed that the top of the hill was a favourite spot; a place where man and dog had sat and shared the silence and the view across North Devon.

I climbed the hill.

That damned hill was longer and steeper than I wanted it to be under the circumstances. I had a small torch with me but with my bag in one hand and the radio in the other, I had to hold the torch in my teeth. Several times I nearly dumped the damned radio which seemed to get heavier by the second. It was, I suppose, built to survive rough and tough conditions and the casing seemed to have been carved out of a solid ingot of iron.

Mrs Gaskin, who was undoubtedly trying to be helpful, kept her much powerful torch directed down the hill. I think it was her intention to light the way but in practice all that happened was that she blinded me. I nearly fell twice when I put a foot into rabbit holes. There must have been a good many rabbits around for there were a good many rabbit holes.

I found Thomas Gaskin slumped on a wooden bench on the grass at the top of the hill. The bench had been placed underneath a small, gnarled oak tree. It was clearly a favourite spot. The vet looked at first as if he were dead or dying. A Great Dane was lying on the floor beside him. The dog was breathing and panting but it too looked moribund. Of the two, however, the dog was definitely in the better condition.

A grave had been dug in the ground about five or six feet away from the bench. There was a pile of soft earth next to it. I supposed that the plan had been to drag the dog's body across to the grave when the deed had been done. If you have to die then it wasn't a bad place to be buried. The damned grave was almost big enough for the dog's owner, let alone the dog.

'That's Nelson, our oldest dog. He has cancer,' explained Mrs Gaskin. 'Tom has been treating him for weeks and tonight he decided that there wasn't anything else he could do and that it was time to put Nelson out of his misery.'

I put down my bag and the radio and picked up a syringe that was lying on the grass. It was around a third full. I then looked around for the ampoule which had contained whatever had been in the syringe. I guessed it was probably pentobarbital – it's a short acting barbiturate and the drug which vets usually prefer when they have to euthanize

18

an animal. Mr Gaskin would have used a hefty dose because the dog was a large one. My guess was correct. The pentobarbital ampoule was nearby, on the bench. And it was empty. A large dose of pentobarbital can stop the heart and shut down the brain within minutes. A single gram of the drug can produce serious poisoning and two grams can kill.

'Were you here when it happened?'

'Yes. We wanted to say goodbye to Nelson together. Thomas put Nelson right next to him, with his head and chest on his leg.'

'How long ago did it happen?' I asked, opening my black bag and taking out my portable sphygmomanometer.

'Oh, just a few minutes before I called you,' replied Mrs Gaskin. 'I ran down to the house and called the ambulance first and they said to call you as well because you would be able to get here quicker.'

I tried to roll up Mr Gaskin's jacket sleeve but I couldn't move it. I then tried to pull his arm out of the jacket but I couldn't do that either. The vet, in his late fifties, must have weighed 20 stone. I had met him a couple of times and knew he was a bear of a man. I'm well over six feet tall and he was as tall as I am but much broader and more strongly built. I doubted if he had ever worked out in a gym but a man who deals with sheep, cows and horses on a daily basis soon develops some serious quantities of muscle. I knew I wouldn't be able to lift him in order to undress him.

Thoughts raced through my mind.

A pentobarbital overdose can be fatal in minutes even when the drug has been taken orally. This hefty dose of the drug had been given straight into a muscle and would act faster. I could only hope that Mr Gaskin hadn't hit a blood vessel by accident and injected the stuff intravenously. His size and weight would work in our favour, of course. A small person, weighing 100 pounds would be in a lot more trouble than a tall, well-built man weighing over 200 pounds. I took out my penknife and cut through his jacket. I then cut through the jumper he was also wearing and ripped open the front of his shirt. Buttons flew everywhere.

'What are you doing?' asked Mrs Gaskin, who seemed rather shocked.

'I need to check his blood pressure and I need to listen to his heart. And I'm going to need to set up a drip.'

There isn't all that much that can be done to treat a patient who has had a pentobarbital overdose. But I did know that I needed to push some fluids into his blood stream. It's the only way to push up the blood pressure and improve the working of the heart. And it is the only way to dilute the drug in the patient's body. I couldn't stop thinking about how crazy it was for a man to die this way.

'Oh gosh, yes,' said Mrs Gaskin. Her voice wavered but she wasn't crying. That, I guessed, would come later. Whatever the outcome there would be tears.

'Tom had Nelson lying on his lap and he was about to give him the injection but he was crying when he had the syringe in his hand. He loves that dog so much. We've had him since he was a puppy. He's 16-years-old and part of the family. Tom was sobbing and at the moment, when he aimed the syringe at Nelson, the dog moved. Tom's hand with the syringe missed Nelson's body completely and went into his own thigh.'

Mr Gaskin's blood pressure was absurdly low for a man of his size.

His systolic pressure was around 85 and his diastolic was only just over 60.

His pulse was feeble; very weak. It felt very thready and unsatisfactory. I didn't bother to count it. I didn't have a minute or even half a minute to waste.

I didn't want to waste time taking his temperature either, but he felt cold. His pupils were constricted and he was drifting in and out of consciousness. Mostly, he was unconscious. Occasionally, he managed to say something though I couldn't tell what it was he was saying.

Suddenly he started to retch and then he vomited a little food.

'Won't that help?' asked his wife. 'They say that when people have had an overdose it can help to make them vomit.'

'It won't help at all, I'm afraid,' I told her. 'Your husband gave himself an intramuscular injection so the drug went straight into his tissues and completely bypassed his stomach.'

In fact, though I didn't tell Mrs Gaskin, I now had a new problem.

Unconscious and semi-conscious patients often choke on their own vomit. It's why patients are put on their side, into the classical recovery position.

But I couldn't get Mr Gaskin onto his side and I needed to make sure that his airway remained open. If he vomited and then inhaled the vomit, we would be in real trouble. His head was slumped to one side too and that wasn't helping his airway.

I did think of dragging him off the bench and onto the grass so that I could put him into the recovery position. But that wouldn't be easy. I had a nightmare thought that if I rolled him off the bench he might just continue rolling down the hill. It wasn't impossible. It was a steep hill. It was dark and getting darker by the minute. I couldn't lift him and I would have to drag him off the bench. Mrs Gaskin didn't look strong so I didn't want to ask her to help. If she tore something or had a heart attack, I would be in even more trouble.

Up until this moment, there had been a little moonlight to help me see what I was doing. The moon now chose to go behind a cloud.

I remembered seeing an advertisement for a new and very powerful torch that could be worn on the head – like a miner's lamp. I'd sworn that I would buy myself one but had never got round to it. I used to have one but it was so weak that it was pretty well useless and I threw it into a drawer. It's astonishing how these incongruous thoughts slip in and out of the conscious mind at the most inappropriate moments.

I opened my black bag and took out an endotracheal tube. I asked Mrs Gaskin to direct her torch onto her husband's face. If I could slip the tube down his throat and into his trachea it would help ensure that his airway remained open. It would provide protection and stop him breathing in anything he vomited. Then I would be able to concentrate on putting up a drip so that I could push in some extra fluids to keep him alive. He was a big man and his blood pressure was already absurdly low and his pulse terrifyingly weak.

And as he drifted back into unconsciousness, I managed to get the tube into place.

Now I had to put up a drip so that I could push some fluids into him.

I looked at my watch. There was still at least fifteen minutes to go before I could expect to hear the ambulance coming. Living in the middle of nowhere is very nice until you have an emergency. And then you're very much on your own.

I suddenly remembered the time I'd had to amputate a man's leg because he'd got stuck between two rocks when the tide was coming in. I had lost my black bag to the sea on that occasion and the bag I was now using was one which the man whose life I'd saved had bought for me as a thank you gift.

I took a needle and some tubing out of my bag and suddenly realised that since we were out of doors, I didn't have anywhere to hang the bag of fluid. In hospitals, the staff always have a drip stand handy – a special device upon which the bag of fluid can be hung. Indoors there is nearly always something you can use. A standing lamp, a bookcase or a doorway will all do very well.

But I was out in the open at the top of a hill. And sometimes the impossible situations simply keep getting more and more impossible.

Then I realised that the bench upon which Mr Gaskin was sitting was underneath a tree.

Thank heavens that Mr Gaskin liked to sit under a tree. Thank you, God, for putting a tree on top of a hill.

It was a small, lonely, windswept, stunted oak. You could see which way the prevailing wind blew by the way the branches had been shaped.

Of course, the tree could not have been put there by God.

There were no other trees around.

And why would a squirrel plant an acorn on top of a lonely hill?

The tree must have been deliberately planted there by Mr Gaskin or some previous owner of the land. It had struggled to thrive but it had survived. Once an oak gets its roots into the ground, it will not easily give up the struggle.

Why the devil were all these unwanted, irrelevant thoughts wandering through my head?

I looked up and could see the silhouette of a perfectly positioned and solid enough branch right above the vet's head.

It took me only a moment to find a vein, slam in a needle and then connect the needle, the tubing and a bag of saline. It felt good to know that I had fluid flowing into his body. It was the only thing I could do to help. I reached up and hung the bag on the branch above us. The branch bowed but held.

And then I had a brilliant thought.

Why didn't I put up two drips?

If I put a drip into each arm then I could push fluid into his body twice as quickly. I'd never seen anyone do that before but I couldn't see what was wrong with the idea.

Mr Gaskin's breathing seemed to be getting weaker and shallower. I didn't like that at all and wondered if I would have to start giving him mouth to mouth respiration.

In an accident and emergency unit in a hospital, a patient with a serious drug overdose of this type would be surrounded by skilled, specialist doctors and nurses. There would be at least half a dozen people checking on his vital signs, giving him fluid, checking his breathing and so on.

Here there was just me.

And I was on the top of a hill in the middle of nowhere.

And it was dark.

At least it wasn't raining.

And then the radio barked at me.

Honestly, that was what it sounded like.

I jumped, Mrs Gaskin jumped and the dying dog jumped. The only one of us who didn't jump was Mr Gaskin.

'What on earth was that?' asked Mrs Gaskin.

'It was my radio,' I explained.

I found the radio (not as easy as it might have been since the radio was the same colour as the grass and in the dark, it was perfectly camouflaged), picked it up and remembered to press R to receive.

It was Patsy.

This was, I suppose, not surprising since there were only two radios on this frequency and she was the only other person to have one.

The reception was quite good though it occurred to me that this might have been because I was standing on the top of a hill.

'The ambulance people just telephoned,' she said. 'They can't get an ambulance to you quite as quickly as they'd hoped. There's been a bus crash in Bideford and everyone is tied up over there. Apparently they did send an ambulance out to Bilbury but unfortunately it went into a ditch.'

'OK,' I said. I then pressed the T button and said it again.

'Can you manage? Is everything OK?'

'I'm going to need more fluid,' I told her. 'Another two or three litres of saline.'

'Anything else?'

'No. I just need more saline. I'm going to try putting up two drips to push through more fluid. But I've only got one litre of saline with

23

me. I'd have been OK if the ambulance had turned up as planned but…' I let the rest of the sentence drift off into nothing.

'Do you want me to bring it round to you on my bicycle?' asked Patsy. She wasn't joking. We only had one motor car and I had it with me.

'No,' I told her. 'That would take too long. I'm going to ask Mrs Gaskin to come and collect the stuff. Put three bags of saline into a box and give it to her when she arrives. No, wait. If the ambulance doesn't arrive, I might need more than that. Put all the bags of saline we've got into the box. That big cardboard box that Patchy used when he brought us the radios is still in the hall. Use that.'

We then did the over and out thing and I turned to Mrs Gaskin.

'I urgently need more bags of saline,' I told her.

'I heard,' she said.

'You know how to get to Bilbury Grange?'

'Yes,' she said. 'But our Land Rover broke down this morning…' I couldn't believe it.

'But don't worry. I'll ride. It will be quicker anyway. I'll go across the fields. I'll leave you the torch.'

And with that she was gone; running down the hill.

I used the radio to tell Patsy that Mrs Gaskin was travelling by horse. 'She won't be able to carry a cardboard box. Put the saline into a rucksack,' I told her. 'There's an old one in the hall cupboard.'

While she was gone, I monitored Mr Gaskin's vital signs. He was now completely unconscious. His blood pressure was still frighteningly low and his pulse was still weak.

Astonishingly, Mrs Gaskin was back in minutes. She even managed to ride up the hill to where I was struggling to keep her husband alive. She passed me the rucksack which Patsy had packed for me.

By the time the ambulance arrived an hour and three quarters later, Mr Gaskin was conscious and talking and I'd used up all the saline his wife had brought from Bilbury Grange.

I still sent him over to the hospital, though.

I wanted them to check him over and keep him under observation for a day or two.

Thankfully, miraculously, he made a full recovery.

And by then one of his partners had given poor Nelson an injection to put him to sleep.

The next time I saw my chum Patchy, I told him that I had no doubt that the radios he had given me had saved a life. If I hadn't known that the ambulance wasn't coming I would not have known to send Mrs Gaskin to Bilbury Grange to fetch more saline.

Sadly, the Gaskin case was something of an exception for the radios didn't turn out to be quite as useful as I had hoped.

The problem was that North Devon is a very hilly part of England, full of hills and valleys, and as a result, radio reception was extremely patchy and unreliable. In the end, we pretty well gave up using the two radios which Patchy had found.

But I have absolutely no doubt that they helped save Mr Gaskin's life.

The Tree Surgeon

For a few weeks we'd had a problem at Bilbury Grange; the house in Bilbury where Patsy and I lived, and where I had my consulting rooms.

The problem was that a branch of a beautiful silver birch tree was blocking the chimney of our dining room at Bilbury Grange.

On several occasions, charred bits of twig from the tree had fallen down the chimney and I really wanted to have the offending branch trimmed away. I was worried that a bigger piece of the branch would fall down and cause a fire.

But several attempts to deal with the problem had proved unsuccessful.

First, I'd tried to reach the top of the tree by ladder. That had proved entirely unsuccessful and even when I'd climbed up to the topmost rung of our longest ladder, I had still been a long way from being able to cut the branch from the tree.

Second, our usual tree surgeon, Mr Rate, who runs a business called 'Special Branch', was away doing something important and no doubt profitable for the Forestry Commission and was working in another part of Devon. Although I had been able to speak to his wife, Amelia, I had not been able to get any idea of when he would be back and available for small, domestic work.

One Sunday, when we were having lunch together, I mentioned our problem to Patsy's father, Mr Kennet. He told me that he was hiring a large JCB digger for a few days. He needed the digger in order to excavate some blocked ditches on his farm, and to dig out the bed of a lake which had become a final resting place for a couple of dead sycamore trees, demolished by a recent storm.

'The model I've hired has a massive reach,' he told me. 'I'll drive it past the Grange on my way to one of my fields. You can climb into the excavator bucket and I'll lift you up to the top of the tree that needs trimming.'

'Will it really go up that high?' I asked him.

'No problem,' he assured me.

'Is the bucket thing big enough to hold me?'

'They're enormous. You could organise a dance in one of those buckets.'

'Is it safe?' asked Patsy.

Mr Kennet, who had a traditional farmer's attitude towards risk, laughed and assured her that I would be completely safe standing in his JCB bucket.

'The last time I rented one of these things I put Mick into the bucket and he cleaned out all our gutters for me. I got him up there and down again without any problems.'

Mick is one of Mr Kennet's farm labourers. He has, over the last few years, broken his right leg once, both arms (once for the left and twice for the right) and his left shoulder blade.

I was not, I confess, entirely happy about the plan but I could hardly say 'No' to my father-in-law's generous offer. We get on well enough but I don't think he's ever entirely got used to the idea of his daughter having married someone who insists on wearing gloves when working in the garden. Mr Kennet has skin the colour, texture and thickness of leather and I've seen him pick up a bunch of heavily thorned rose stems without flinching.

Still, his kind offer was a way to get rid of our little tree problem.

And what could possibly go wrong?

I'd climb into the bucket on the end of the JCB digger's arm. Mr Kennet would pull a lever or press a button or whatever you do with these things, and I would be raised up to the top of the tree. I would cut off the branch that was hanging over our chimney. Mr Kennet would then bring me back to earth. I would climb out of the bucket, thank him and wave goodbye as he trundled off to clear ditches and dredge lakes.

I had half forgotten about the offer when the telephone rang at 6.15 a.m. one morning.

'I'll be with you in five minutes,' said my father-in-law. 'You can trim that little branch that's giving you trouble. Get your loppers ready. Oh, and you'll need some wellington boots because the JCB bucket is still a bit muddy.'

He rang off.

I leapt out of bed.

'Who was that?' asked Patsy, sleepily.

'Your father. He's bringing his JCB round so that I can cut that branch over the dining room fireplace.'

'When?' demanded Patsy, sitting up in bed.

'In less than five minutes!'

'Oh crumbs! Don't be late! You know what Dad's like.'

Unlike most other farmers in Bilbury, my father-in-law tends to do everything at top speed, and he gets terribly upset if he has to hang around and wait. Since he had doubtless hired the huge JCB by the day, and had probably paid a small fortune to do so, he would not, I knew, want to waste a minute.

I looked around the bedroom for my clothes. I normally keep a set of clothing by the side of the bed, ready for emergency calls during the night.

'Where are my trousers and shirt?' I asked Patsy.

'Didn't you have to go out during the night?'

And then I remembered. Patsy was absolutely right. In fact I'd been out twice.

First, I'd had an emergency call to visit the Southams. Mr Southam had cut himself with a saw. His wife had bandaged it up but the bandage had come off and the wound had started bleeding again. I'd put in a few stitches. It had been raining heavily and since I'd had to park the car and walk a quarter of a mile to their cottage, I'd got back home soaked to the skin and muddy up to my knees. I had thrown all my clothes, including the pyjamas I had been wearing underneath, straight into the washing machine.

The second call had been a false alarm.

Mrs Watson, who was having her first baby, thought she was going into labour. But she had been merely suffering the painful consequences of eating half a jar of pickled onions.

Once again I'd come home soaked, and those clothes had also gone into the washing machine.

'Where's my dressing gown?' I asked.

'I put it into the wash yesterday. It was covered in dog and cat hairs.

I opened my wardrobe, wondering what else to wear. This was, I suspected, going to be a dirty job and I keep my gardening clothes in the potting shed. There really wasn't time to go and fetch them. I have never been someone who acquires a lot of clothes. All I had left

28

in the wardrobe were my best jacket and trousers. If I got those muddy, I wouldn't have anything to wear for the morning surgery.

'Just put on my dressing gown,' said Patsy. 'It's due for a wash anyway. And it'll keep you decent. You can't go out there naked.'

This seemed sensible. It would take no more than five minutes for Mr Kennet to lift me to the top of the silver birch, for me to cut off the branch that needed removing, and for him to lower me back to the ground.

Patsy threw me her dressing gown and then started rummaging in her dressing table. 'And put these on,' she said, handing me a bright blue pair of swimming goggles.

'Swimming goggles? Why do I need these?'

'Because we had a fire in the dining room last night and for some reason you put on a huge log not long before we came to bed. The fire will still be smoking. And if you're hanging around a couple of feet away from the chimney, you'll get smoke in your eyes and you won't be able to see what you're doing. I don't want you falling out of that digger bucket because you can't see anything.'

Patsy was clearly still unhappy about the plan.

I must admit that I wasn't too keen on it either. I'm not one of those unfortunate souls who freezes if they have to go half way up a stepladder but I've never had much of a head for heights.

The swimming goggles seemed a good idea.

I put them on.

And then I rushed downstairs, found my tree loppers, put on my green Wellington boots (I'd have preferred black but Peter only had green ones when I'd bought that pair) and dashed outside. I got there just in time because Mr Kennet was parking the JCB close to the Grange and to the tree which he had correctly guessed needed attention.

'What the hell have you got on?' demanded Mr Kennet.

He seemed surprised to see me wearing a pink, fluffy dressing gown and a pair of bright blue swimming goggles. The dressing gown was clearly several sizes too small for me. The sleeves finished six inches before they got to my wrists.

'It's Patsy's,' I explained.

'I'm pleased to hear it,' said Mr Kennet, drily.

'It'll only be for five minutes,' I assured him. 'And there won't be anyone about at this time in the morning.' I didn't bother to explain about the swimming goggles.

With some difficulty, I climbed into the JCB bucket. It was, as I had been warned, very muddy and wet.

And just then it started to rain again.

It wasn't one of those light showers that you can ignore. It was heavy, serious rain which came down as suddenly as if someone up in the heavens had turned on a shower tap. And the wind, an easterly, was strong and gusting stronger. I am never much good at guessing the speed of a wind but this was moving the trees – not just the smaller branches and the twigs but the larger branches too.

'I am always conscious of an uncomfortable sensation now and then when the wind is blowing in the east,' said Mr Jarndyce in Bleak House.

I knew what he meant.

'You'd better put this on!' said Mr Kennet, rummaging around behind him and then tossing me a shiny, bright yellow sou'wester. 'It'll go nicely with that dressing gown.'

I caught the waterproof hat and put it on. At Mr Kennet's suggestion, I tied the string under my chin to make sure it didn't blow off. The item might have its uses but whoever designed the sou'wester had a malicious sense of humour for there is no more comical piece of headgear in the world.

Mr Kennet then played around with the machine's levers and a minute or two later, I was up at the height of our chimney and able to cut off the branch which was causing the problem. While I was there, I also removed one or two smaller branches which looked as though they might become problematical at some time in the near future. Patsy had been right. The chimney was still smoking and I was glad I was wearing the swimming goggles. The smoke made me cough. Up at tree top height, the wind seemed even more noticeable, though I suppose that this was because sitting in the JCB excavator bucket, I felt exceptionally vulnerable.

However, everything had gone perfectly to plan and I called down to Mr Kennet to let him know that I'd finished what I had needed to do.

A couple of minutes later, I called back down again to remind him that I was ready to go back down.

'Can't work out how to bring you down!' yelled Mr Kennet. 'Getting you up there was easy enough but Pete, one of my guys, usually operates this thing and I'm buggered if I can bring the bucket back to earth. It's one of these levers but I can't remember which one. I don't want to just take my chances in case I tip up the bucket and throw you out by mistake.'

I thought at first that he was joking.

I called to tell him that it was the best joke I had ever heard while stuck in an excavator bucket in a high wind but that having enjoyed the gag I would be able to appreciate it more if he would take me back to earth as quickly as possible. It was, however, so windy that I doubt if he heard more than half of this.

'I'm serious!' he shouted. 'I can't for the life of me remember which lever brings the bucket back down.'

Feeling very vulnerable and now utterly soaked, I peered down at him in disbelief.

'The quickest thing to do will be to drive to the field where we're due to be working,' shouted Mr Kennet. 'Pete will be there. He'll get you down in a jiffy. No problem.'

I couldn't help thinking that these things always happen to me.

However, there wasn't much point in worrying about it because I could do absolutely nothing about my situation. Stuck in the bucket of a JCB digger, suspended chimney pot high, I was entirely in the hands of my father-in-law. I could only hope that I hadn't done anything to annoy him too much.

When we had been stationary, the bucket in which I was now stranded had been extremely stable. But once the JCB started to move along the Bilbury lanes, the bucket began to sway rather alarmingly. In fact, it was swaying so much that I actually began to feel a little seasick. I had to crouch down, half kneeling, half sitting in the muddy water at the bottom of the bucket, and gripping the sides of the bucket as if my life depended on it, which I suppose it probably did.

And still the rain kept coming down. And the level of the muddy water in the bucket kept rising noticeably. Since I was crouching, the water poured into my Wellington boots and soon the only part of me that was dry was my head; safely ensconced in my father-in-law's sou'wester.

From time to time, I popped my head out of the bucket in order to see where we were.

We travelled slowly, of course. Large JCB diggers aren't designed to race and they don't exactly break any speed limits.

The difficulties were compounded by three things.

First, our lanes in Bilbury are very narrow and have high hedges which make it difficult to manoeuvre or, indeed, to see where you are or what is coming.

Second, Mr Kennet wasn't a very experienced JCB driver.

Third, with the bucket up in the air, Mr Kennet had to keep swerving around tree branches.

Oh, and did I mention that it was raining?

Actually, it wasn't just raining – it was the sort of weather that would have made King Lear sit up and take notice. And I was just thinking that all we needed was a clap of thunder and a flash of lightning, when the Good Lord obliged by providing more than ample quantities of both – treating the whole of Bilbury to a free son et lumière spectacle.

It must have taken us half an hour to cover a mile.

It was on one of the occasions when I had my head out of the bucket, trying to see where we were, that I noticed that we were passing the Duck and Puddle, Bilbury's only public house.

Frank Parsons, the landlord, was outside the pub supervising an unusually early delivery of best bitter from the brewery. The driver of the dray was skilfully rolling the barrels to the chute leading down into the pub's cellar.

Frank, noticing a huge JCB passing by, looked up and saw me. He immediately yelled at Mr Kennet and asked him to stop.

'Is that you, doc?' Frank called, peering uncertainly through the rain.

I confirmed that I was, indeed, me.

'What the devil are you doing up there? Is it carnival week? Why are you in fancy dress?'

'It's a long story,' I explained.

'While you're up there,' said Frank. 'Can you see if we have a slipped slate on our roof? Water has been coming into one of the guest bedrooms.'

I looked at the pub's roof. There was, indeed, a slipped slate. The slippage had left a gap about four or five inches wide, plenty big enough to enable water to enter the pub and do a considerable amount of damage to a bedroom ceiling. The roof was not lined with wood or with felt and I could see clearly into the loft.

'I can see it,' I said.

'Can you push the slate back into position?' yelled Frank.

I reached out of the bucket as far as I could but I couldn't quite reach the slate that needed repositioning. 'I'd have to climb out and onto the roof,' I told him. 'And the roof looks very wet and pretty slippery.'

'Oh, you'll be fine,' said Frank, offering all the reassurance of a confident man standing on terra firma.

'You climb out onto the roof and sort out Frank's slate while I go and get Pete to show me which levers to pull to get the bucket back down again,' shouted my father-in-law, who had climbed out of the cab to see what was happening.

Gingerly, I clambered out of the JCB bucket and crawled onto the flat roof of one of the pub's dormer windows. From my vantage point on the small area of flat roof, I could fairly easily reach the slate that had slipped. I really didn't like being up on Frank's roof very much at all but Frank is my friend and I wanted to help.

As I listened to the JCB trundling away along the road, I pushed and pulled at the slipped slate and gradually managed to jam it back into position. You can do that sometimes with slates. Of course, they only stay where they've been put until they decide to slip out again but you can sometimes manage a repair this way that lasts years. Frank doesn't tend to think in terms of years, anyway. He'd be happy if the water stopped coming through the guest bedroom ceiling for a month or two. It's difficult to rent a room when there's a bucket by the side of the bed and a steady drip, drip of rain water interfering with the bucolic peace and quiet which the visitor was expecting.

When I'd got the slate as firmly fixed as was possible, I sat on the flat roof of the dormer window and waited for my father-in-law or Pete to return with the JCB and its bucket.

And I waited.

And I waited.

Realising that Patsy would wonder where I had got to, and why it was taking me so long to cut a small branch off a silver birch tree, I asked Frank to ring Bilbury Grange and let my wife know that I'd hit a bit of a snag but would be home soon.

And as I sat on Frank and Gilly's roof, it soon became clear that the JCB was being used for whatever it had been hired to do and I had been forgotten. Meanwhile, the rain was getting heavier again. And the wind now seemed to me to be something between a gale and a hurricane. I decided that my account with my father-in-law was well in credit.

Meanwhile, the village of Bilbury had woken up and people were moving about.

By half past eight, Thumper Robinson and Patchy Fogg had appeared on the road below my perch.

'Why are you sitting up there?' asked Thumper.

'It's the only flat piece on Frank's roof,' I replied. 'If I sit anywhere else I'll slide off and come to a very sticky end.'

Soon both Thumper and Patchy were offering advice and a commentary on my costume. I guessed, correctly as it turned out, that they had both been telephoned by Frank.

And it seemed from what they said that it was the first time they'd ever seen anyone sitting on the flat roof of one of the dormer windows of the Duck and Puddle public house wearing a pink but soggy dressing gown, green Wellington boots, blue swimming goggles and a yellow sou'wester; although by this time, the blue swimming goggles were dangling round my neck and I had untied the cord holding on the yellow sou'wester since I seemed to remember once laughing at someone who had his hat tied under his chin with a piece of string. It's not a dignified look.

Summoning up every last vestige of my badly damaged dignity, I told the pair of them, and the rest of the crowd which had gathered and which was growing by the minute, that if they really hadn't ever seen anything similar then they'd led insular and sheltered lives and needed to get out more.

It occurred to me that in a town or a city, a man sitting on a roof would probably attract little or no attention. Unless there seemed to be a chance that he might jump to his death, passers-by would simply assume that he was some sort of eccentric; perhaps a harmless lunatic; perhaps a madman who, for some unexplained reason, preferred to sit on the roof rather than in an easy chair in front of the television set. The green Wellington boots, the blue swimming goggles, the yellow sou'wester and the fluffy, pink dressing gown would have confirmed all suspicions of any combination of lunacy and eccentricity.

Frank brought out the longest ladder he could find but it wasn't long enough. The top rung was about four feet below me and there was absolutely no way I was going to accept his suggestion that I dangle off the edge and wiggle my feet about until I felt the ladder with my toes.

To be honest, I wouldn't have climbed down that ladder even if it had reached the roof. It was a wooden ladder and at least a quarter of the rungs had been eaten by woodworm and some of them were missing completely. The remainder of the rungs would probably turn to powder if anyone trod on them. Frank only keeps the ladder so that he can tell the local council that he has suitable emergency equipment available for the rescue of any paying guests who might be trapped as a result of a fire.

Thumper suggested that Frank open the window just below me so that I could swing down off the flat roof and into the bedroom. I laughed at this suggestion and as I did so, I sincerely hoped that the laugh was capable of being described as 'derisory'. A monkey could have probably managed the manoeuvre but I was already worrying about how I was going to get back into the JCB bucket if my father-in-law ever remembered to come back for me. Any manoeuvre which required more in the way of gymnastic skills was way outside my limited repertoire.

At twenty to nine, Frank threw up a metal weight with a piece of strong cord attached. He had to do it four times but eventually I managed to catch the weight. Frank told me to take hold of the string and let down the weight, which I did. He then tied a small wicker shopping basket to the other end of the cord and told me to haul up the basket. I was quite delighted when I found that the basket contained several slices of buttered toast and half a mug of coffee. The mug had been full of coffee when it had started its journey but all the jerking on the cord had resulted in a considerable amount of spillage. I didn't really mind that half the coffee had been spilt because I was conscious of the fact that if I drank too much my bladder would need emptying and although part of me found the idea of emptying it over the small crowd below distinctly attractive, the more rational part of my brain told me that this would not be something that would be easily erased from village memory. Mind you, I was pretty sure that it was going to be some time before I lived down the story of how I came to be marooned on the pub roof wearing green Wellington boots, a bedraggled, pink dressing gown, blue swimming goggles and a yellow sou'wester which I no longer really needed because it had finally stopped raining. If I'd been wearing anything underneath it, I would have taken off the pink, fluffy dressing gown which was soaking, very absorbent and extremely uncomfortable.

I heard someone down below, I think it was one of the Beresford brothers, say that I was up on Frank's roof as a bet. Someone else said he had heard that it was a forfeit I was paying in lieu of a gambling debt.

And then I heard Mrs Trenchmore say she knew for a fact that I was up there for charity and that I had only chosen to sit on Frank's roof because I didn't have a long pole with a barrel fixed to the top of it.

I remembered those pole sitters.

The fashion started in the United States in the 1920s. A stuntman climbed up a flagpole and stayed there for hours, though no one seems certain just why he did it. Within days, there were people up flagpoles all over America. It must have seemed as though half the nation was sitting at the top of poles. The idea never really caught on outside the United States though the practice did have something of a revival in the 1950s when one or two exhibitionists competed to see just how long they could sit up on top of their poles. They didn't actually sit on the top of the poles, of course. They had little platforms built, about the size of the dormer roof on which I was sitting. They had food and drink sent up to them and usually tied themselves to the pole so that they could sleep without dropping off.

Mrs Trenchmore's certainty about my being up there for charity, quickly became the default diagnosis and soon people were not trying to decide what I was doing on Frank's roof but what charity I was doing it for. It quickly became accepted wisdom that I was raising money for our local hospital and Frank, showing a surprising turn of speed, darted indoors and came out three minutes later with a yellow, plastic bucket and a large piece of brown cardboard upon which he had written the single word 'Donations'.

Mrs Harrod said she wasn't going to give a penny and didn't care who knew it because she thought it was rather irresponsible of me to be sitting on the roof of the Duck and Puddle when it was time for me to be doing the morning surgery, and did I really expect her to climb up onto the roof just so that she could obtain a new prescription for her two way stretch, double strength, flesh coloured, elastic stockings.

Peter Marshall, proprietor of Bilbury's only shop, turned up and wanted to know why I was sitting where I was.

I told him what I'd already told Thumper, that it was the only flat area on Frank's roof and that if I tried sitting on the bits that sloped, I would slide down and that I didn't really want to do that.

Peter then wanted to know if I would take advertising.

He said he'd heard that someone had telephoned the local television station and that they were sending someone round to film me. He said he would make a generous donation to my charity if I held up a sign promoting his special offer on hand-cut kindling. The discovery that if I stayed where I was, my discomfort would end up as the light relief item at the end of the local television company's evening news programme added a new layer of panic to my discomfort.

By ten past nine that morning, the crowd included quite a few people who would have been at Bilbury Grange for the morning surgery if I hadn't been sitting on Frank's roof, and to my astonishment I found myself giving medical advice to people down below.

Miss Broderick showed me her elbow and wanted to know if her psoriasis looked any better to me. Since I could hardly see her elbow, let alone her psoriasis, I had to tell her that I needed to see her at the surgery. Mr Lincoln told me that his ankle still wasn't better and would I give him another sick note. He said a week would just about do it nicely. I had to tell him that I didn't have any sick notes with me. Mr Nightingale wanted to know if I would syringe the wax out of his ears if he shinned up the drainpipe. And Mrs Oliver told her nine-year-old to say Ahhhhh and wanted to know if I thought his tonsils were inflamed.

'Do you want me to go to Bilbury Grange and collect your prescription pad?' asked Thumper who was having difficulty not laughing.

'I've got forty feet of rubber tubing in the garage,' said Patchy. 'Shall I fetch your stethoscope? I could use my rubber tubing to extend the length of it and you could listen to people's hearts and chests while you're up there.'

This suggestion occasioned considerable amusement and many ribald comments which I ignored with as much dignity as I could muster. Two workmen who had rested their bicycles against the pub wall wanted to know if I was expecting to have to examine any interesting chests.

And then Mrs Wilkins said she wanted to know what I was wearing underneath the dressing gown and Mrs Oliver said she would have thought a doctor would have owned a dressing gown that fitted him properly and Mrs Jones said that for what it was worth she could pretty well confirm that she'd been keeping a close eye on me, especially when I moved my legs to avoid getting cramp, and was certain that I hadn't got on anything at all underneath the dressing gown.

I told my pal Thumper that if he didn't go and fetch Mr Kennet and his ruddy JCB digger to get me down very soon, I would certify him as suffering from an unpleasant communicable disease; something deadly which would require men wearing white suits and breathing apparatus taking him away and keeping him in an observation room for at least three months.

And so Mr Kennet and his JCB machine rescued me just moments before the television crew arrived.

It was a messy, ungainly and woefully undignified business.

Once the bucket on the digger was back down at ground level, I clambered out and accepted Thumper's offer of a lift back to Bilbury Grange in his truck.

'It's been blowing a gale up there,' I said to Thumper, as I got into the truck.

Thumper looked at me. 'It didn't seem much more than a stiff breeze,' he said.

'Well it was at least a gale up on the roof,' I insisted. 'It may have been a hurricane.'

He had the sense not to argue with me.

'Where on earth have you been?' asked Patsy when I walked in through the front door. 'Why did Frank ring me? What were you doing at the pub at this time in the morning?'

She then burst out laughing.

'What are you laughing at?' I demanded.

'You look a fright!' said Patsy.

I took off my green Wellington boots, removed the yellow sou'wester and unslung the blue swimming goggles from around my neck.

'That dressing gown is about ten sizes too small and the colour doesn't suit you,' said Patsy. 'Let's get you upstairs to the bathroom before any of the patients see you.' She laughed again. 'What on earth would people say if they'd seen you dressed like that?'

I didn't like to tell her the truth just then.

I thought I would explain later how that particular horse had long ago bolted from the stables.

Not So Trivial

I was sitting having a cup of coffee at the end of a long surgery and Patsy, who was preparing our lunch, had the radio switched on.

An eminent doctor was talking on the wireless about medical problems.

I don't remember much of what he said (he was very boring and long-winded) but I do remember that he stated quite categorically (and rather pompously) that doctors should not waste their valuable time on trivial medical problems.

He was, as you might imagine, a doctor who hadn't held a stethoscope, a syringe or a sphygmomanometer for the best part of a quarter of a century. He was one of those doctors who earns a very good living sitting on committees and boards and acting as a consultant and advisor to a wide variety of groups.

His argument was that the sort of problems which he described as trivial should be dealt with by nurses, auxiliaries or even clerical assistants.

When I heard this doctor talking, I was reminded of my predecessor, mentor and friend Dr Brownlow, who said that he thought it was a crying shame that all the really important decisions in medicine were being made by administrators, bureaucrats and politicians – people who had absolutely no day to day practical experience of what patients need, or how they are best diagnosed and treated. He said that there were far too many people in the medical establishment who spent their days running round in circles, never looking where they were going, but always pretending to be making progress.

When I heard that eminent practitioner, who was doubtless a stalwart of the medical establishment, pontificating about the insignificance of selected medical problems, and then sniffily dismissing them as 'trivial', I almost threw my coffee cup at the wireless.

I disagreed violently for several reasons; but mainly because I believed that it was a very dangerous attitude.

The truth is that there are no trivial problems in medicine.

Problems which a doctor might regard as relatively insignificant, and definitely not life-threatening, might still be a real worry to a patient.

And a problem which might appear to be trivial may be hiding a really important health problem.

Moreover, I believe that by attending to relatively simple medical tasks, things which could perhaps be handed over to a nurse, a doctor is able to build up his relationship with his patients. This is important because, in due course, the strength of that relationship might prove to be vital if the patient acquires a serious or life-threatening disorder. The relationship between doctor and patient is all about trust.

I was able, without much thought, to come up with several incidents which proved my point that it is foolish for doctors to hand so called 'trivial' problems over to nurses or auxiliaries.

So, for example, there was Mr Oliver Padgett.

Mr Padgett came into the surgery complaining of indigestion.

'I wonder if you could give me something stronger than the stuff I can buy at the chemist?' he asked.

Now, indigestion is almost certainly one of those health problems which the eminent practitioner on the wireless would doubtless be inclined to dismiss as 'trivial' – easily within the remit of an assistant who could hand out a packet of antacid pills or simply arrange for a prescription to be written out. But is it always so easily dismissed?

I asked Mr Padgett, who was in his forties and rather overweight, how long he'd had indigestion.

'Oh, a few months,' he told me. And he proceeded to give a perfect medical history of a man with indigestion. His pain only came on after he had eaten. It seemed to go away if he swallowed a little antacid. And so on and so forth.

I was tempted to succumb and write out a prescription for something to ease his indigestion pain.

But some instinct told me that things might not be quite as simple as they appeared to be.

'Do you get any other symptoms?' I asked him.

'I get a bit breathless,' he said. 'But I put that down to wind in my stomach.'

'Anything else?'

'A bit sweaty occasionally. But the pain is pretty bad sometimes so it's not surprising that it makes me sweat.'

'Whereabouts is the pain?'

'Right across my chest,' he replied, without hesitation.

And at this point, the warning bells began to ring because the pain of indigestion is usually much more specific. Patients sometimes point to their stomach with one finger to show just where they feel the pain.

'Does the pain go anywhere else?'

'I get a pain in my arm sometimes.'

And now the alarm bells were ringing so loudly that they were probably audible in the next county.

'Do you only ever get the pain when you eat?'

'Well, actually, I get it several times a day. It is sometimes when I'm eating.'

'But sometimes when you're not eating?'

He nodded.

'And the antacid medicine helps the pain?'

'Oh, yes.'

'Do you do anything else to ease the pain?'

'I sit down and take things easy for a while.'

'And then the pain goes?'

'Oh yes.'

'But it could be sitting down and resting that helps get rid of the pain – rather than the antacid?'

'I suppose it could.'

And, indeed, so it proved to be.

Mr Padgett was suffering from angina and heart pain. His problem was anything but trivial.

If he had simply been given a bottle of antacid and sent on his way then there is a good chance that within a few weeks, or possibly months, he would have probably had a huge heart attack and died.

Miss Kenshaw was another patient whom the eminent doctor would doubtless have preferred to pass onto an aide or some kind.

A gentle, maiden lady in her mid-50s, Miss Kenshaw came to my surgery complaining that she could no longer hear very well.

'I work as a telephonist in Barnstaple,' she told me. 'And having good hearing is vital for my work.'

She was clearly worried about losing her job. It was obvious that her work was terribly important to her.

A peep into her ears showed that both of them were pretty well blocked with wax. I got out the brass tray and the large brass syringe which I was at the time using to syringe wax out of ears, and I managed to remove an enormous quantity of the stuff from her external auditory canals. To be honest, I was surprised that Miss Kenshaw had been able to hear anything at all.

A lot of doctors tell their practice nurse to do the ear syringing.

They consider such simple work to be beneath them. But I always preferred to do these things myself. A doctor can build up a good relationship with a patient by helping him or her to hear again. It's one of those simple jobs which produce a large dividend in terms of goodwill and a good relationship.

But, when I'd finished clearing out Miss Kenshaw's ears, I could tell that there was something else still worrying her.

I sat her down and told her I wanted her to wait a while before leaving the surgery. Patients can sometimes feel a little dizzy after they've had warm water squirted into their ears.

And while she was sat there, I asked her if there was anything else she wanted to talk to me about.

I was hoping that she tell me what I sometimes think of as the 'sting'.

(The sting invariably comes at the end of a consultation. After discussing some relatively minor problem, something which eminent practitioners would probably dismiss as 'trivial', nervous patients will often say 'by the way' or more commonly 'while I am here' and then introduce the problem they've really been worrying about all along. This second problem will invariably be something complex which will involve a full medical examination and a good deal of brain work. The doctor, who thought he was ready to go on to the next patient, will find himself starting the consultation all over again. This sort of thing often happens because the patient is nervous and too frightened or embarrassed to discuss their 'big' worry. The 'trivial' problem is introduced as a 'foot in the door', an opening gambit, designed to 'warm' up the relationship between doctor and patient.)

At first, Miss Kenshaw denied that she was worried about anything else.

But I knew her well enough, and I'd been a GP long enough, to know that there was something she wasn't telling me.

Family doctors need to get as good at ferreting information out of some patients as parents are at squeezing the truth out of their children.

And how people say things can be just as important as the things they say.

Dr Brownlow, my predecessor and the man who taught me more about general practice than anyone else, explained this to me. He called it listening to the mood as well as the words and he argued that with some people the mood can be even more important than the words.

And, sure enough, Miss Kenshaw eventually told me what was worrying her.

'I think I might perhaps have asthma,' she said. It came out as a confession as much as anything. 'Several times recently I've suddenly noticed that I get short of breath. It happens quite suddenly.' The words came out in a rush and the relief was almost palpable.

'There are no pains?'

'Oh no.'

'How long does the shortness of breath last for?'

'It varies. But usually just a few minutes.'

'And how often has it happened?'

'A dozen times, I would say. I think it's asthma because my brother used to have asthma when he was small. He's gone now, God bless him. He died in a motor car accident.'

'I'm sorry,' I said. I remembered seeing in her notes that her brother had died. His accident had happened long before I'd come to work in Bilbury.

'It was some time ago.'

'Have you noticed anything else abnormal?'

'I get clammy and sweaty sometimes. It can't be the change of life because I went through the menopause a few years ago.' She paused and looked at me. 'I get very tired when this happens.'

'But you don't have any pain.'

'Well, I do sometimes get a pain in my shoulder and my neck. But that could be arthritis. I injured my shoulder when I fell while hiking last summer. I went to the Lake District for a fortnight.'

'Do you get any pains in your chest?'

She smiled. 'Oh no, doctor. There isn't anything wrong with my heart.'

'And do you get the pain in your shoulder and neck at the same time as you're clammy and sweaty?'

She thought for a moment. 'Yes, I think so.'

'Do you have the shortness of breath at the same time?'

'Yes, sometimes I do. But sometimes I get the shortness of breath by itself without the pain or the sweating. Although then my pulse does feel as though it's racing.'

I took her blood pressure and I listened to her heart. I couldn't find anything wrong.

'I want you to go to the hospital and have an electrocardiogram,' I told her. 'Just to check out your heart.'

'Do you think I might have a heart problem?' She sounded surprised and anxious.

'I can't find any signs of heart disease,' I assured her. 'But those symptoms could be signs of heart trouble. We need to check it out.'

'But I haven't had any chest pains at all!' she said, clearly puzzled.

'Men usually get chest pains when they have heart problems,' I told her. 'But women are sometimes different. They can have heart attacks without any chest pains. It may well be that there's nothing wrong with your heart. But it would be safer to check it out.'

And it turned out that it was well worthwhile sending Miss Kenshaw to the hospital.

The electrocardiogram showed that Miss Kenshaw did have some heart abnormalities, and the consultant who saw her concluded that she had suffered a number of minor heart attacks. The consultant and I worked out a gentle diet and exercise regime to improve her heart, and slowly the symptoms stopped troubling her.

But if I hadn't syringed her ears, I would not have known about her heart trouble until she'd had a major heart attack.

And that could well have been too late.

I honestly doubt if any of that would have come to light if Miss Kenshaw had merely come to the surgery, seen a nurse and had her ears syringed in a routine sort of way.

Doing relatively small things for patients (syringing ears, removing stitches, checking on blood pressure, taking blood, weighing patients who are on a diet) are tasks which are often delegated to nurses, aides or even to completely untrained staff.

I think this is a terrible mistake.

It is my belief (and I know this is probably very old-fashioned and certainly out-of-date) that a doctor who is prepared to look, to listen and to be patient can learn an enormous amount about his patients when performing these small and often routine tasks.

The Bridle Path

The area in and around Bilbury is criss-crossed with footpaths, tracks and bridle paths. Some of these pathways are old and have been used for hundreds of years. Some were created by sheep or wild goats wandering hither and thither, not always knowing where they were going (or why) and not always taking the shortest route between here and there.

Some of the old tracks and paths have fallen into disuse because they no longer mark a route which is used regularly or used at all.

But, as old tracks and paths disappear, so new ones appear.

Some paths are new and are created for new and often personal reasons.

So, for example, when the Ponsonby-Futtocks moved into Willow Tree cottage, the family's eleven-year-old son, Darren, developed a friendship with Edward Teach, a boy of the same age, who lived with his parents in Laurel Cottage. Now, these two cottages are a mile and a half apart if you go from one to the other by road but less than a third of a mile away if you go across the fields. During the summer holidays, the boys ran across the fields so often that they eventually wore a new path of their own and no one objected or would have dreamt of objecting. The farmer who owned the land didn't mind as long as the boys kept to the sides of the fields and shut any gates they opened.

(Neither of the boys opened any gates, of course. What eleven-year-old boy opens and shuts a gate when he can climb over it or clamber over the fence alongside? And both boys knew enough about the lore of the countryside not to make gaps in hedges. Sheep, in particular, are good enough at doing that on their own; they don't need any help from humans.)

And both sets of parents preferred their sons to cross the village through the fields rather than along the lanes.

We don't get much vehicular traffic in Bilbury but the lanes are narrow, giving pedestrians very little room to get out of the way, and it is a regrettable truth that many drivers, particularly those from outside the village, drive far too quickly.

A trip across the fields was both quicker and safer.

And when Pamela Lightner and Edgar Branson were courting, they wore a distinctive pathway between their parent's homes. However, when Miss Lightner and Mr Branson became Mr and Mrs Branson, and set up home together, the pathway was no longer used and within a year, it had disappeared from view.

For years, no one in Bilbury had bothered to make a proper up-to-date map of all the paths and bridleways. Paths which were not used just disappeared and new paths which were needed just appeared. I don't think any landowner ever objected to a new path appearing as long as crops weren't damaged, livestock weren't endangered and gates were not left open.

Occasionally, someone from one of the organisations which represents walkers and ramblers, usually an earnest, rather self-important enthusiast from a city such as Bristol or Exeter, would wander into the village and, with unwelcome officiousness, demand that we produce a proper map of all the historical pathways in, through and around the village. They would come armed with photocopies of old deeds and ancient maps and, sometimes, old minutes of council meetings and planning reports and they would also forcefully demand that we clear all the unused paths and then maintain them in good order.

I'm afraid we never really welcomed these folk.

We thought our rather fluid and informal system worked very well.

As villagers, we didn't see the point in re-opening any path which was now covered in brambles and nettles and which didn't connect any two places which needed to be connected. It seemed a lot of work and disruption for no real purpose.

We welcomed the strangers' enthusiasm for the countryside and we were delighted that they showed an interest in our village but their requests (which were usually phrased more in the style of demands) were less welcome. Pedantry does not always benefit the people it is supposed to benefit.

Things changed for the worse when Mr Cinnamon Brooke came to live in the village.

Mr Brooke was a retired company director who had, we were regularly informed both by him and his wife, been a Very Important Person in the city. He had sat on numerous boards and chaired many meetings and had met and socialised with many other Very Important People. He had attended charity auctions and had spent much of his shareholders' money on making charitable contributions to 'good causes'. He had also arranged for considerable sums of company money to be given to all the leading political parties. It was, so it was widely said by Mr Brooke and his wife, only a matter of time before his generosity with other people's money was rewarded with a knighthood or maybe even a peerage.

When they arrived in Bilbury, Mr and Mrs Brooke bought 'Combe House', a rather splendid but dilapidated old house on the edge of the village and they imported builders and decorators from Bristol to do the necessary renovation work.

Not surprisingly, this did not go down too well with local workmen and not a little complaining was done in the Duck and Puddle and other North Devon hostelries.

Still, the work got done, and the restored house (which was, with a staggering lack of imagination renamed 'Four Winds') did look very smart.

When the various workmen eventually left the scene of their various fiscal crimes, 'Four Winds' had a new roof, working electrics, efficient plumbing, central heating (for the first time in its life), a brand new, state of the art burglar alarm, a conservatory and an indoor, heated swimming pool complete with a Jacuzzi and a Scandinavian steam room.

Mr Brooke quickly made it clear that although he was a newcomer to the village, he regarded himself as someone we should all listen to and within two months of moving into the newly refurbished 'Four Winds', he had submitted a number of recommendations both to the Parish Council and to the County Council.

The most important of his recommendations was that a full map of footpaths and bridleways in the village of Bilbury should be compiled and that all footpaths and bridleways should be cleared and well signposted. 'There should,' he said, 'be plenty of signs throughout the village, showing visitors just where footpaths began and where they ended.'

Locals complained that they liked the village as it was and didn't want it covering with metal signs which would, if Mr Brooke's instructions were taken to their conclusion, make the village look like a motorway junction.

One of Mr Brooke's first demands was that a sign be placed at the two ends of a bridleway which goes between fields near to but not belonging to the Duck and Puddle public house. The local council, keen for an easy life and eager to shut up Mr Brooke, agreed to have large signs installed.

It has to be said that the signs were not, however, entirely successful and their erection not entirely without incident.

On the Saturday immediately after they had been erected, I drove past the end of the bridleway and noticed that two Japanese tourists, a man and a woman, were sitting on a weather battered wooden bench which has been there for as long as I can remember. They each had a rucksack and a camera. Since there was no cinema in the village, the bench has long been popular with courting couples and the oak slats were well decorated with carved initials. I remember once noticing that someone had carved 'HB loved GA hear' on the top slat of the back of the bench and being mildly amused by the fact that one of the protagonists had later added the word 'Twice' to this simple declaration. The specificity of the initials and the spelling error meant that most of us knew the names of the two protagonists.

Three quarters of an hour later, as I drove back from the visit I had made, I noticed that the couple were still sitting on the bench. They had taken out a packet of sandwiches and a flask but they seemed to be waiting for something. There is a bus stop close to the bench and since I was worried that they might not be aware that in Bilbury buses are slightly rarer than green woodpeckers, I stopped to ask if I could help. (In fact, on most days of the year anyone who wants to catch a bus from Bilbury has to walk to Blackmoor Gate and then catch the Lynton bus into Barnstaple. The bus stop in Bilbury is more ceremonial than practical.)

'Do you knowing when the next wedding people is due?' asked the Japanese woman brightly.

'Wedding?' I said, rather stupidly.

'We like take photos of weddings,' said the woman. 'They very romantic occasions.'

I must have looked as puzzled as I felt for the woman then pointed at the newly erected sign, just behind my head. I turned round to look at it. 'Bridle way' it said.

'Ah,' I said. 'I think you may have misunderstood.'

I tried to explain the difference between a bride and a bridle. 'You may see a horse pass by but you are unlikely to see any brides,' I said.

They clearly did not understand for they just nodded and smiled and when I left them, they had resumed their picnic lunch.

I hope they didn't stay there too long waiting for the bride who would never appear.

Mr Brooke's enthusiasm for properly signposted footpaths and bridle ways continued unabated.

In an interview with a local newspaper, Mr Brooke insisted that he had no interest whatsoever in going into politics. ('I am particularly uninterested in entering politics on a local level,' he was quoted as saying, 'for there is no doubt that my talents and my experience would be wasted on a small stage.') However, it was widely suspected that Mr Brooke was still desperate for some sort of recognition in the New Year's Honours List, or the Queen's Birthday Honours List (or possibly both) and that his misplaced enthusiasm to make his mark on village life was designed to boost his chances of becoming Sir Cinnamon Brooke or, possibly even, Lord Something or Other.

And so, as a result of Mr Brooke's efforts, there was a far larger turnout than usual at the next meeting of the Parish Council.

These events are usually rather desultory affairs, attended by no more than half a dozen people and a stray dog or two, but this one was different. Just about everyone in the village was crowded into the St Dymphna's Church Hall for it had been announced that the Clerk to the Council would publish a new, interim map of all the paths and bridleways found to date within the village boundary and that photocopied maps would be distributed at the start of the meeting. (There are three churches in or close to Bilbury: St Dymphna, St Damian's and St Crispin and St Ermentrude. The only one with a church hall is St Dymphna.)

The details of the new map had been kept surprisingly confidential and we all turned up for the meeting feeling rather nervous.

Would any of us discover that a previously unrecognised path ran across our land? Would we be required to put in stiles or kissing gates?

It was expected that the meeting would be, to say the least, 'rather lively' and that there could well be some protests and a little more noise than is usual.

Patsy's father, who is one of the largest landowners in Bilbury, was extremely concerned. He has always made sure that those pathways which are used regularly are kept clear and suitable for use. And he has always repaired stiles and so on at his own expense. He readily admits that there is some self-interest in this for if walkers use the stiles and follow the proper pathways, far less damage will be done to his fields and fences. But he was worried that more paths and bridleways might have been discovered.

The meeting had not even started before the first protest was made.

And it came from an entirely unexpected quarter.

A bald, fat man in a brand new three piece Harris Tweed suit walked to the front of the hall and waved one of the newly printed maps at the Clerk to the Council. Many of us had never seen him before but we all knew who it was.

'What is the meaning of this?' demanded a very red-faced Mr Brooke, pointing at something on the map he was holding.

We all examined our maps to see if we could spot what had got him so excited.

The Clerk to the Council looked at the map which Mr Brooke was holding.

'Oh yes, Mr Brooke,' said the Clerk. 'That's an old bridleway which we discovered.'

'But this is a nonsense!' cried Mr Brooke. 'This isn't on our deeds or any of the paperwork we received when we bought Combe House.'

'No, that's the problem with some of these old pathways,' said the Clerk, regretfully. 'They appear on some old documents but not on others.'

As more of us managed to find our place on the map, and see what it was that Mr Brooke was complaining about, the hall became full of titters. Gradually the tittering segued into giggling and then the giggling turned into outright laughter.

'But this is absurd!' complained Mr Brooke, who was now so red-faced that he looked as though he might burst into flames or even explode.

'It's certainly inconvenient,' said the Clerk. 'I can see that it is an inconvenience.'

'Bah!' said Mr Brooke, so furious that speech seemed to have deserted him. 'Bah and balderdash!' I'd never heard anyone say 'balderdash' before. But he did. And with that he turned round and stalked out.

The meeting never really recovered after that and those of us with an inclination to do so repaired to the Duck and Puddle.

We all agreed that it was one of the most wonderful things any of us had ever seen.

The new map showed that a centuries old bridleway passed straight through the middle of Mr Brooke's conservatory and his new swimming pool.

Mr Brooke complained to anyone and everyone, and his protests were reported so widely that it was generally agreed that any chance he might have had of appearing in one of the honours lists disappeared entirely. He became a laughing stock in the tabloid press and columnists and cartoonists had great fun at his expense.

In the end, the Council agreed to allow Mr Brooke to put a bridle path around the side of his conservatory and swimming pool. But the path enabled walkers to look into both buildings, and destroyed the privacy that Mr Brooke claimed was so important to him.

No other significant or unduly inconvenient new paths or bridleways were found and the rest of the village rested easy.

And, after Mr Brooke's disaster, it seemed clear that there would be no more investigating of hidden or forgotten footpaths. Mr Brooke was certainly not in the mood to encourage any more investigations. Who knows what else would turn up on some old piece of long-forgotten parchment?

There was, however, some continuing surprise at the route taken by the bridleway which went through Mr Brooke's garden. No one in the village could remember ever hearing of such a path and it was difficult to see why it would exist – since it did not connect any two points in the village which could possibly need connecting.

'I didn't know about that bridleway, did you?' said Thumper to Frank one day when we were all sitting in the snug at the Duck and Puddle.

'No,' said Frank. 'I'd never heard of it. And I thought I knew everything about this village.'

'Who found the map showing that old bridle path going through Brooke's land?' asked Thumper.

'Oh that was me,' said Patchy Fogg, who had kept quiet until that moment.

We all looked at him.

'You found a map with that old bridle path on it?' I said.

Patchy nodded.

The important document had, he said, been hidden amidst a pile of old maps and mortgages and it dated back to around 1860.

He had, he admitted, slipped it into a folder of maps and documents at the council offices.

Now Patchy has for many years been able to lay his hands on all sorts of useful, old documents. He has, for example, always been able to 'find' old documents showing that a bed was once the property of William Shakespeare or that a desk was a favourite piece of furniture once owned by Charles Dickens.

In addition to being a very good friend of mine, Patchy is my brother-in-law. He is married to Adrienne who is Patsy's sister and Mr Kennet's other daughter.

And Mr Kennet had been very relieved when the search for paths and bridleways came to a sudden and fortuitous halt.

It was probably wise of Patchy to slip the map into that folder of documents at the council offices – thereby hiding its source.

Privately, I couldn't help wondering if my brother-in-law might not have been earning himself some brownie points with his father-in-law.

The Cadwalladers

Their names were Brenda and Binky Cadwallader. They were both in their 60s and they had been together virtually all their adult lives.

He was called Binky, and he had the wide-legged gait of a man who has spent his life working as a sailor; constantly bracing himself against the rolling deck. However, the gait was misleading. As far as I knew, he had never been to sea. He had certainly never worked as a sailor. The fact was that he had a wide-legged, cautious way of walking because he had a large inguinal hernia which he steadfastly refused to have repaired. He wore a truss only on Sunday mornings, and on those important Christian festivals, such as Christmas and Easter, when he attended church. (I had another patient, Paddy Fields, who walked the same way. He had a massive hydrocele which he refused to have treated.) Apart from the hernia, Binky was in good health; a wiry, agile, muscular man. He was a good man, a good husband and a good friend. He was the sort of fellow who would turn out at 3.00 a.m. to help a friend and think of it not as a favour done, a tick on some celestial score sheet, but a genuine pleasure.

She was called Brenda and she was built on generous proportions. She had started life as a skinny little girl with a noticeable limp. But she had blossomed and grown into what is sometimes known in the politest dressmaking and corsetry circles as a 'full-figured woman'.

When she laughed, which was often, she wobbled all over, rather like a blancmange which needed more time to set or required more of whatever it is that gives blancmange its firm and sturdy qualities.

She stood and walked like a woman who had spent a good deal of time riding horses, or who was, perhaps, no stranger to the obstetrics ward and the delivery room. But I don't think she had ever ridden a horse and she had certainly never had any children. Her gait was the result of a congenital hip problem which had never been properly treated.

All things considered, she was a woman who was built for comfort rather than speed.

When they went for a walk together, the Cadwalladers were an ungainly looking couple.

However, their meeting and courtship was a romantic story in itself.

At the age of 16, he had run away from home, a cruel place by his account, not worthy to be called a 'home', and had become a roustabout with a travelling circus. From what Binky told me I gather that his father was a cruel man through stupidity. On the other hand his mother was cruel not because she didn't know any better but because she enjoyed being cruel; she apparently used to take a strange pleasure from her cruelty.

Binky told me several things about his parents which appalled me.

For example, his parents ate fish and chips for tea every evening but Binky and his sister had dripping sandwiches for their evening meal on six days a week and they had sugar sandwiches on Sundays.

At weekends in the summer, the two parents used to send Binky and his sister to the shops to buy two ice creams. But the ice creams were for the parents, not for the two young children. Binky and his sister would be expected to hurry home before the ice creams melted and hand them over; one to their mother and one to their father. They would then sit and watch as the ice creams were consumed.

I thought that was one of the saddest stories I'd ever heard.

Binky once summed up his parents by saying that his father used to blow his nose with his fingers and his mother didn't mind.

At the circus, Binky slept rough, lived rough and worked hard but it was, he said, a million times better than his home life.

Brenda, on the other hand, had been brought up in a very traditional, middle class home in South Wales. Her parents had great ambitions for her.

When Brenda was a young girl, it was fairly unusual for girls to go away to university but both her parents and her school teachers had encouraged her to think of taking a degree.

Binky and Brenda had met when the circus had visited the town where she lived.

He had been a worldly wise 18. She had been an innocent, naïve girl, two years younger.

There had been no broken hearts and contrary to what you might expect, the girl had not been used and discarded. The boy and the girl fell in love and then the circus left town. He was illiterate and so there was no chance of their staying in touch. There were no letters and no telephone calls. Those were, remember, days when the telephone was used only on very special occasions.

But the romance did not die.

Surprisingly, perhaps, this unlikely couple stayed true to each other.

And when the circus returned to her home town the following year she was waiting for it to arrive.

The roustabouts always arrived first, of course, because they had to erect the Big Top and make things ready for the animals and the performers.

And when the lorries which carried the roustabouts, the canvas and the poles rolled into town, Brenda was there to meet them. The young couple had one more week of each other's company. Fortuitously, it was a school holiday, the last summer of Brenda's school days.

The circus toured all year round (in the winter it went to Southern France and Italy) and since the roustabout hadn't had a proper holiday for two years, his boss allowed him as much time off as he could. The boy and the girl went for long walks in the local parks. They held hands. They had exquisite picnics. She lent him her brother's bicycle and they took day trips to local landmarks. And she taught him to read and write so that they could keep in touch.

It seems almost unbelievable now but this strange courtship went on for another two years.

She made sure she went to a university in a town which was on the circus's itinerary. And while she was at university, she spent the whole of her summer holidays travelling round the country with the circus.

When she graduated, the first girl from her school to go to university, the first to receive a degree, she had only one ambition: to marry Binky, her true love.

The inevitable objections which her parents had raised at the outset of the romance had long since disappeared.

And so the young couple married.

She obtained a post as a school teacher in Exeter and he gave up the circus and took a job as an apprentice plumber. He had learned some circus skills. He could ride a horse bareback, he could juggle and occasionally he put on white paint and baggy trousers if one of the clowns was ill. But he had seen enough of circus life to know that it was not for him, and it was not what he wanted for his new bride. He wanted a house and a garden for Brenda. It was important that the house had an upstairs. Everyone who worked for the circus lived in a caravan. And caravans don't have an upstairs.

He was still young and he was keen to learn the plumbing trade. He did well. When his boss retired, the young, former roustabout started his own plumbing business. There is always a demand for good plumbers who do honest work at fair prices. In the evenings, Brenda looked after the books for him, for although he could read and write he was hardly numerate.

When they reached 60, they both retired. They had worked hard and they decided they had earned some years of autumn sunshine. They bought a cottage in Bilbury, a village they had first discovered a decade earlier when they had been on holiday in nearby Berrynarbor. They lived there, with two cats called Hither and Thither, and hardly ever spent even half a day away from their home.

Binky grew flowers. They were his passion. 'We can buy all the vegetables we need,' he said. 'But we can't buy all the flowers I want. I want a garden and a house filled with flowers. I want our lives to be filled with colour and perfume. I want to be able to give my wife armfuls of flowers.'

While Binky cultivated flowers, and did so with gusto, vigour and justified pride, Brenda kept bees.

When she bought her first hive, she knew nothing about bee keeping. But within two years, she had become an expert apiarist. She had three hives and got on so well with her bees that she never wore the mask, gloves and gown which are usually regarded as an essential part of the beekeeper's kit. Amazingly, she was rarely stung.

A normal hive will produce between 25 and 30 pounds of excess honey in a season but Brenda Cadwallader's hives each produced well in excess of three times that, and her three hives produced nearly 300 pounds of honey a year. A garden full of flowers made sure that the bees were well supplied with pollen.

She and her husband used honey for all their baking and cooking needs where most of us would use sugar.

Every time I saw her, Brenda reminded me of the benefits of honey over sugar. It is, she said, far less likely to cause stomach problems, it provides energy and supplies iron, calcium and many other essential minerals which aren't in sugar. She pointed out that fruits stewed with honey keep for longer and that cakes made with honey stay moist for longer. And she offered to help Patsy and me set up a hive or two if we wanted to produce our own honey. I talked to Patsy about it, we were convinced and later on we did, indeed, have a couple of hives of our own.

The Cadwalladers were a lovely couple, still very much in love; so close and committed to each other that they were rarely separated. Since their marriage, they had not spent one night apart.

They both had good health and professionally I saw them only rarely. Binky had his hernia, which had become like one of the family, and Brenda had her limp. But they coped well.

And then, at the age of 62, Brenda had a nasty scare.

She came to see me complaining of a chest infection and while listening to her lungs, I found a small lump in her left breast. It was very small, had clearly defined edges and it wasn't attached to the tissues beneath or to the muscle. There were no lymph nodes to be felt in her axilla. I was convinced it was a harmless fibroadenoma, sometimes called a breast mouse, but some things in medicine are always worth a second opinion and a breast lump is high on the list. The surgeon whom she saw in Barnstaple agreed with my diagnosis but because Brenda Cadwallader was still worried, he agreed to remove the lump.

If an operation can ever be described as 'minor' then this was that operation.

Mrs Cadwallader was in hospital for less than half a day and the laboratory confirmed that the lump which had been removed was, as both the surgeon and I had surmised, entirely harmless.

This should have been the end of it.

But Mr Cadwallader was deeply troubled and he came to see me a week or so after his wife had been to the hospital. He had done a little reading about breast lumps and he wanted to know what they could do to help spot any lumps which might appear in his wife's breasts in the future.

I explained to him that it would be perfectly easy for his wife to examine her own breasts once a week and, at his request, I explained precisely how she should do this. I pointed out that each quadrant of each breast should be examined in turn and that both axillae, the armpits, should also be checked for enlarged lymph nodes. I even wrote out some notes so that Binky wouldn't forget what to do when he got home.

At first, Brenda Cadwallader was reluctant to examine her own breasts. I gather she told him that she would feel embarrassed to lie down on the bed quite naked and palpate her own bosom.

And so Mr Cadwallader had a bright idea. He suggested that to make the whole thing more fun he should lie down beside her and they should both palpate their breasts. If either of them found anything odd, he said, the other could be called in to provide a second opinion; an amateur opinion it is true, but a second opinion nevertheless.

Mrs Cadwallader laughed at this suggestion and pointed out, with considerable accuracy, that Mr Cadwallader didn't have much in the way of breast tissue to examine. Mr Cadwallader readily agreed with his dear wife that in terms of the scenery being offered to view, he would definitely be getting the best of the bargain. Having conceded this point, he added that they could add a little spice to the proceedings by going ahead with examining each other's breasts anyway, regardless of any need for a second opinion. She laughed again and was won over. And so they started examining their breasts.

Since these things are best done as a regular ritual (or else they are put off or forgotten completely) the pair set aside a few minutes every Sunday, after luncheon, for their weekly lump check. They undressed, lay down on the bed and went through the programme I had outlined and they did it with deliberate care.

It was on the third Sunday that a lump was found.

It was a very small lump, hardly anything more than a pea, but they both agreed that it was something. They decided that they would make a note of the exact position of the lump and check it again the following week.

The following week they both agreed that there was still a lump to be felt that, moreover, they thought that the lump had grown in size. And it did not feel anything like the fibroadenoma which had

60

been excised from Mrs Cadwallader's breast so recently. It was harder and it did not move about so easily.

There was another difference, too.

The new lump was not in either of Mrs Cadwallader's breasts and nor was it in either of her axillae.

The new lump which they had found was underneath Binky Cadwallader's left nipple.

The following morning, the Monday, they were in my surgery.

'Do you think it's cancer?' asked Mrs Cadwallader. She had tears in her eyes and a tremor in her voice.

'It could be,' I told them. 'We need to get it checked out. The good thing is that you've found it very early. The lump is still tiny. I'll ring one of the surgeons and get you seen as soon as possible.'

'Can men get breast cancer?' asked Binky. 'I thought only women got breast cancer.'

'Men can get breast cancer,' I said. 'But it's nowhere near as common as it is in women. For one thing, women have much more breast tissue than men. And for another thing, breast cancer can be influenced by the amount of oestrogen hormone circulating in the body – and that is a hormone which is found in much greater quantities in women than in men.'

I pointed out that most men who develop breast cancer seek help only when the cancer has really developed and is very difficult to treat.

I picked up Mr Cadwallader's medical records and looked through them, trying to see if there might be a clue as to why or how the cancer had developed.

'When you were young they thought you had tuberculosis,' I said, spotting something I hadn't seen before.

'One of the men working in the circus had TB and I shared a caravan with him for a year. I had my chest X-rayed loads of times but they never found anything.'

'How many times did they X-ray you?'

'Oh, for a year or so I was X-rayed every month. The circus boss was paranoid that everyone in the circus was going to get TB. One of the big attractions, a trapeze family, left when they heard about Billy's tuberculosis and the guy who looked after the elephants was threatening to leave. So the boss insisted that the two of us who had lived with Billy, the guy who had TB, should be X-rayed regularly.

Every time we went to a big city, we went to the local hospital and had X-rays done. Doctors used to do a lot of X-rays in those days.'

'That would have been in the 1930s?'

'Yes, I suppose so.'

'But you never had tuberculosis?'

Binky shook his head.

'Could all those X-rays have caused the lump?' asked Brenda. I could not help noticing that she didn't want to use the word 'cancer'.

'It's possible,' I agreed. 'The notes don't say how many X-rays were done. But having too many chest X-rays can cause breast cancer. Indeed, it's one of the reasons why I'm not terribly fond of women having too many mammograms. There's a risk that the very process of X-raying the breasts could actually cause breast cancer.'

Binky Cadwallader was seen two days later by the same surgeon who had operated on his wife. The surgeon thought that the lump was cancerous and less than a week later, Binky went into the hospital to have the lump removed.

To everyone's relief and delight, the operation was a complete success. Histology showed that the lump was cancerous but there were no signs at all that the cancer had spread.

At the hospital, the surgeon offered to repair Binky's inguinal hernia while he was under the anaesthetic (an unusual two for one offer if ever there was one). Binky thanked him but turned him down, saying that the hernia had become a friend and he would miss having it around. Actually, it probably wasn't a bad decision. Inguinal hernias don't usually kill anyone, but the treatment of them sometimes does.

I couldn't help wondering whether Binky would have ever spotted the lump behind his nipple if he and Brenda hadn't begun examining their breasts as a routine. If he hadn't found the lump for, say, six months then the outcome could have been very different.

And there's an odd thought: Brenda Callwallader's harmless breast lump had saved her husband's life.

Gilly's New Cupboard

Gilly Parsons, the landlady at the Duck and Puddle, had ordered a new cupboard and four of us were sitting around in the bar staring at it. There was her husband, Frank Parsons, Patchy Fogg, the antique dealer, Thumper Robinson (whose job description is impossible to summarise in a few words) and myself.

'When she said she'd bought a new cupboard for the kitchen, I stupidly thought she'd bought a new cupboard for the kitchen,' said Frank rather sadly.

When he is unhappy, Frank looks rather like a bloodhound – one of those dogs with long faces, floppy ears and sad, sad eyes though of course, Frank doesn't have floppy ears.

'She showed me a picture in the catalogue and it looked very much like a cupboard.'

'That doesn't look much like a cupboard,' said Patchy, nodding in the direction of the stuff Frank had emptied out of the box in which it had been delivered. 'It looks like a box of kindling and a packet of screws. Why does everyone keep buying this rubbishy stuff? I could have found you a solid, wooden kitchen cabinet for a fiver. Any size you like, beautifully fitted doors, shelves and real dovetail joints – proper craftsmanship.'

'What sort of wood?'

'Any wood you like: pine, mahogany, walnut, oak. I've got a really nice oak cabinet in the van. Suit you perfectly. Gilly would love it. You can get really nice, old furniture for a song these days. No one wants old-fashioned brown furniture. But it's lovely stuff. Ask the doc.'

'It's true,' I confirmed. 'Patchy has helped Patsy and me buy tons of furniture. Proper stuff that looks like it's supposed to look when you buy it. Decent furniture that you can kick or walk into without it falling apart,' I said. I looked at the pile of bits on the floor and shuddered. 'I hate those things that you have to build by yourself,' I added.

I had tried on more than one occasion to put one of these fabricated pieces of furniture together.

'Though, I'll say one thing for the people who make this flat pack furniture,' I added, 'they do give you loads of spare bits.'

Frank, Thumper and Patchy all looked at me.

'Spare bits?' said Thumper.

'Every time I've tried to put one together there have been tons of bits left over,' I said. 'Bits of that thick cardboard stuff they use instead of wood, little knobbly things, screws and loads of little bits of plastic. The last time I tried to put one of these things together, there was probably enough left over to make something else. I think they always give you spare bits as a sort of 'thank you' for expecting you to finish making the thing yourself.'

'What were you making?'

'Patsy said it was another bathroom cabinet,' I said. 'I tried one some time ago and it ended up on the bonfire, so Patsy persuaded me to buy another one from a different company. It was a disaster. I'm pretty sure that what they sent me wasn't a bathroom cabinet at all. I think they'd sent something else by mistake.'

'So, what was it?'

'I'm not sure. We never did work out what it was supposed to be. It didn't have a bottom or a door and the bit where I put the knob wouldn't open. I followed the instructions to the letter but that bloody knob was a real nuisance. It stuck out of the back and made it impossible to fix the whole thing to the wall.'

Thumper laughed. I have no idea why. Thumper isn't perfect. He once tried to cut his own hair. He ended up wearing a woolly hat for a month.

'At least they gave you extra bits,' said Frank. 'I wonder if we've got spare bits with this one?'

'I bet you have,' said Patchy. 'As the doc says, everyone always has bits left over.'

'It says here that all you need is a screwdriver and this little metal tool thingy,' said Thumper, who was reading the sheet ambitiously labelled 'Instructions'. He held up a piece of metal which looked like a bent nail.

'And you always need a hammer,' I said. 'You definitely need a hammer. I always use a hammer whenever I'm putting anything together. We bought a photocopier for Miss Johnson to use and I had to use a hammer on that.' Miss Johnson is my receptionist and secretary. She was also my predecessor's receptionist and secretary and can remember him doing his rounds in a horse drawn doctor's buggy or on horseback.

'Did it work?' asked Patchy.

'The hammer? Yes, the hammer worked perfectly well. It's one of those hickory shafted hammers which Peter sells. I've never had any problems with it.'

'What about the photocopier.'

'No, the photocopier didn't work properly. Actually, it didn't work at all let alone properly. I think they sent us the wrong lead or perhaps it had a faulty circuit board. And there was a big crack in the plastic where two bits were supposed to fit together.'

'That wouldn't have been where you used the hammer, would it?'

'Possibly,' I admitted. 'But you had to use a hammer because the bits didn't fit together unless you hit them. It doesn't matter, though. The thing has got a flat top and so Miss Johnson uses it to display her cyclamen plants. We didn't really need a photocopier anyway. I let Miss Johnson order it because she'd been on about needing one for months.'

'Who the hell had the idea for selling cupboards and stuff in bits?' asked Frank.

'I read about a company which sells houses in a kit,' I said. 'You order a house and they send it round in bits on the back of a lorry. It probably saves postage costs. They sell cars in bits too – sports cars mostly. You order a flashy new sports car and the postman brings it round in his van. I expect they'll be selling babies in bits before too long. You just flick through the catalogue and order whatever sort you fancy.'

'And then you glue it all together when it arrives,' said Thumper.

'Precisely!' I agreed. 'Just think of the mess and pain it will save. I don't expect they'll use glue, though. There will probably just be bits that connect together. You'll slot the legs into the pelvis and then click the head onto the neck. Like putting together one of those Lego kits.'

We were all quiet for a while as we thought about the future. To be honest, it was not a future with which we felt particularly comfortable. In Bilbury, we still sometimes struggle to accept that the 20th century has arrived and seems absolutely determined to make its mark on our lives. We don't like to think of what the 21st century might bring.

'You probably won't believe this but the Normans brought over a castle in kit form when they first came to England,' said Patchy.

'The Normans?' said Frank, frowning. 'Who are the Normans? I don't think I know the Normans. Are they local?'

'The Norman Normans,' said Patchy, patiently.

Since his stroke, Frank sometimes has difficulty in remembering things. But there are, of course, many things which he hasn't forgotten but doesn't know because he never knew them. Gilly reckons that once he'd learned to read and write, Frank stopped concentrating at school. She says he'd have come top in firing ink pellets and pulling pigtails but was probably bottom in everything else. Frank says he can't remember.

'Is that the Normans who came over for the Battle of Hastings?' I asked.

'Ah, that would be 1066,' said Thumper, showing off. He looked very pleased with himself. I would bet that Thumper couldn't name a single other famous date in history. This is a man who can't even remember his wife's birthday or their anniversary. In December, he only knows it's Christmas because he makes a few quid delivering Christmas trees and cutting mistletoe out of the trees on my father-in-law's farm.

'That's the ones,' agreed Patchy, as though Normans had been coming over every couple of years. 'The Normans who came over in 1066.'

'Long before my time,' muttered Frank. 'I told you I didn't know any people called the Normans. I hate it when people boast about when their ancestors came here. It's like people boasting about coming over from America on the Mayfly.'

'Mayflower,' I said. 'And it went the other way.'

'What do you mean 'it went the other way'?'

'It went from Plymouth to America,' I explained. 'It was full of pilgrims.'

'Was it? Did it? Are you sure?'

'Pretty sure.'

'Crumbs,' said Frank. 'You live and you learn, don't you? I could have sworn it was called the Mayfly and came over from there to here.'

'The Mayfly was a British airship,' said Patchy. 'It was like the German Zeppelins. I once bought some photographs of it.'

'Crumbs,' said Thumper. 'I didn't know we had any Zeppelins of our own. So what happened to the Mayfly?'

'It never flew,' said Patchy. 'It fell apart before they could get it into the air.'

We all sat quietly for a moment, reflecting on this long-ago failure.

'Still we beat the Germans in two wars and in the 1966 football World Cup,' said Frank cheerily.

Thumper decided that we should celebrate these victories by ordering more drinks. Thumper ordered a pint of his usual. Patchy had another white wine. And I reluctantly agreed to take another small malt whisky.'

'A single?' asked Frank.

'Not that small,' I told him. A single whisky hardly covers the bottom of the glass.

Frank poured us all drinks and was about to pour himself a whisky when Gilly, his wife, appeared. I don't know how she does it. She always knows when he's about to pour himself a drink.

Gilly didn't say anything but just looked at him.

Since Frank had his stroke, Gilly had made it her responsibility to look after his health. She limits his consumption of alcohol and fatty food and his blood pressure had stayed low for some months.

Frank put the whisky bottle back but kept the whisky glass and poured in half an inch of concentrated orange juice. He hates the taste but sips it and says he can convince himself it's whisky.

Just as she was about to leave, Gilly turned back. 'How's that cupboard coming along?' she asked.

She knew darned well how well it was coming along. The bits were all spread over the carpet in the snug.

'We're working on it, love,' said Frank. 'The boys are giving me a hand.'

'So I see,' said Gilly. 'Very good of them.'

'It needs a lot of thinking about,' I explained. 'These build it yourself cupboards can be tricky.'

'Yes, doc,' said Gilly. 'Patsy did tell me about your talents in this field.' She looked at me and half smiled. 'I'm sure your experience will help Frank enormously. But perhaps we could have the knobs on the front this time?'

She then disappeared.

'I don't know what she was talking about,' I protested. 'I put the knob exactly where the instructions said to put the knob. Mind you, it didn't help that the instructions were in Swedish. I think it was Swedish but it might have been something else.'

'The Normans who first landed at the English town of Hastings on the southern coast came over the Channel from Normandy in Northern France,' continued Patchy when Gilly had gone. Patchy is not easily distracted from a tale he is determined to tell.

'Aha! Don't tell me,' said Thumper. 'That's why we call them the 'Normans'.

'Spot on!' said Patchy. 'But the odd thing is that the Normans were originally Vikings who lived in Scandinavia. They only became Normans because a French King called Charles the Simple had given a big chunk of Northern France to a Viking chief called Rollo. Charles hoped that if he gave the Vikings a bit of France then they might stop attacking the rest of it.'

'This is all taking us somewhere, I hope,' said Frank, who has the attention span of a butterfly on a sunny day.

'It is,' Patchy assured him. 'When the Normans arrived at Hastings, the archers were first off the boats. They were followed by the knights, all armed and mounted on their war horses, and finally the carpenters disembarked.'

'Did you say the carpenters?' I said, not sure that I'd heard properly. 'How do you know all this stuff?'

'The carpenters,' confirmed Patchy. 'I read a book about it. Creasy's *The Fifteen Decisive Battles of the World*.'

'Must be a new book,' said Frank. 'I haven't come across it.'

'Published in about 1850,' said Patchy.

'Before my time,' said Frank.

'Is this all true?' asked Thumper.

'I promise,' said Patchy, crossing his heart with the hand containing his white wine. A little of the wine slopped out onto his trousers. 'It's all true. Each archer carried a bow and a quiver full of arrows. The knights were wearing their hauberks and had their shields slung round their necks. They had swords at their sides and carried raised lances.'

'What the devil is a hauberk?' asked Thumper.

'Armour,' replied Patchy.

'I hope this is going to get somewhere soon,' said Frank. 'What about these damned carpenters of yours?'

'They all had axes and planes and adzes,' continued Patchy.

'They'd need hammers,' said Thumper.

'You can't build anything without a hammer,' I confirmed.

'They had all their tools fitted onto their belts,' said Patchy. 'They probably had hammers too.'

'One of those leather belts with pouches Peter Marshall sells?' enquired Thumper. 'They look good but he bought them from a wholesaler who went bust and they're all sized 'very small'. I think they were designed to fit little Japanese workmen.'

'Those are the things,' continued Patchy. 'And while the archers and knights looked for people to shoot or slice, the carpenters looked around for a good spot to put up a castle.'

'This will eventually get us back to furniture, won't it?' said Thumper.

'It definitely will,' laughed Patchy. 'Because the thing is that when I said that the carpenters were looking for somewhere to put up a castle, that's exactly what I meant because they'd brought their castles with them. On board their ships they had three ready-made castles.'

'You're kidding!' said Frank. 'Like that ruddy build-it-yourself furniture?'

'Exactly!' answered Patchy. 'They brought with them three flat-pack castles in bits, all in wooden pieces, shaped and ready to be put together. And, as soon as they'd found a nice flat piece of land, they carried all the bits ashore and put them together with the aid of the pins they'd also brought with them. Packing must have been a nightmare. But, of course, they didn't have customs people in those days. You sailed up to the shore, got off the boat and there you were.'

Patchy explained that the castle walls and so on were all pierced so that they could be connected together.

'And they had barrels full of pins – all cut and ready to use. Before evening had set in, the carpenters had finished. They then put their stores away before they sat down and had dinner in their cosy new castle.'

'Are you pulling our legs?' asked Thumper.

'I'm not,' said Patchy. 'It's all in the history books.'

'I wonder if they had bits left over,' I asked.

'Almost certainly,' said Frank.

'And I wonder if their castles fell down,' I said. I turned to Patchy. 'Is there any history of their castles falling down after they'd put them up?'

'Not that I know of,' said Patchy.

'They probably brought some glue with them,' said Frank. 'There probably weren't any decent glue shops in Hastings in those days.'

'Did they have glue in those days?' asked Thumper.

'Of course they did,' said Frank. 'The Egyptians must have had glue when they built the pyramids.'

'Yes, but that was in Egypt,' Thumper pointed out. 'We're talking about southern England.'

'I think the pins probably worked just fine,' said Patchy. 'They just banged them into place and built their castle.'

'Using hammers,' I said.

'Almost certainly,' agreed Patchy.

'So they had hammers as well as the axes and whatever else you said.'

'I'm sure they did.'

'So,' said Frank. He took a sip from his concentrated orange juice and pulled a face.

'So,' said I.

'What are we going to do with all this stuff?'

We all knew he was talking about the bits and pieces of the unassembled cupboard.

'I've got an oak cupboard in the van,' Patchy reminded us. 'Much nicer than this one will ever be. Two shelves, two doors and proper handles. Why don't I bring it in?'

'How much is it going to cost me?' asked Frank.

I'll give it to you,' said Patchy. 'As long as you throw that boxful of junk away,' he nodded in the direction of the prefabricated cupboard. 'Do something useful with it.'

'Like what?' said Frank.

'Burn it,' said Patchy as he disappeared through the door.

Three minutes later, Patchy came back into the snug carrying a cupboard.

'It looks heavy!' said Thumper, as Patchy struggled in.

'It's a well-made Victorian cupboard,' I said. 'The Victorians made furniture to last. And oak is a heavy wood.'

'Don't bother to help,' said Patchy, breathlessly. 'Just sit there and watch me struggling.'

'OK,' said Thumper. 'Thanks. We will.'

'You seem to be managing fine,' I said.

Patchy put down the cupboard and bent forward, hands on knees, gasping.

'You're not as fit as you were,' I told him.

'Thanks,' said Frank, examining his new cupboard. 'It looks nice.' He opened the doors. 'Bit dusty inside.'

'Nice?' said Patchy. 'Dusty? I'll take it back if you don't want it.'

It was, I have to admit, a very good looking cupboard.

'No, no,' said Frank quickly. 'I'm just kidding. I'm not heavily into cupboards but as cupboards go it looks really good. Very smart. I'll give it a wipe with a damp rag and it'll be perfect.'

'Can I burn this lot?' asked Patchy, picking up some of the make-it-yourself cupboard that was lying on the floor.

'Certainly,' said Frank.

Patchy tossed a small armful of compressed cardboard onto the fire. Thumper picked up all the screws and bits of metal and gave them to Frank who put them into his pocket. Not wanting to do nothing, I picked up more compressed cardboard and added it to the blaze.

'This faux wood burns quite well,' said Patchy.

'Foe wood,' said Frank. 'What's foe wood? You mean it's an enemy of the real stuff?'

'Something like that,' said Patchy.

Frank fetched some crisps from behind the bar. We opened the little blue packets and salted our crisps and then we sat and munched and sipped and enjoyed the blaze.

'I like these little packets of salt they put in with the crisps,' said Thumper. 'Opening them and salting your own crisps is a nice thing to do.'

'I hope they don't ever stop putting them in with the crisps,' I said. 'Crisps wouldn't be the same without them.'

71

Ten minutes later, Gilly appeared. 'How's my cupboard coming along?' she asked us.

'It's all done,' said Patchy.

'It's finished, love,' said Frank. 'It looks good doesn't it?'

Gilly looked at the cupboard on the snug rug and frowned. 'Is that it? It doesn't look like the picture in the catalogue.'

'It's good solid oak,' said Thumper. 'Last you for a lifetime. You'll never need another cupboard.'

'It's got a few dents in it,' said Gilly.

'They were there when we unpacked it,' said Patchy. 'They put them in to age the item. It's like faded jeans and distressed leather. But we've varnished it for you. The varnish is still a bit tacky so don't examine it too closely just yet.'

Gilly frowned. 'Are there any bits left over?'

'Left over?' I said.

'You four would have bits left over. You always have bits left over.'

'I've got some spare screws and things,' said Frank. He pulled a small handful of screws and metal things from his pocket and showed them to his wife.

'Is that all you had left?'

'Nothing else,' said Frank. 'We managed to use up everything they sent.'

'It looks very solid,' said Gilly. 'It's better than I'd expected to be honest. These items of furniture that come in bits are usually flimsy and a bit rubbishy.' She turned to leave.

'Glad you like it,' said Patchy.

'The fire is going nicely,' said Gilly as she left. 'Something is burning well.'

'Do you think she knows?' asked Thumper, after she'd gone.

'Of course she knows,' said Frank.

'Women always know everything,' said Patchy. 'And they only pretend they don't know when it suits them.'

We finished our crisps.

We all knew he was right.

But it was nice of Gilly to pretend.

The New Barmaid

It was early afternoon and Thumper, Patchy, Frank and I were sitting around a blazing log fire in the Duck and Puddle. I'd done my house calls for the day. The practice receptionist, Miss Johnson, was holding the fort back at Bilbury Grange and knew where I was if she needed me. Patsy was at her mother's where they were busy bottling pears. Thumper, Patchy and I were doing what we did best: nothing much.

I did, however, have a notebook on my lap because in theory I was trying to prepare a short talk on pigs which I'd promised to give to the local Women's Institute.

My supposed expertise on matters porcine was founded entirely on the fact that we were the adopted parents of Cedric, the largest pig in the village. Cedric belonged to a lovely American couple who had won him in a 'Bowling for the Pig' game of skittles at the Duck and Puddle. They had wisely decided not to try to take him back with them to the United States and Patsy and I had happily agreed to look after him.

Patsy had also been roped in to give a short lecture to the Women's Institute. She had agreed to give a talk entitled 'Parsnips – and their round the year role in the kitchen'. I didn't know much about pigs but I knew less about parsnips, so I was glad she was doing that talk.

So far, my notebook contained the word 'PIGS' written in block capitals at the top of a fresh page. The date of my talk was still far enough away for me to be quietly confident that if I waited long enough, either the rest of the talk would materialise without my having to think too much about it. Either that or the invitation would, for some reason, be cancelled.

Both Patsy and I had been roped into talking to the Women's Institute by Patsy's mother, Mrs Kennet. It was her turn to be secretary of the Institute and her major responsibility as holder of this important position was, it seemed, to arrange speakers for the Institute's once a month get-together.

I don't know what these meetings are like in towns and cities but in Bilbury, the Women's Institute meetings usually turned out to be a bit of a knees up. It had for years been the custom for attendees to bring with them bottles of home-made wine, and home-made wine in Bilbury tends to be capable of loosening the top of your head if you drink too much of it.

Members of the Institute who attend meetings in other parts of the country probably content themselves with a slice of seed cake and a cup of tea. In Bilbury, the meetings ended up with a fairly extensive wine tasting. And the wine certainly seemed to make things go with something of a swing. A year earlier, an illustrated lecture on traditional Russian dancing had ended rather dramatically. The speaker, an estate agent from Exeter, had brought swords with him so that he could demonstrate the memorable sabre dance which enlivens the final act of Khachaturian's ballet Gayane. Unfortunately, sabres and home-made wine do not mix well. The estate agent had removed a large bunion from his right foot, and three traumatised members of the Institute had required lengthy bed rest.

My mother-in-law is a wonderful woman, kind and always thoughtful, but she has a way about her that means that I find it difficult to say 'No' when she asks me to do something – such as giving a talk on pig keeping.

So I had a notebook on my knees in case anything occurred to me.

Thumper, who was definitely not attempting to prepare a lecture for the Women's Institute, was drinking a pint of a new beer from a local brewery. The beer was called 'Old Harrison's Anticipated Strong Bladder Water' and Thumper reckoned it was 'distinctly passable' but that he would need to try a few more pints before he would be able to give a properly considered opinion. Thumper doesn't like to rush into things.

Most of the beer sold in North Devon is potent stuff and this brew did not appear to be any exception.

Visitors from towns and cities where the beer is often watered down and frequently not very strong to start with are sometimes surprised by the strength of our local beer.

'Alcool hash no effect hat haul on me,' insisted an insurance and pension fund salesman from Middlesex. He had come to Devon in the hope of persuading locals to give him regular chunks of money in return for insurance policies. He'd have done better to try to persuade the cormorants on the coast to hand over their fish. He had tried to drown his sorrows in local beer. He had, I remember, chosen a brew called 'Old Restoration' which was Thumper's standard choice.

'Get down off the table before you fall and break a leg,' said Frank.

'Hime purfickly safe,' insisted the insurance salesman.

'No, you're not,' said Frank. 'Not with your trousers round your ankles like that.'

It was only at this point in the conversation that the salesman realised that he was in a state of dishabille. He never did remember that he had climbed onto the table to perform an impromptu striptease. He did not seem to be a bright fellow and Patchy, who had at the time been reading a biography of the Duke of Wellington, suggested that if the man had entered an IQ contest with a shop window mannequin, then the competition would have been a 'damned nice thing – the nearest run thing you ever saw in your life'.

Patchy was drinking a tumbler of 'Sheep Dip' (a Devon delicacy which looks and tastes like whisky but which appears on the business accounts of many a North Devon sheep farmer without, as far as I am aware, ever coming anywhere near to a sheep's foot) and I was, for a change, nursing a glass of Wellington Brandy (promised, by the proudly English distiller to be stronger and more palatable than Napoleon Brandy). This had been recommended to me by Patchy. Frank was sipping a glass of a lemon cordial. Frank has high blood pressure, which is pretty well controlled at the moment, and he had a stroke a little while back. To protect his health, Gilly, his wife, allows him just one alcoholic drink a day and she is very strict about this. Generally speaking, Frank prefers to have his one allowed drink in the evening rather than at lunchtime.

Gilly had just passed through the snug on her way to the kitchen at the back of the pub. She'd been into Barnstaple and was carrying several bags of shopping. She had stopped to show to Frank a boxful of new china mugs. They looked unusually delicate and expensive for a public house. 'But we've already got dozens of mugs!'

complained Frank when he saw them. It wasn't a real complaint. Frank worships Gilly and loves her so much he said nothing when she put up new chintz curtains in the snug. He didn't even mutter a protest when she made half a dozen cushions with the leftover material. 'Yes,' replied Gilly, 'but these are for showing and not for drinking. Aren't they smart? I thought I'd put them onto the top shelf of the Welsh Dresser.'

And then she was gone.

When Gilly had disappeared to unpack and arrange her mugs, the three of us returned to watching Frank, who was sorting through a pile of mail which he had on his lap. He had already placed a small number of items of mail in a neat pile on the brass bound Captain's table before us. There was still ample room for us to stand our glasses, on the rare moments when we weren't actually drinking from them. Frank was tossing the rest of the mail, most of it unopened, into the fire.

'Did all that mail come today?' asked Thumper, incredulously.

'Good Lord, no!' answered Frank. 'There is a month's mail here. I always like to let it build up a bit. If you look at the stuff every day, you end up spending most of your time reading letters and then answering them. I'm a bit soft like that. Once I've opened an envelope, I always feel obliged to reply. This way, most of the mail is out-of-date before I get to read it so I don't have to bother with a reply.' This was quite a long speech for Frank.

He tore open an envelope and showed us a letter from his bank manager in Barnstaple. 'See, look at this one,' he said. 'He wanted me to go to a meeting with him two weeks ago. It's now out-of-date so I can throw it away.' He screwed up the letter and the envelope and tossed them both onto the fire which consumed them hungrily.

'Bright thinking,' said Patchy. 'I always used to try to deal with the mail before I did anything else in the day. But then suddenly, one fine spring day, I realised that if you give priority to all the crap in your life then you never have a chance to get round to the good things or the fun things, do you? I used to go sea fishing a lot and I'd promised myself that the next time we had a fine day, I'd go off and drown some bait. But at 11.30 in the morning, I was still on the phone trying to sort out some problem with an electricity bill. I'd been on hold for 20 minutes so I put the phone down, collected my rod, put together a picnic and buggered off down to the beach for the rest of the day. The thing is that the crap never ends, does it?'

No one bothered to reply to these rhetorical questions.

I too shared Frank's dislike of paperwork.

The problem is that the inconsequential and the unimportant have a tendency to take over our lives and you need to be constantly alert to make sure that they don't. If humans are wiped off the face of the earth, I believe that all that will remain will be cockroaches, bindweed, nettles, ivy, brambles and paperwork. The administrators who create the paperwork will survive anything – even a nuclear blast. The fact is, however, that no one ever received thanks or achieved greatness for keeping neat accounts (or, as Patsy says, for plumping up their scatter cushions).

'It's bills I hate,' said Thumper with the quiet status of a man who has never in his life paid a bill that wasn't printed in red. He was so emphatic that he waved his beer mug around and spilt some of it. He frowned for he hated spilling beer as much as he hated paying bills.

'I like getting letters from my brother,' I said. 'Opening a letter from him is like opening the front door and having the sun burst in. He's always rather jolly and he writes marvellous letters. He only writes once or twice a year, mind you.'

'I didn't know you had a brother!' said Thumper.

'I haven't seen him for years,' I said. 'He's quite a lot older than me. He emigrated to Canada years ago.'

'Is he a doctor, too?' asked Patchy.

'Oh no,' I said with a laugh. I don't really know why but I found the idea of my brother being a doctor rather comical. 'He was never in the slightest bit academic.'

I sipped at my brandy and thought about my long lost brother. Patchy poked the fire, provoking a flurry of sparks. Frank continued to sort through his mail. It occurred to me that although I was fond of my brother in a co-sanguine, standard sibling sort of way, my real brothers in life were sitting within a few feet of me.

'I can't stand bills,' muttered our landlord. 'I get loads of them. I suppose everyone does.' He held up an envelope on which was stamped the logo of the TV licensing people. The envelope also carried a message which appeared to be intended to intimidate. 'Look at this!' he exclaimed in disgust. 'I've already put three more of these on the fire. These people don't seem to have anything to do except send me threatening letters.'

'What is it?' asked Thumper. 'Who's it from?'

'The TV licensing people,' explained Frank.

Thumper looked at him and frowned. 'The who?'

'You know,' said Frank, 'those people who threaten to come round to make sure you've bought a TV licence.'

'I bought our TV,' said Thumper, clearly puzzled. 'I paid £4 for it. You can get colour on it when the wind's blowing hard from the south west.'

Knowing that the prevailing winds in North Devon are from the south west, and can have a powerful effect on television aerials, we all nodded.

'You still have to buy a licence,' said Frank. 'At least you're supposed to.'

'A licence for the television? They make you buy a licence if you have a television?' He laughed at the absurdity of this.

'I think they do,' said Patchy. He looked at me. 'Have you got one?'

'Television?'

'No. Yes. But have you got a licence for it?'

I shook my head. 'They send me a lot of those letters and I keep meaning to,' I said. 'But the letters demanding money are so aggressive that I always feel I have to ignore them.'

'They're never going to come round to Bilbury to see if we've got licences,' said Frank.

'I never answer the door unless I know who it is,' said Thumper, who didn't. 'How many times have you opened the door to an unexpected visitor and had a pleasant surprise?'

'I bought a television licence once,' said Patchy. He looked around, saw our looks of astonishment and lowered his head. 'It was years ago,' he explained, embarrassed. 'I was very young and naïve then.'

'I still can't get my head round this,' said Thumper, leaning forward. 'You're serious? We're supposed to buy a licence to watch television? We are supposed to buy a licence even when we own our television set? And with all the adverts they put between the programmes these days?'

'Don't the licensing people send you letters?' asked Frank.

Thumper shook his head. 'I don't think so,' he said. 'Mind you, the dog eats most of our mail before I get to see it.'

'That sounds like a good excuse for not paying bills,' I said.

'So it is. I never thought of that!' grinned Thumper.

We all sipped at our drinks.

'I can't get used to life in the 1970s,' muttered Thumper.

'I think they've had TV licences for quite a while,' said Frank.

'Bloody outrageous,' said Thumper. He took a man sized sip of his beer. 'This is good stuff, Frank,' he said. 'I'm pretty sure I'm definitely going to like this one. What's it called again?'

Frank nodded and told him, pleased that the new beer was getting the seal of approval. Frank always reckons that Thumper has taste buds which reflect the taste of the average man in Bilbury. If Gilly makes a new pie, she always makes sure that Thumper tries it first before she puts it on the menu.

'I was in my early twenties,' explained Patchy. 'We all do stupid things in our early twenties, don't we?'

'Don't worry about it,' I told him. 'We'll forget about it eventually.'

'Everywhere you turn they want money for something or other,' said Frank. 'They'll be making us buy licences for our cars soon.'

We all looked at him.

'They don't, do they?'

We all looked at him, wondering if he was taking the piss. But he clearly wasn't.

'I'm afraid so,' said Patchy.

'Don't for heaven's sake tell Gilly,' said Frank. 'She'll worry about it.'

We promised we wouldn't. I sometimes think what a good thing it is that Frank long ago grew through and way beyond any manifestation of embarrassment.

As Frank continued to sort through his mail, we chatted, as friends will, of this and that, of cabbages and kings.

Patchy told us that a fellow in Lynton who operated a small removal company had been hired to move a Bechstein grand piano out of a cottage in Lynmouth and to take it to a terraced house in Plymouth. None of us could imagine why anyone would want to move anything from Lynmouth to Plymouth but we agreed that the explanation had to be either love or money.

The basic problem they had was that the front door to the cottage was narrow and the hall leading to the front door had a bend in it. The difficulty was exacerbated by the fact that the piano was, of course, exceedingly large. The removers decided that instead of merely moving the piano in a suck it and see sort of way (the usual method favoured by removers everywhere), they would have a plan. They would hire a local carpenter to make a plywood replica, reproducing not the detail of the piano but merely the size, and then work out a way to take the piano out of the cottage without doing any damage to the valuable piano or the cottage.

'What happened?' I asked him. 'Sounds a good plan. Did it work?'

'Unfortunately, not,' said Patchy. 'They carpenter made a plywood replica of the piano but it was so large that he couldn't get it out of his workshop. The removers gave up and knocked a hole in the cottage wall.'

Thumper told us that a pal of his, who is an undertaker, was driving through Ilfracombe recently, on his way to pick up a customer in Combe Martin, when an elderly woman ran out into the road and waved for him to stop.

'Ernest isn't dead yet,' she screeched at him. 'But I'm pretty sure he will be ready for you to collect next Wednesday. If you're around this way then just call in. It'll save me the price of a phone call.'

Temporarily chastened by this reminder of our own mortality, Patchy emptied his glass and decided it was time to order fresh drinks. It was not necessary for Frank to take a break from feeding the fire with unwanted mail (of which there seemed to be an inexhaustible supply) because he and Gilly had hired a barmaid to assist them in running the Duck and Puddle and she had now reappeared behind the bar.

It is, I think, fair to say that Arcadia Blanchardine did not look like a barmaid. Mind you, she didn't look much like an 'Arcadia' either.

If you were a film maker in Hollywood and you'd asked Central Casting to send along a barmaid, you would have been disappointed if they'd sent Arcadia Blanchardine. She had none of the qualities which were traditionally regarded as standard equipment for a barmaid in the 1970s. She was not charming, seductive or voluptuous. She was not a woman for whom the words 'buxom', 'flirtatious' or 'friendly' had been coined. More appropriate adjectives would have been 'forbidding', 'harsh', 'grim', 'starched', 'chilly' and 'hostile'. These are not qualities which were usually associated with the welcoming nature of an English hostelry. Ms Blanchardine did not have a winning smile and she and badinage were 'strangers who had never met 'ere in passing cross the distant moors'. Merry quips were not her forte and the general attractiveness of the Duck and Puddle was not enhanced by the thick, baggy, mustard coloured polo neck jumper which she wore every day, whatever the weather and however warm it was in the snug at the Duck and Puddle. She wore the jumper, which did not appear to have ever been washed, together with a pair of industrial strength blue jeans which were about four or five sizes too large for her.

'This Englishwoman is so refined she has no bosom and no behind,' wrote Stevie Smith and, apart from the 'refined' bit, it might have been Ms Blanchardine of whom she was writing.

'Give her a break,' said Frank, when Patchy commented that he would like to see her smile occasionally. Frank always tries to see the best in people. 'I think she would probably be a really nice person if she wasn't such a mean, self-centred and rude individual,' Frank added, not meaning to be critical.

Frank would have probably described Nero as a nice chap, who played a pleasant tune with his fiddle but was perhaps a bit careless with matches. It was Frank, bless him, who told me that Mussolini had a pet lion, of which he was inordinately fond, that Hitler was devoted to a pet dog called Blondi and that without Stalin's enthusiasm, the AK47 would have probably never been made.

It was nigh on impossible to estimate Ms Blanchardine's age.

She wore her hair in a style which was more commonly associated with squaddies in the army and if she wore any make-up it was in such small quantities that it was not visible to the naked eye.

That is all in the way of setting the scene and introducing you to Ms Blanchardine. Most of it didn't matter a damn, of course and none of this is intended as criticism for, like Frank, I always try to see the best in people, but merely as an introduction to an important addition to village life.

The only thing that did matter was that instead of greeting customers with a welcoming smile, she met them with a sour look.

'What do you want?' was her standard salutation and it was delivered with all the emphasis on the third word. The result was that the customer, whether a regular or a stranger, was made to feel something of a nuisance.

Ms Blanchardine somehow managed to make it clear to all and sundry that she had more important things to be doing with her time than serving customers. These crucial, private and confidential activities were not detailed but their existence was implicit.

'May I ask how you selected your new barmaid?' I asked Frank a few days after she had arrived at the pub. The object of my enquiry was down in the cellar reconnecting a new barrel of Old Restoration to the tap which brought beer to the thirsty. The Duck and Puddle does not have a large clientele when measured in numbers but those customers for which it caters are renowned for their proclivity for feather spitting.

Frank sighed and shook his head rather sadly. 'We advertised in the local paper and asked the Labour Exchange to send us details of suitable applicants. We said we'd prefer someone with experience in the hotel or pub trade but that we would, if necessary, hire someone without any knowledge of the business. Do you know how many people wanted the job?'

'No idea. A dozen? Half a dozen?'

'One,' said Frank. 'Ms Blanchardine was the only one who was interested. She had no experience and admitted that she only wanted the job because she thought it would help her find a husband.'

I stared at him in disbelief.

'That's what she said,' said Frank with a shrug. 'Gilly interviewed her and Ms Blanchardine told her that she had been single long enough and that she had decided to marry.'

'But why did you hire her at all?' I asked him.

'Gilly said we needed help in the bar,' said Frank. 'She doesn't want me working too hard because of that stroke I had and at meal times she has to be in the kitchen preparing food.'

Sure enough, Ms Blanchardine quickly made it clear that she had not been joking when she'd told Gilly that she was in Bilbury on a husband hunt.

Apart from her standard 'What do you want?' her only other question to customers was 'Are you married?' This query, of course, was reserved for male customers. Female customers received only the 'What do you want?' and a glare. Ms Blanchardine didn't like having other women in the bar. She clearly regarded them as unwelcome competition.

Whenever she found an unmarried male customer, Ms Blanchardine would attempt to smile. Unfortunately, smiling was not a skill she had mastered and the result was a tooth-baring grimace which exhibited years of dental malpractice for no useful purpose. Invariably, she would accompany the 'smile' with another of her favourite lines which was: 'I'm single too'.

Peter Marshall, our local shopkeeper, became a prime target for her smile and mildly implied promise but Peter, who had only recently avoided a rather unpleasant matrimonial affiliation with a predatory mantis, who had got as far as making a unilateral decision to distribute around the village an extensive wedding present list, was more than a match for her clumsy wiles. After her inquiry as to his marital status, Peter glared defiantly and added: 'And I shall make damned sure I remain that way, too.'

Ms Blanchardine's other main target had been the newly appointed vicar of St Dymphna.

Frank reported that when she discovered that the Reverend Michael Micklemass was married, and had seven and two thirds children, she went into a moody decline which lasted for the best part of a week. She had, apparently, rather set her heart on becoming a clergyman's wife. She told Frank that she thought she was well suited to the role of becoming a pastoral guide for lost souls of Bilbury, though Frank said he thought she perhaps underestimated the wider demands of the role and might find herself stretched if required to give lessons on jam making to the Young Wives Group or required for 'bonniest baby' judging duties at the summer fete.

When Frank told me of Ms Blanchardine's ambition I was, I confess, reminded of an entry in Arnold Bennett's diary for August 10th 1899.

'I have just remembered a saying of Mrs Dunmer, our new housekeeper at Witley,' wrote Bennett. 'She said to me: 'There's a lot of old maids in this village, sir, as wants men. There was three of 'em after a curate as we had here, a very nice young gentleman he was, sir. No matter how often the church was opened, those women would be there, sir, even if it was five times a day. It's a sign of a hard winter, sir, when the hay begins to run after the horse.''

'Could we have four refills, please?' asked Patchy politely. Patchy is always polite to everyone and claims he has even been known to address traffic wardens with a respectful finger to the brim of his hat. (No one has seen evidence of this and there are some who suspect that two fingers may be involved.)

'What do you want?' asked Ms Blanchardine, who, unlike Frank, never made any effort to remember what her customers were drinking.

Visitors who called in to the Duck and Puddle once a year would be astonished when, as they walked through the door, Frank would greet them and then ask if they wanted their usual. Ms Blanchardine either didn't have much of a memory or didn't believe in exerting it overmuch.

As usual, Ms Blanchardine managed to make her inquiry sound like an accusation. She spoke in the manner of a harassed mother addressing a troublesome six-year-old or an irritable and irascible head teacher responding to an infant pupil's request for information.

Patchy told her what we were drinking. Normally he would have invited her to have a drink herself but we had all abandoned that custom since Ms Blanchardine would invariably reply 'I'm not thirsty so I'll take mine directly from the till.' And she would duly add the price of a triple malt whisky to the bill. None of us actually saw her drink anything though we did see and hear her eat for she had an insatiable fondness for pork scratchings. She would, said Frank, get through a dozen large packets a day without paying for any of them.

In due course, Ms Blanchardine announced that our drinks were ready.

'Your drinks are here,' she shouted.

Even when the bar was quiet and she had nothing else to do, she would never take drinks to a table.

'I was hired as a barperson,' she told Frank, when he suggested that it might be a good idea if she were to put drinks onto a tray and take them over to customers. 'I have bad feet and I wasn't hired to cart drinks about the place like a skivvy.'

The result was that if he was in the bar (and where else was he going to be?) Frank would be the one who would take the drinks across to the table where the customers were sitting.

There was no doubt that life in the Duck and Puddle wasn't anywhere near as joyful now that Ms Blanchardine was behind the bar. We tried to ignore her dark and looming presence but it wasn't easy. 'I always feel she's watching to make sure we don't misbehave,' muttered Thumper, when Frank collected our drinks from the bar and put them down on the captain's table.

Patchy and I nodded agreement and picked up our fresh drinks.

'This is good stuff,' said Thumper, as he began his fresh pint of Old Harrison's Anticipated Strong Bladder Water. He savoured the liquid, allowing it to remain in his mouth for a while in the same way that a wine or whisky drinker will hold a favourite tipple on tongue and palate. 'Do you know,' he said to Frank, 'I think I would definitely put this one into my top three favourite beers.'

Frank, who still chose the stock for the bar and always took great care when selecting new beers for his customers to enjoy, nodded his appreciation of Thumper's vote of confidence. 'What would the other two be?' he asked. 'Old Restoration would be one, I assume?'

'Oh yes,' said Thumper, who claims he has probably drunk enough Old Restoration to fill the Estuary at Bideford. 'The Old Restoration would definitely be in there. And I'd have Wilkinson's Prize Double Pigman's Drench as my third.' He thought for a moment. 'If I were allowed a reserve it would be 'Charles Wells Bombadier'.'

Thumper is, we all know fond of this particular brew as much for its name as for its malty taste. The beer is named after Bombadier Billy Wells who was, as a boxer, the first British holder of the Lonsdale belt but who is now more widely remembered as the well-muscled fellow banging an oversized gong at the start of the wonderful British films which were made by the J.Arthur Rank organisation.

'I'd have the Old Restoration and this new one from Old Harrison,' said Frank. 'But my third would have to be Rudman's Singular Stout.'

'Ah yes,' said Thumper. 'So many beers…'

Patchy said that if he had to choose three drinks for the rest of his life he would choose any decent claret from the Chateau Mouton

Rothschild, Sheep Dip whisky and a nice cup of tea. Thumper immediately told him that this was cheating since he was only allowed alcoholic drinks in his top three. Patchy then said he'd have a decent bottle of Dom Perignon as his third choice.

No one was much surprised when I chose three malts as my favourite alcoholic drinks: Laphroaig, Bunnahabein and The Macallan (always preceded by the definite article); with Cardhu a very respectable reserve.

'If you could only have one meal for the rest of your life what would it be?' asked Patchy. 'It doesn't have to be nutritional or balanced or any of that stuff. What would you not like to live without?'

'Gilly's steak and kidney pudding with buttered mashed potatoes and sliced carrots,' said Frank instantly.

'A fried breakfast,' said Thumper firmly. 'Bacon, sausage, egg, tomatoes, mushrooms and hashbrowns.'

'Pancakes covered in sugar and liberally splashed with lashings of lemon juice,' said Patchy, unexpectedly.

'Your turn,' said Frank, looking at me.

'Hot buttered toast,' I said, after some thought. 'Using a toasting fork on a sparking log fire.'

There were groans at my rather unimaginative contribution.

'What about you, Ms Blanchardine?' asked Thumper, turning towards the bar. None of us, not even Frank, had been given permission to call her by her Christian name. Frank had tried once but had been heartily reproved.

'I don't like silly games like that,' she said sniffily. 'We all need a properly balanced diet. There's no point in just picking one meal. You're grown men, you should be able to find better ways to spend your time than playing silly games.'

That rather put a stop to our silliness and so we sat quietly and watched the logs blazing in the fireplace. A two-foot long piece of silver birch was now burning very nicely and looked set to last for an hour or so.

'Have you nearly finished sorting through your damned mail?' asked Patchy, looking across at Frank who had just tossed a bunch of advertising circulars and a water bill onto the fire.

'Nearly done,' said Frank, holding up the handful of mail which remained. 'And then I'm finished with the mail for another month!'

It seemed an excellent policy.

I found myself wishing I could do the same.

Unfortunately, medical reports and laboratory investigations tend to require rather more urgent treatment.

Still, I respected Frank's method of dealing with his mail and admired it greatly from afar.

'Hot buttered toast,' mumbled Thumper, looking in my direction.

I grinned at him and shrugged.

'We could make paper aeroplanes with some of those leaflets,' Patchy said to Frank.

Thumper and I looked him. I picked out a leaflet advertising central heating and quickly made a very decent dart. I tossed it across the room and watched with pride as it floated behind the bar.

Ms Blanchardine made a loud tutting sound and stalked out of the snug.

'It's better without her in here,' muttered Patchy.

We spent the next fifteen minutes making paper darts.

Ms Blanchardine, who could hear us having a good time, did not return.

Beneath us, down in the Duck and Puddle cellar, we could hear Ms Blanchardine doing something noisy. She also appeared to be shouting abuse at a barrel of beer. I couldn't help thinking that this was all going to end in tears.

'Bit of a spoilsport, isn't she?' said Thumper.

'Into each life some rain must fall,' said Patchy.

'The Ink Spots,' said Frank. 'Great song.'

'Henry Wadsworth Longfellow,' said Patchy. 'Great poem.'

We sat and watched the fire for a while. When the flames began to die down, Frank threw on another assortment of circulars and final demands.

The Bilbury Snitch

We had not had a policeman living in the village of Bilbury for several years.

The problem (if that is how you want to describe it) was that the crime levels in Bilbury were not high enough to merit our having our very own resident constable. During the last year when we had a resident constable, there had been very little major crime.

A bucket had been reported stolen but was later found to have been blown into a ditch during one of our not infrequent winter storms.

And Mr Brooke, a newcomer to the village whom we have already met, complained that, although admitting he had no proof of the theft, he believed that some of his apples had been taken.

Mr Brooke, a former Very Important Person in the City of London, was a pompous and self-important fellow whose small but bountiful orchard produced far more apples than he could ever eat. He claimed that he believed that his apples had been stolen by a gang which was working for a cider maker in Taunton. When the police investigated the theft, it was found that the two dozen apples which Mr Brooke claimed were missing, were rotting quietly in the lush undergrowth beneath the trees in question.

And then there was the case of Mrs Banbury and her failing memory.

I don't know whether this happens in other villages but in Bilbury, people seem to hide all sorts of stuff in all kinds of odd places for a variety of different reasons.

I once had a patient called Hodgson who was a retired accountant who kept a sizeable hoard of gold sovereigns packed into a bird box at the bottom of his garden. He chose sovereigns because, since they officially count as currency, there is no capital gains tax to be paid when they are sold. You'd be surprised at how many sovereigns you can cram into a bird box. The thing was so heavy that it had to be supported with a piece of wood nailed onto the tree underneath it.

The ex-accountant was so worried about forgetting that he had put them there that he told everyone he knew what he'd done. The coins were still there when Mr Hodgson died and his executors emptied the box.

And then there was Hilda Perkins. Mrs Perkins was a sweet, old lady who kept her jewellery in a hollowed out loaf which she kept in her freezer. She was a widow and lived alone and when she became bedbound in her late 90s, I visited her once a week, just to check on her and to make sure she was eating and breathing satisfactorily. She had terrible arthritis and a heart which misbehaved whenever the weather changed. Two neighbours took it in turns to take her food.

Every time I visited Mrs Perkins, she asked me to fetch the hollowed out loaf so that she could check that the jewels were still safely hidden. The jewels were all paste and almost worthless but they were important to her. I never let on that I knew that they were paste. On the contrary, I always treated the jewels as though they belonged to the Queen and were on loan from the Tower of London.

And another patient of mine, the aforementioned sweet, old lady called Mrs Banbury, persuaded her nephew to stuff bits of jewellery and a few gold coins into the hollow pole which suspended the curtains in her living room.

It was, I suspect, an idea she'd got from one of the many crime novels she read.

When the nephew emigrated to Australia, Mrs Banbury completely forgot where her treasures had been hidden and there was no one around to remind her.

After being unable to find them in her underwear drawer (the 'safe' place she had used for over 50 years) she called in the police and reported that she had been robbed.

It took Constable Hobbling (who was our local representative of the constabulary at the time) three days to discover that the jewels had not been stolen at all. However, before the happy conclusion to the enquiry, the investigation caused some considerable concern in the village. I know of two people who, as a result of the investigation, actually started locking their doors at night and carried on doing so for the best part of a month.

(Hollow curtain poles, the sort that carry curtains on large rings, have been used to store all sorts of strange things. I heard about a family in Barnstaple who were so upset at being thrown out of their rented accommodation that they hid bits of fish in the hollow curtain poles they left behind. They had been thrown out of their home because the landlord believed he could make more money by doing some renovation work and then renting out the property to wealthier clients. The stale fish did what stale fish tend to do and, as a result, the house stank. The landlord, whose renovations had not included replacing the curtain pole, couldn't find the cause of the offensive odour, or anyone prepared to live in the smelly house. After a weary and disappointing six months, he gave up the struggle and decided to sell the house cheaply. By this time, the family who had been thrown out had managed to scrimp and save enough money for a deposit. They bought the house from which they had been evicted and threw out the curtain poles. As far as I know, the landlord never found out what they'd done. I only found out about it because the man who had hidden the fish was a cousin of Gilly's and she delighted in telling the story.)

The only other crime problem of any significance we had in Bilbury was a spate of thefts which were so small and insignificant that the duty sergeant at the police station in Barnstaple insisted that they didn't even warrant labelling as petty crime.

But at the time there is no doubt that the thefts were worrying.

I should, perhaps, point out that these crimes were not directly involved in the main theme of this account but are included here because, as I believe experienced and accomplished authors are wont to say, they help to set the scene and they provide essential background embroidery. As you will have already noticed, this chapter is exceptionally well embroidered.

The thefts had two things in common.

First, the items which were stolen were all taken from outhouses, barns, sheds, garages and so on.

Second, the items were pretty well worthless and it was the fact that someone had taken the items which was the worry, not the disappearance of the things themselves. None of us likes the idea of a malfeasant stranger wandering onto our property and fingering our possessions – worthless though they might be.

The thief had had an easy time of it.

Most rural properties are well served with what are, I believe, known as 'storage facilities' and this is as true of Bilbury as anywhere else.

Space is not at a premium in a village, in the way that it is in town and suburban gardens, and whereas the average town dweller has to store his lawnmower, garden tools, old suitcases, malfunctioning electrical equipment and boxes of old accounts at the back of his garage or, maybe, in a small garden shed, rural properties are usually so well served with storage space that nothing is ever thrown away.

Bilbury Grange, for example, is blessed with 17 barns, outhouses, stables, linhays and sheds. I know this because I once counted them.

If you added in coops and field shelters and the buildings which have crumbled away and are now little more than foundations, then the number would be even greater.

Many of these buildings had been of little or no practical value for some years.

I think that our predecessors at Bilbury Grange had a policy that when a barn or stable was beginning to look ropey, and had lost a good part of its roof, they would simply build a new one. It was, to be fair, probably cheaper and easier to build something else rather than to attempt to do repairs to a structure that had been weakened by woodworm and wet rot (and possibly even a touch of dry rot) and then battered into submission by the storms and gales which are as much a part of North Devon as the moors, the combes and the rock-strewn coastline.

Some of our outbuildings were more or less empty but several were stuffed to the rafters with bits of old machinery, rotten coils of rope and unopened bags which contained heaven knows what because the labels had long since rotted away.

The one thing all these edifices had in common was that, whether sound or not, they remained forever unlocked.

House dwellers in a town or a city will almost certainly lock their garage, if they have one, and most probably have a stout padlock on their shed. Even in the suburbs, house owners are apprehensive and cautious through necessity and experience. But I don't think any garage in Bilbury was ever locked, and the idea of putting a padlock on a shed door would have caused much merriment had it been mooted in the Duck and Puddle.

Given this, and the fact that the items which disappeared were of little or no value or consequence, it was, in its own small way, a miracle that anyone noticed that things were disappearing.

It was, I think, my dear friend Thumper Robinson who first mentioned that something of his had gone missing.

We were sitting in the snug at the Duck and Puddle one day when he mentioned, out of the blue, that someone had stolen a rusty bucket with a hole in the bottom which he had been planning to use to help force some rhubarb. He wasn't concerned about the loss of the bucket, it would have been impossible to put a monetary value on it, but about the fact that someone had snuck into a shed in his garden and taken it.

Patchy then mentioned that he had experienced a similarly strange theft.

In his case, an intruder had entered a store shed he used for unsaleable junk and had taken an old bicycle saddle which had been sitting on a shelf. Patchy has an encyclopaedic knowledge of every item in his inventory and he'd noticed the absence of the saddle instantly. It had, he said, been the space on an otherwise crowded shelf which had attracted his attention.

Frank said that he'd lost an old, plastic milk crate which he kept in an alleyway behind the pub. He regularly used the crate to help him reach up and un-block a stretch of guttering on a low roof. Because of its position, the guttering was regularly filled with leaves and other debris. Frank said he couldn't understand why anyone would steal a scruffy, old milk crate which was of little value to anyone who didn't have guttering which needed un-blocking.

Listening to these tales of modest woe, I remembered that I had noticed that an old trowel had been taken from our greenhouse. I'd only spotted that the trowel had gone missing because the handle had been loose and I had put the trowel to one side, intending to bind the handle back into place with some baler twine. The blade, the scoopy shaped metal part of the trowel, was perfectly serviceable so it had seemed a pity to throw it away. Having lived in the country for some years, I had acquired country ways and was always reluctant to throw away anything which might still be serviceable. I had filled a barn and a half with bits and pieces which didn't appear to have any future use but which I had kept simply because 'you never know when it might come in handy'.

None of us cared about the items which had disappeared. They had neither sentimental nor monetary value. But we cared very much about the fact that someone had entered our properties and taken them. No one likes to feel that the sanctity of their home, albeit a peripheral part of it, has been invaded.

Even so we wouldn't have bothered to report the thefts if it had not been that, by coincidence, the local constable, P.C. 'Peculiar' Clarke, was in the Duck and Puddle at the time, enjoying a lunchtime pie and a pint. (P.C. Clarke had taken over from Constable Hobbling who had retired to grow organic mushrooms in a large, dark barn in the Black Mountains.)

'Peculiar' had removed his helmet so that he could honestly claim that he was not in uniform, and therefore could not be accused of drinking while on duty. He overheard us talking and, since he hadn't had any crime to deal with for nearly nine months, became quite excited by what he described as a 'serial thief'.

A rural policeman without any crimes to solve will grasp at anything which allows him to convince his superiors that he is needed where he is and should not be shunted off to do something which requires daily confrontations with villainous individuals carrying knives, bludgeons and shotguns. 'Peculiar' Clarke was no coward but he had enough brain underneath his helmet to know which side his bread was buttered.

('Peculiar's real name, when he squeezed his size 8 helmet onto his oversized cranium, crammed his size 12s onto his bicycle pedals and rode around the village looking for crime, was P.C. Archibald Clarke. For reasons lost in the far distant mists of time, he was known to everyone as Peculiar. No one, least of all Archibald, was offended by this and local youngsters regarded him as a fierce upholder of the law and a stern protector of low-hanging fruits and nuts. Scrumpers, if caught and recognised as established recidivists, could expect to have their ears boxed, regardless of age or size. In those days, it was perfectly legal and proper for police officers to box the ears of minor miscreants. This saved the courts a good deal of work and enabled offenders to continue with their lives without having to contend with the burden of a criminal record.)

P.C.Clarke finished his pie, put his helmet back on, took out his notebook, licked his pencil and took our statements.

He then began his enquiries.

To begin with, P.C. Clarke's prime, and indeed only, suspect was a local man called 'Nutty' Slack, who lived in a tin shack on Exmoor and who had a fine collection of utterly worthless items stored under a tarpaulin next to his home.

Operating on the principle that a collector, however simple his tastes, however mean his ambitions, will be innately ruthless and greedy, will stoop as low as is required, and will stop at nothing in order to enhance the size and quality of his agglomeration, P.C. Clarke visited Mr Slack's abode and, although not armed with a search warrant, requested permission to 'take a look at the stuff what you got tucked under that tarpaulin'.

The items which had disappeared were not, however, in Mr Slack's collection and genuine and fulsome apologies were proffered and accepted.

Constable Clarke was so stumped that he had to issue a verbal announcement (in the Duck and Puddle) that he 'was pursuing enquiries' and that 'an arrest was expected imminently'. As Thumper pointed out, this clearly meant that Constable Clarke didn't have the foggiest idea where to look, or whose collar to feel.

And then, to everyone's surprise, the culprit confessed.

And to everyone's even greater surprise, the culprit turned out to be the Reverend Micklemass, the new vicar of St Dymphna's church.

According to P.C.Clarke, the vicar explained that he was depressed because the church needed essential repair work doing to the roof and he had no idea how he was going to pay for it. His depression had deepened when the grave digger had retired and the Church Council had decided to hire a man with a motorised digger to dig graves. What had doubtless seemed a good idea at the time, quickly turned into a disaster when the man with the digger succeeded in digging up a couple of yards of the sewer pipe which served the vestry washroom and lavatory.

With no prospect of ever finding the funds to repair all these structural problems, the vicar had sunk into what John Bunyan might have described as 'a slough of despond'. He had, he reported to P.C. Clarke, been told by one of the Bishop's aides that the diocese had no funds to spare and that if he could not raise the money himself then the church would have to be closed, shuttered, abandoned and deconsecrated.

The vicar had taken this badly for it seems that, for a clergyman to lose his church, is a disaster on a par with a captain losing his

94

ship. The vicar had, it seemed, chosen to distract himself from his predicament by wandering around the village taking things that did not belong to him. His story was so strange that it was clearly true. All the purloined items were found, neatly stacked, in a corner of St Dymphna's crypt.

At a meeting held in Constable Clarke's front parlour, all those who had been victims of the vicar's pointless kleptomania agreed that they were not interested in asking the police to pursue the case. We agreed, indeed, that we would not give any evidence if the case were taken to court.

Constable Clarke was, of course, slightly disappointed by the disappearance of his case but even he agreed that there was absolutely nothing to be gained by locking up the vicar.

Moreover, now that the problems of St Dymphna were out in the open, it became clear that we needed to club together to find some help. Cedric 'Bill' Stickers, the part-time grave digger, was persuaded out of retirement by the promise of a small pay rise and he was given a modest bonus to repair the damaged sewer pipe. We persuaded the vicar to set up a roof restoration fund and to plan a series of fund raising events. With hope filling his heart, the vicar became a changed man.

Nine months later, Constable 'Peculiar' Clarke retired, left the police force and moved out of Bilbury. The Chief Constable decided that there was no need for him to be replaced.

P.C. Clarke took early retirement and purchased a delightful cottage and a small market garden of around seven acres in South Bugford, a tiny hamlet of no more than a dozen houses. There, in peaceful isolation, he and his wife grew cabbages and kept a small flock of llamas and alpacas. I gather that neither activity kept them in champagne and caviar (not even the Polish champagne sold by Peter Marshall) but they were fortunate in that a police pension, while not providing for luxury, is reliable in that it arrives every month, come rain or shine, and in a part of the country where prices are relatively low and expensive distractions fairly uncommon, the Clarkes were, I gather, extremely happy with their lot. I kept in touch with them, since South Bugford is so small that it does not have its own resident doctor and both Peculiar and his wife, Lucy remained on my list of patients. Indeed, I was rather flattered by the fact that Mr and Mrs Clarke came to see me before they bought their cottage and told me that they did not intend to move to South Bugford unless I was able to assure them that they could remain on my list. It was for them a big step for they had both lived in Bilbury all their lives. Before they took the plunge and bought the cottage in South Bugford, they had rented a terraced cottage on the Barnstaple road.

We had thought nothing much of it when Peculiar chose to hang up his handcuffs and truncheon and the Chief Constable decided that Bilbury would no longer have a resident policeman.

None of us thought of Bilbury as a suitable location for gangs of Train Robbers to hide out and plan their next heist. And we had little concern that outsiders would swoop on the village and systematically work their way through local properties. Our experience was that visitors usually got lost even in daylight and we were quietly confident that if burglars swooped on Bilbury after dark they would probably be found, two days later, wandering around the lanes, lost, bewildered and disorientated.

We knew that it would take at least half an hour for a police car to reach us from Barnstaple but we had, I suppose, grown rather complacent and we weren't in the slightest bit worried by this.

And then another batch of problems started.

These were different.

This time there were no thefts involved.

And my chums and I all found that we had become the lawbreakers.

Over the centuries, the British Parliament has continually added new laws to an already adequate stockpile. But they have put nowhere as much effort into getting rid of old and useless laws as they have put into drafting and enacting new and useless laws. As a result, Britain is packed to the courtroom ceiling with daft laws which have accumulated over the centuries and never been repealed.

It would, perhaps, have been a good idea if someone had introduced a law insisting that every time a new law was introduced, one of the old ones would have to be discarded. But law-makers like making laws and don't like unmaking them, and so Britons have been left with an almost endless conglomeration of bizarre and trivial legislation.

So, for example, there is a law which forbids women to eat chocolate on public transport and there is another which makes it perfectly legal to shoot a Welsh person with a longbow in the Cathedral Close of Hereford as long as you do the shooting on a Sunday.

It is illegal to fly a kite in London but perfectly legal to do it outside London. And it is illegal to clean your doormat in the street or to clean it after 8 o'clock in the morning. (It is, one assumes, a hanging offence to clean your doormat in the street and to do it after 8 o'clock in the morning.) It is illegal to be drunk or tiddly in charge of a horse or cow and it is illegal for a landlord to allow someone to get drunk in their pub. It is illegal to carry a plank along a pavement and illegal to 'handle salmon in suspicious circumstances' (though the law is woefully unhelpful about the nature of the circumstances which might be regarded as suspicious). It is Illegal to slide on ice or snow in the street (a law which must surely mean that virtually every child in the country is a criminal). And it is illegal to have a pigsty in front of your house though perfectly legal to have one around the back.

You get the idea.

By the 1970s, England had become awash with rules and regulations and with laws and statutes.

It is sometimes difficult to see where a rule ends and a law begins but since anything the Government defines as 'not being allowed' is usually punishable in some way I always find it safer to regard all rules and regulations as laws and to leave the semantics to those who live in ivory towers and only write about these things rather than having to live with them.

And if breaking a law is a crime, and the person doing the law breaking is a criminal, then Bilbury suddenly became a hotbed of criminal activity.

The crimes of which we were accused had two things in common.

First, they were all rather trivial.

Second, the criminals were all individuals who might reasonably be described as seemingly respectable members of the community.

I write from first-hand experience for I was one of the alleged criminals, though my crime, and my encounter with the very long arm of the law, comes a little later in this account.

The first strange thing that happened was that my father-in-law, Mr Kennet, received a visit from P.C. Gerald 'Squeaky' Dors, a constable sent by the police station in Barnstaple.

The constable, who was as embarrassed as he should have been by the nature of his errand, told Patsy's father that the station sergeant had received a report complaining that Mr Kennet had (and here the constable referred to his notebook so that he could read the charge as it had been given to him by the station sergeant) 'knowingly allowed nuts of several varieties to fall onto the road thereby endangering the lives of members of the public'.

After he had checked his diary to make sure that this wasn't an April Fool's Day joke, Mr Kennet asked who had made the complaint and exactly what nuts were involved and why their presence on the highway might be considered a menace to traffic.

'I'm afraid I am not at liberty to identify the identity of the complainant,' said P.C. Dors, using the jargon of his profession, (a jargon which means that policemen always 'give chase' when criminals flee, and never 'run after' them), 'but I gather that the nuts in question are predominantly of the hazelnut variety though according to the complainant there may also have been nuts of the walnut variety and nuts of the horse chestnut variety involved.'

Mr Kennet, who is as law-abiding a citizen as I have ever met, and a man whom I have seen run for a quarter of a mile to chase down a used sweet paper which had slipped from his hand, insisted on accompanying the constable to the lane in question so that the nature of the offence could more accurately be assessed.

And there they were.

The offending nuts, generously scattered on a road surface which was more weed than tarmacadam, were largely hazelnuts though in patches there were also walnuts and horse chestnuts to be seen.

'But the trees overhang the road,' explained Mr Kennet. 'How am I supposed to stop the nuts falling from the trees when they are ripe?'

Mr Kennet went on to explain that the entire field was protected by a Tree Protection Order and that the order had been imposed when the local council employee whose job was protecting trees, had decided that the field contained too many notable trees for him to mark them with individual Protection Orders.

'It is a criminal offence for me to cut down any of these trees,' said Mr Kennet. 'It is a criminal offence for me even to cut a branch off a protected tree.'

'Indeed it is, Mr Kennet, sir,' said the constable. 'I am cognisant of these circumstances and it would, as you say, be quite against the law for you to interfere with these protected trees. But unfortunately, sir, littering is also an offence and since the trees clearly belong to you and the nuts which they have dropped have fallen onto the public highway, there is no doubt that you are, technically at least, in breach of the law as it stands.'

At this point, Constable Dors, not a bad fellow and one of the best skittle players in North Devon, removed a large, red handkerchief from his trouser pocket and mopped his brow. He would have felt much more comfortable boxing ears or talking firmly to an individual who had been riding a bicycle without the appropriate illumination than he felt discussing the legal implications of fallen nuts.

'The tree protection officer wanted to protect the beech trees, the horse chestnut trees and the walnut tree,' explained Mr Kennet. 'But since there were so many trees involved, he thought it simpler to slap the protection order on the whole field. This means that even the hazel trees are now covered. I can't cut any of them any more than I cut any of the beech trees or the horse-chestnut trees or the walnut tree.'

'Exactly, Mr Kennet, sir,' said P.C. Dors.

'So what do you suggest I do?'

'I can't rightly offer you legalistic advice on that point,' admitted the constable. 'But there seems no doubt in my mind that the presence of the nuts on the highway must be considered an offence. Normally, it is not something we would bother about but since there has been a formal complaint made by a complainant it is out of our hands as you might say.'

'But the squirrels will move all the nuts and bury them,' pointed out Mr Kennet.

P.C. 'Squeaky' Dors agreed with him but said, with some sadness it has to be admitted, that this did not alter the fact that an offence had been committed and that there would have to be a trial and since there couldn't be a trial without a prisoner, well, Mr Kennet could probably see where this was going, couldn't he?

Indeed, Mr Kennet could.

And so the majesty of the law proceeded on its way as it is wont to do and in due course Mr Kennet was fined £5 and reprimanded by magistrates who probably wondered privately why the hell the police didn't spend their time on more worthwhile activities but who, in public at least, had little choice but to express their dismay that an English highway should have been besmirched in such a way by a man whom they all agreed was old enough to know better.

A junior reporter from the Barnstaple paper managed to get seven inches of copy from the story, though this was doubtless only to justify the work of the subeditor who was responsible for writing the paper's headline and who was probably quite pleased with the caption 'Police Go Nuts'.

An editorial, written by someone with a large amount of tongue and a small amount of cheek, suggested that Mr Kennet, and all other tree owners in the county, might now feel the need to hang nets underneath their trees in order to catch the falling nuts.

'Moreover,' wrote the editorialist, 'there will be much concern throughout the region during the next few weeks since several million leaves are likely to be falling onto roadways, pavements and other public areas without giving warning and with, apparently, no regard for the requirements of the law.'

Within less than a week of Mr Kennet's bizarre encounter with the local constabulary, it was the turn of Frank Parsons, the landlord of the Duck and Puddle, and as genial and kindly a fellow as you could hope to find were you to wander the length and breadth of the country in search of geniality and generosity.

Frank's crime was, so he was told by another police constable from the same station, was that he had allowed customers in his public house to sing rousing choruses of 'Happy Birthday' and verses of several other assorted songs during what was described by the authorities as 'a noisy evening on licensed premises where there was no licence for public entertainment'.

To say that Frank was shocked by this complaint would be like saying that Red Riding Hood was startled when her granny took off her bonnet.

Frank's astonishment was exacerbated by the fact that the Duck and Puddle has no neighbours close enough to have been disturbed by the singing. Moreover, all the customers who had been in the pub at the time had been singing lustily. So, wondered Frank and Gilly, who on earth had complained?

Once again, the authorities, in the person of the rather weary police constable from Barnstaple could offer no name. 'I'm afraid I can't divulge that information which is of a confidential nature,' said the police officer who had, like his colleagues, been well trained in the art of using 12 words when two would do.

Frank's crime was rather more serious than Mr Kennet's since Frank had a licence to lose.

However, the police wisely decided that since this was Frank's first known offence, and that a conviction in the magistrate's court would inevitably lead to his licence being investigated and possibly suspended, they would let him off with a warning.

The relief was tempered by the thought that whoever had complained once could easily complain a second time.

Moreover, it was quickly decided within the village that the complainant who had reported Frank was very probably the same complainant who had reported Mr Kennet's errant nuts.

And so identifying the complainant became a priority.

Before we could do this, however, things quickly became farcical and complaints fell upon the village like autumn leaves.

Someone complained that Olive Robinson, Thumper's aunt had a chimney which smoked occasionally, and the police were dispatched to warn her that failure to abate a smoky chimney is an offence. She was sternly warned that something needed to be done before the fire was lit again.

Thumper, who had a set of chimney cleaning brushes and who had already intended to sweep his aunt's chimney, was furious. He was extraordinarily fond of his aunt, a sweet and gentle lady, and he was enraged that someone would report her to the police.

Two householders were warned for lighting bonfires in their gardens and someone reported Sidney 'Skinny' Arbuckle for riding a bicycle after dark without a working front lamp. Skinny's response, that he ate a lot of carrots and consequently had excellent night vision, although regarded as imaginative and original, did not protect him from a stern talking to and an official warning.

On two separate occasions, Peter Marshall, the proprietor of the Bilbury village shop, found himself being quizzed by men and women representing various departments of the local council.

A man in a blue suit, who had six coloured pens clipped securely into one of those funny little pen holders fixed onto his breast pocket, announced that there had been a complaint about Peter's opening hours.

For as long as anyone can remember, Peter has had a sign above his shop door which promises that his emporium is 'Open all Hours'.

However, the man from the council reported that his colleagues had received a complaint that the shop was only open between 7.00 a.m. and 12.00 midnight.

Peter had protested that if a customer rang the doorbell at 3.00 a.m. he would open the shop, even if it were only to sell a parsnip or a packet of budgerigar seed. Amazingly, this is quite true.

In the end, the man from the council only went away when Peter changed the notice to read 'Open all Hours (Between midnight and 7.00 a.m. by appointment)'.

A woman in a grey trouser suit, who carried a clipboard and a plastic briefcase and was accompanied by a male assistant in the sort of white coat usually associated both with laboratory technicians and dentists advertising toothpaste on television, announced that the Trading Standards department had received a formal complaint that the weighing scales which Peter used to measure out produce he was selling were out-of-date and therefore likely to be inaccurate.

The woman and her assistant had brought with them a set of digital scales and they proceeded to test Peter's Victorian weighing scales (which relied on the items being purchased being placed in a metal bowl on one side of the scale, and metal weights being placed on a platform on the other side of the scale).

To everyone's astonishment, and to Peter's delight, the test showed that the Victorian scales were perfectly accurate.

Peter, who was about to celebrate by putting up a large sign announcing to the world that his scales had been tested, checked and approved 'by the appropriate authorities' was slightly startled when he was subsequently visited by another two representatives of the same council department,(who were, on this occasion, accompanied by three police officers), and served with a summons for selling produce in imperial weights rather than in the metric weights which the EU had ordered the United Kingdom to adopt.

Peter protested that it was the first he'd heard of any such law but the council officials were adamant and, in due course, the local newspaper reported that a Mr P Marshall of Bilbury had been ordered to pay a £10 fine for selling parsnips by the pound instead of the kilogram.

Peter was told that although his imperial scales were still in excellent working order, he had to purchase new scales measuring goods in metric units. Peter duly bought the scales but used them only when selling fruit and vegetables to strangers. When selling fruit and vegetables to locals, Peter continued to weigh and sell in imperial units.

And then it was my turn.

My offence, it turned out, was that I had allegedly attempted to chop down a fully grown beech tree without having first obtained permission from the council to remove said tree from our land.

The police, in the person of P.C. Dors, told me that the complainant had seen me up a ladder and that I had been observed attempting to cut through the trunk and fell the tree without obtaining the necessary authority.

'Is this the tree I am accused of trying to chop down?' I asked 'Squeaky' Dors who was, once more, the constable delegated to drive to Bilbury and to investigate the crime.

'I believe it is, doctor,' agreed the policeman, consulting a small map with which he had been supplied. The map, which seemed surprisingly accurate, contained details of Bilbury Grange and all the trees in the vicinity. The constable counted the number of trees in the lane, repeated the calculation, and then confirmed that the tree to which I was referring was the tree which I had allegedly attempted to remove.

'Would you like to take a look at the tree and see if you can find any damage?' I suggested.

'Squeaky' Dors examined the tree.

'I can see no sign of any damage to said arboreal item,' he admitted, at last. He took a notebook and a pencil from his tunic pocket. 'The trunk appears to be unharmed.' He licked the lead end of his pencil and wrote laboriously in his notebook. (Why, I wonder, are policemen the only people on the planet who feel it necessary to lick the business end of a pencil before using it?)

'Exactly,' I agreed. 'But you will be able to see that the ivy which was climbing the tree has been cut.'

I explained that the ivy which had climbed up the trunk of the beech tree had begun to cover the crown of the tree. I pointed out that when that happens the ivy can stop the tree from breathing and the weight of all the ivy can bring down weakened branches.

And so, with some reluctance, I told 'Squeaky', I had cut through the ivy.

I don't like cutting ivy because it provides food and home for an enormous number of insects. But there are times when surgery is necessary.

'Yes, doctor,' said the policeman. 'I can validate that there is evidence showing that the ivy has clearly been severed. I would surmise that the severing was, all things being equal and on the face of it, probably performed with a sharp implement of some kind. A knife perhaps? ' He licked the lead of his pencil again and made another note.

'Secateurs,' I said. 'And I think it is not illegal to remove ivy from a tree.'

'No, doctor, it is not at this time considered felonious to remove ivy from a plant of any kind, up to and including a plant of the arboreal family.'

'I cut through the ivy with a pair of secateurs,' I told him. 'It would, you will agree I am sure, be difficult to cut through a fully grown beech tree with a pair of secateurs.'

I would have produced the secateurs as evidence but sadly I had dropped them while completing the task of cutting through the ivy. And the makers of my secateurs had cleverly made their products in green. This ensured that if they were dropped then they were easily lost in the undergrowth. I always felt that they did this on purpose, in the same way that potato peelers were made in 'potato peeling brown' so that the peelers got thrown away with the peelings.

'It would indeed, doctor,' said the policeman. 'I wouldn't like to try it.' He put the pencil and the notebook back into his tunic pocket and then buttoned the pocket to make sure that the notebook remained secure.

And that was the end of my short lived career as a criminal. The case against me was dismissed for lack of any supporting evidence that I had attempted to chop down the tree.

There was, however, no escaping the fact that for me, as for Frank, this could have been a difficult business.

The General Medical Council, the body which regulates doctors working in Britain, does not take kindly to doctors being found guilty of criminal conduct – however minor or unrelated it may be to their professional responsibilities.

And, bizarre as it may sound, there is no doubt that if I had been found guilty of attempting to cut down a tree without permission, I would have been reported to the GMC and the consequences could have been dire.

I have it on good authority that neither logic nor good sense is a quality which is highly valued in the decorated halls of the medical profession's disciplinary body.

All had ended well on this occasion.

But there was no escaping the fact that, in the same way that the village had previously harboured a very petty thief, it was clear that we now had a petty sneak in Bilbury.

And the sneak was turning out to be far more trouble than the thief – and far more dangerous. Losing an old trowel with a wobbly handle isn't quite in the same category as losing your livelihood.

Understandably, and quite properly, the police were not going to tell us the identity of the sneak who was making our lives so difficult and so Frank, Patchy, Thumper, Peter and I decided that we had to do something about this particular problem ourselves.

'We must all hang together or, most assuredly, we shall all hang separately,' said Patchy, quoting Benjamin Franklin. Patchy could borrow an apposite quote as easily as he could 'borrow' a history for a desk or a double bed.

We decided to meet at Bilbury Grange one afternoon in order to discuss how best to expose the sneak.

'There's no point in meeting at the Duck and Puddle,' Patchy had pointed out. 'If the sneak is sitting there in the corner, or pops in to the pub for a pint, they'll overhear us. We need to discuss this in privacy.'

And so Patsy made three dozen sandwiches and two dozen large vegetable pasties and did some extra cake baking.

My friends all have what are usually known in polite circles as 'hearty appetites' and although Frank had been on a diet since he had his stroke, he still had an appetite which qualified him as a doughty and determined trencherman.

Patchy, Thumper, Peter and Frank always eat well at Bilbury Grange.

This is largely because Patsy is an excellent cook who also understands the need for quantity, but also because the three of them are so polite that they rarely, if ever, refuse an invitation to 'have another' and would all feel that they had offended the hostess if they left anything uneaten. The result is a competition between, on the one hand, my friends who are determined to eat everything that is available in order to prove that everything available was excellent and, on the other hand, Patsy who is eager to make sure that the comestibles are supplied in more than adequate quantities and who would, I suspect, only really be pleased if she could defeat the appetites of the devouring horde.

For the record, when I told her about the planned meeting, my wife made, in addition to the sandwiches and pasties previously mentioned, a fruit cake, a sponge cake filled with cream and homemade raspberry jam and a seed cake. She also baked four dozen rock cakes, four dozen butterfly cakes filled with cream and covered with little bits of chocolate, and four dozen almond macaroons (a particular favourite of Patchy's).

'There are going to be six of us!' I exclaimed, when I saw how much food she had prepared. 'You, me, Frank, Peter, Patchy and Thumper!'

'I know,' said Patsy, looking worried. 'Do you think I should have made more?'

I smiled and gave her a hug.

'The sneak is clearly someone in the village,' said Patchy, when our informal meeting began.

The very thought made us all deeply miserable. But what alternative explanation could there possibly be?

'And probably someone with an axe to grind,' said Thumper.

'It could just be someone with a nasty, vindictive streak,' said Peter. 'We need to stop them before they dob one of us in to the tax people.' He shuddered, visibly. Peter does not harbour great fondness for the tax authorities.

There was silence for a few moments as we contemplated this possibility; something that was, for Peter and Frank in particular, if not exactly a fate if not worse than death then a fate more daunting than walking ten miles without shoes on a stony road. Patchy was investigated by the tax authorities a couple of years ago, and the tax inspector was so confused by Patchy's accounts that he was reported to have been off work for six months. Thumper does not trouble the income tax authorities who do not seem to be aware of his existence.

The silence was broken only by the quiet munching of sandwiches and vegetable pasties. I can't think of anything much that would put my pals off their food. The cakes had yet to appear.

'So, what's the plan?' asked Frank, taking a temporary break from demolishing a six inch long pasty.

'We need to think of something that would excite our sneak,' said Thumper. 'And then perhaps give us a clue to his identity.'

'No,' said Patsy quickly. 'We need a number of 'somethings' that would excite the sneak. And we need to leak these 'somethings' to one suspect at a time.'

'What do you mean by 'somethings'?' asked Frank.

'A false accusation, a bit of gossip, a rumour – anything that our sneak can report to the authorities,' explained Patsy. 'So, for example, we could tell one suspect that Peter was selling mouldy parsnips and we could tell another that he was selling rotten turnips.'

'There's nothing wrong with my parsnips!' said Peter immediately. 'And I've never sold a rotten turnip in my life!' He paused and looked around the room. 'Not knowingly anyway,' he added.

Frank put the rest of his vegetable pasty into his mouth.

'Not deliberately anyway,' said Peter. 'Definitely not deliberately. I'm surprised at you Patsy – making accusations like that.'

'It wasn't an accusation!' said Patsy. 'It was merely an illustration of what we could do – just a suggestion. You would, of course, be able to show that you weren't selling mouldy parsnips or rotten turnips but the nature of the complaint would tell us the identity of the sneak. We could say that Patchy was selling fake Shakespearean beds or that my husband had been speeding on the road to Barnstaple.'

'Maybe we need to think up accusations that are a little less dramatic,' I said gently.

We all agreed that Patsy's idea was a good one though it was generally agreed that we'd tone things down a tad so that there was no talk of faulty parsnips, fake beds or speeding motor cars.

So over the next hour or so, we worked out a host of false rumours, tittle-tattle, gossip, scuttlebutt and bits of hearsay that we thought might trigger the Bilbury Snitch to continue their nasty sneaking – and invite the attention of the local constabulary without there being any risk of what Peter called 'consequences'.

And then, once the sandwiches and vegetable pasties were gone, we worked our way through Patsy's wonderful collection of cakes.

By the time we'd finished, and it was the hour for me to get ready to start the evening surgery, we were well pleased with our plans and we were confident that we'd soon identify and expose the Bilbury Snitch.

'I didn't prepare enough food,' said Patsy, when everyone had gone.

I looked at the plates on the two low tables in our drawing room. They were all empty. Only crumbs remained.

'Frank could hardly move when he left,' I pointed out. 'And the others were absolutely stuffed. They eat everything you make because they worry you'll be hurt if they don't.'

'I'll make more next time,' said Patsy firmly. 'Maybe I'll do a chocolate cake as well. And some of those coconut and cherry cakes that Thumper likes. I didn't have any cherries this time.'

'However much food you make, they'll eat it all,' I warned her.

'Oh no they won't!' said Patsy firmly. 'I'll get my mother to make a few cakes as well. Perhaps I can persuade her to bake a couple of her caraway seed cakes and a batch of her special rock cakes.'

'There will definitely be some of those left,' I promised.

Patsy's mother is an excellent cook but when she makes 'rock cakes' she has a tendency to take the first half of the name rather too seriously. I have seen three people break teeth on her rock cakes. And I don't think it is unfeeling of me to say that Mrs Kennet's caraway seed cakes, although undoubtedly made with love and a good deal of caraway seed, are what might reasonably be described as 'an acquired taste'.

I didn't mention any of this but, nevertheless, Patsy threw a cushion in my direction.

I ducked.

But I need not have bothered.

The cushion missed me by miles but missed Ben, asleep on a chair, by less than a foot.

Ben opened an eye, looked around to see what had happened, closed the eye again and went back to sleep.

And so we began what Patchy insisted on calling 'Operation Snitch Exposure'.

Thumper, Patchy, Frank, Peter and I spread silly rumours far and wide in the vain hope that someone would take one of them seriously and make a complaint to some authority or other.

But nothing happened.

Absolutely nothing happened.

We knew that the Bilbury Snitch was someone who either lived in the village or who visited Bilbury regularly.

At our meeting at Bilbury Grange we had, with great reluctance, compiled a short list of possible suspects.

It wasn't pleasant to think that someone we knew could be responsible, and that the Bilbury Snitch could be someone living in our midst, but there was no alternative explanation, and no other way to deal with what had become a very serious threat.

But none of our rumours triggered a call from the authorities.

We were close to despair, waiting to see who next in the village would be the victim.

In the end the snitch was uncovered by a serendipitous accident; a fortuitous happenstance. And all our clever scheming proved to be quite unnecessary.

It was Gilly Parsons, Frank's wife, who unmasked the snitch. And the snitch was not one of the suspects we had put on our list.

Gilly was walking from the kitchen to the bar when she happened to hear someone on the telephone.

'She was talking very quickly and she was whispering,' said Gilly. 'And that attracted my attention because I'd never heard her whisper before. It sounded very strangely conspiratorial.'

The snitch was, as you will have doubtless guessed but we did not, Arcadia Blanchardine, the newly hired barmaid.

Gilly overheard her telephoning the local police to report that the landlord of the Duck and Puddle public house was growing marijuana plants in his back garden.

It was nonsense, of course. There were no marijuana plants anywhere near the Duck and Puddle though there was a large amount of mint, which looks like cannabis to an uninitiated eye, near to the back door. Gilly has several varieties of mint growing in her herb garden.

But because the accusation was a serious one it had to be taken seriously and it meant another journey to Bilbury for Constable Dors.

This time, however, Frank and Gilly were forewarned, forearmed and ready for the visit.

Once Constable 'Squeaky' Dors had established that the garden was free of illegal plants, Frank and Gilly told him the identity of the caller who had made the false claim and Ms Blanchardine was formally warned for wasting police time.

'I don't like this place,' she told the Constable and the Parsons when she was confronted. 'The people are all so damned nice to one another.'

'But don't you think that it makes everyone happier if people are kind to one another?' said Frank.

'Kindness and happiness aren't all they're cracked up to be,' snapped Ms Blanchardine very sourly. 'There's more to life than being nice to people and having a good time. Besides, I like complaining about people. It's sort of my hobby. I think of it as a public service.'

Frank and Gilly then suggested that Ms Blanchardine might like to continue practising her hobby in some other part of the country. Frank took out his cheque book and gave her a month's salary in lieu of notice.

Ms Blanchardine was apparently quite surprised at being fired. 'You're letting me go just because of this?' she said.

'Yes,' said Gilly, through gritted teeth.

'Hrmph!' said Ms Blanchardine as she headed upstairs to pack. 'Rotten place anyway,' she was reportedly heard to mutter. 'There's not one man here that I'd choose to marry.'

The Duck and Puddle was once again without a barmaid.

But Bilbury was without its snitch.

There was some noisy celebrating in the Duck and Puddle that evening. We sang loudly and Frank stayed open thirty minutes after his official closing time.

The Psychiatrist Who Ran Away (Part 1: The Awakening)

I'd had a busy morning and the last patient of my extra-long morning surgery was a man in his fifties whom I was pretty sure I had never seen before. He certainly wasn't a local resident and I was pretty sure that he wasn't anyone who had been to see me in the past.

He was a spindle-shanks, he had a prognathous chin and he came into the surgery wearing a dark purple watch cap.

I'd seen several of those hats before and I knew where he'd bought it.

When he removed the hat, I could see that he was balding, but had a bushy and rather unkempt ring of hair remaining. He looked as though he hadn't shaved for a day or so. It didn't look like one of those skimpy, little beards that are sometimes fashionable among those who want to look wild and reckless without actually being wild or reckless, it simply looked as though he hadn't shaved. He was also wearing a pair of what are, I believe, called 'aviator shades'. He took these off and placed them in his breast pocket.

I don't know anything about fashion but even I find that it isn't difficult to differentiate between cheaply and shoddily made clothes and well-made and probably expensive clothes. Although I could tell that he was dressed in what had been quite expensive clothes, he somehow managed to look like a tramp. His tweed jacket had burn marks down the lapels on both sides and his tie was covered in a variety of food stains. A quick glance enabled me to identify egg yolk and tomato ketchup. The buttons of his matching waistcoat had been pushed through the wrong buttonholes, giving him a uniquely lop-sided sort of look. And when he'd walked into the consulting room, I couldn't help noticing that the trousers of his tweed suit showed signs of his having knelt in something oily.

The funny thing is that despite all this, he still managed to look as though he was accustomed to having a certain amount of authority over his life. It wasn't difficult to guess that he had a job which gave him a certain amount of power.

I said good morning and invited him to sit down.

He sighed, looked around the room, nodded to me, moved the chair reserved for patients, for no apparent reason that I could discern other than that he wanted to establish some degree of control over his surroundings, and sat down.

I didn't have the faintest idea what was wrong with him but I got the distinct feeling that he hadn't come in to see me because he had a twinge in his knee or a slightly annoying tickle in his throat.

'My name is Eckersley, Pelham Ronald Eckersley,' he said. 'I am 56-years-old, I am a consultant psychiatrist and I have run away.'

I was rather startled by this introduction and I'm afraid I just rather stared at him for a moment. It was, of course, the admission that he had run away that had rather surprised me.

'Where have you run from?' I asked.

'London. I have a consultancy at one of those mildly snotty teaching hospitals and a private practice in an extraordinarily snotty part of Harley Street,' he said. 'I've been sat in your waiting room for several hours, by choice I would add. I arrived early but, realising that my requirements would probably need a good chunk of your time, I instructed your receptionist to allow all your other customers to take their turn ahead of me.'

I looked at him. I had seen runaways before but they had invariably been under the age of twenty. I had never before seen a grown man who'd run away. I had certainly never before seen a psychiatrist who had run away.

'I have committed no crime,' he went on. 'And I have no close family or, indeed, close friends and so there was no one to lie awake last night wondering whether I was safe.'

'But, it is presumably reasonable to assume that people will have noticed that you've disappeared, and that at least one of them will report your disappearance to the police.'

'Oh, yes, I expect they will. But they won't report my disappearance because they care about me or are concerned for me. If there is a search, it will be because my colleagues feel that my absence could embarrass them and adversely affect their plans to restructure the hospital's administration and management. We are in the throes of reorganising ourselves. My colleagues reorganise

112

things every few years. I'm on the restructuring committee. I can't imagine why or how it happened but I'm the chairman of the committee. The rest of the buffoons on the committee are the sort of idiots who believe in rules. Believe me, the place where I work is packed to the ceiling with bifarious pettifoggers. There are more humbugs working there than you'd find in an old-fashioned sweet shop.'

'Bifarious pettifoggers?'

'Laughably crooked shysters.'

'Thank you.'

'Have you ever noticed that people who are over committed to regulations spend their whole lives teetering on the very brink of absurdity? In practical terms, my position means I am the restructuring committee. I can choose the builders we appoint and the competitors for the work would, no doubt, be happy to reward me handsomely. I have already had to return several generous bribes. They didn't call them bribes, of course, but that was what they were. One major building company wanted to me give me a five year contract as their Mental Health Advisor. I would, of course, have been given an absurdly generous honorarium and no responsibilities whatsoever.'

'Is that why you've run away? The stress of the committee work?'

'Good heavens, no! There's an awful lot of cobblers talked about stress these days. Many of the patients I saw in my practice were locked in fear of torment by their own paranoia. They had no idea about the real nature of stress. There was an Australian cricketer called Keith Miller who was the best all-rounder Australia ever had. In the 1950s, after a pretty gruelling Test Match, he was asked at a press conference whether he had found the day stressful. Miller, who flew planes for the Royal Australian Air Force during the Second World War, laughed at the suggestion. 'Stress?' he said. 'I was playing cricket! Stress is when you're flying over Germany with a Messerschmitt up your arse.''

I smiled. I remembered the quote.

'Myself, I prefer to live in a comfortable state of ataraxia,' continued Dr Eckersley. 'The truth is that I don't give a damn how they restructure the hospital. In my not unlimited experience, these reorganisations take place every few years at all similarly sized institutions. They are usually a result of one faction's attempt to gain power over existing managers or over another faction. I have no idea how or why I became chairman. I suspect it was probably because too many other people wanted the job and I was lumbered with it because I was the only person who didn't want it.' He pulled a pipe out of his pocket, examined it, thought about it, and then put it away. 'The big problem these days is that it is impossible to tell the good guys from the bad guys. Indeed, in public life there don't seem to be any good guys any more. I can't name one politician alive today whom I respect and whom I regard as entirely, or even mostly, decent and honourable. I don't mind betting that you can't either. Can you name one public figure you regard as a leader and whom you would follow into war, comfortable in the knowledge that you were doing the right thing?'

I didn't say anything, partly because it seemed clear that the question was rhetorical but also because I couldn't think of anything to say. The conversation seemed to be continuing quite well without any input from me.

'Difficult, eh?'

'Difficult,' I agreed. 'But you didn't run away because of the lack of honour among modern politicians. Why did you run away?'

'Excellent question, doctor! I thought you'd get round to asking me that. I ran away because I am fed up with my life. Or should it be 'fed up of my life?' I really don't care. I realised that my life was utterly pointless and without joy. There I was, enjoying the present and still thinking that I was the future and then suddenly I woke up and found that I was the past. And none of it was any fun!'

'Ah!' I managed to squeeze into the conversation. I also managed a nod.

'I have been meandering through life for a long time,' continued Dr Eckersley, 'and yesterday evening I suddenly realised, at long last, that if you wait for the right time and the right place to make a change then whatever you are planning or hoping for will never happen because the right time and place will never coincide. And so I seized the moment and fled. Carpe diem, as our old friend Horace used to say. Memento mori as someone else said.'

There was a superficial brashness about him but it wasn't difficult to see that underneath the brashness he was very glum.

'But what were you fleeing from?' I asked. I seemed to be asking the same question time and time again without getting anything resembling an answer.

'I was running away from my life. I've had enough of it. I am, to put in popular parlance, fed up to the back teeth.'

'In what way are you fed up?'

'If you knew my life then you would not be foolish enough to ask that question. But you don't know my life, do you?'

'No,' I agreed.

'All day long people come to me with their problems,' he complained. 'I know you could say that your job is the same but it isn't. You sit here in your rather wonderfully old-fashioned consulting room and you see a parade of real people with real problems. You know most of the people you see because you live amongst them. Sometimes you can help them. You stitch them up, or you give them some antibiotics or you give them a diet sheet or an exercise programme to follow. You can make a difference. I envy you for that.'

'But you see patients with psychiatric problems,' I pointed out. 'You see people with real mental health problems – depression, anxiety and so on. You can help them get better. Doesn't that make you feel good?'

'Oh no, no, no, no!' said Dr Eckersley emphatically. 'I don't have a normal practice. I have, for some reason, become known as a doctor who deals with fashionable neuroses. Celebrities of all kinds come to see me in their droves. Actors, actresses, film producers, film directors, television personalities, politicians – they all stumble through my door, weighed down by self-concern. Most of them seemed to live in an uncomfortable hinterland which lies between their memories, which are full of fear and inevitably decorated with regrets and recriminations, and an equally forbidding mixture of fearful anticipations. They rarely seemed to live in the present. And while they generously shared with me their eternally maudlin and self-obsessed thoughts, their chauffeur driven limousines clogged the hospital car park or were double parked outside my rooms in Harley Street.'

'The wonder of my job was that I was not only allowed to ask these celebrities all sorts of impertinent questions but it was also tacitly understood by all parties, even the politicians, that I was entitled to honest answers. If a journalist from *The Times* or *The New York Times* had dared even to imagine asking questions of such impertinence, he would have been blackballed by Hollywood for a lifetime and a half without the option.'

'But couldn't you see some patients with real problems?' I asked.

'Not a chance. The hospital administrators loved having all these celebrities in the hospital. They were convinced that some of the glamour rubbed off on the institution and, indeed, on them. And since I was the jam pot which attracted these wretched people, I was regarded as unique and irreplaceable. I was constantly pressured to see more and more celebrities. The tabloid newspapers described me as 'The Shrink to the Stars'. When the broadsheets mentioned my name in connection with one of my celebrity patients, they invariably described me as 'the world renowned celebrity psychiatrist'. As a result, I myself became a little bit famous. And within the upper reaches of my own speciality, I was renowned for inventing a disorder which I described as 'justifiable rational paranoia'. No psychiatrist is worth his salt until he has invented a new disease. And my disease is 'justifiable rational paranoia'.'

'I'm sorry to have to ask,' I said hesitantly, 'but what exactly is 'justifiable rational paranoia'?'

'It is a condition resembling paranoia but based on genuine and reasonably based fears and suspicions,' said Dr Eckersley. 'All my celebrity patients suffered from it. The nub of it is the concept that it isn't clinical paranoia if the bastards really are out to get you. I saw a lot of politicians who suffered from it. And I saw company chairmen and chief executives with it. They had to pay more to see me because they weren't famous and did not bring kudos to the hospital.'

'It all sounds very...' I began, and then realised that I wasn't sure what I had intended to say.

'That sums it up very accurately,' said Dr Eckersley very quickly. 'It is very something.'

'Important? Satisfying?'

'Sadly, it is neither of those. It is lucrative, yes. No one ever paid their own bills, of course, so I put a nought on the end of what would be absurd. Film studios paid the bills for the celebrities. Companies paid for the executives. And taxpayers paid the bills for the politicians. But the work was neither important nor satisfying. Nor, I fear, would I describe my work with medical students as important or satisfying. Did I mention that I am an Emeritus Professor of Clinical Psychiatry at the teaching hospital next door to the godforsaken place where I work?'

'No,' I said. 'I don't think you did.'

'Well, I am. Maybe I live too many lives. Do you remember that Oscar Wilde quote?'

"For he who lives more lives than one, more deaths than one must die.' Do you mean that one?'

'That's the one. Maybe I'm dying bit by bit. I hate my work as a psychiatrist. And I have grown to hate the whole educational process.'

He stopped for a minute and just stared at me. It was rather disconcerting. 'How long did your education last?'

I frowned and thought. 'About twenty years, from start to finish.'

'A quarter of a decent lifetime?'

'I suppose so.'

'And how much of the stuff you learned has been of any use to you?'

I laughed. I knew what he meant. I remember the years I spent being educated with mixed feelings.

'You think that the entire educational process was pretty much a waste of time, money and energy, don't you?'

'Sometimes, I do.'

'What were the two most important things you learned?'

'How to read and how to write,' I said, without hesitation.

'Exactly, and once you had managed to learn how to read and write you were force fed information which you were made to digest and then regurgitate. Much of that information was of limited or negligible value. You will have spent much of your two decades of formal education learning and repeating information which has been of absolutely no value to you in your life. The modern educational process exists to filter and grade students in order to decide whether or not they are suitable to be promoted to the next level of the process. The final result is a certificate which is supposed to provide the owner with a ticket into the world of well-paid employment. But the whole irrelevant nonsense could be replaced with a single well devised intelligence and personality test and our education could be over by the age of six at the latest. We could then begin an apprenticeship for our chosen career.'

117

'But at medical school I learned a great deal.'

'Did you? Did you really? I'm willing to bet that you have already forgotten most of the stuff you were forced to learn at medical school. You were, were you not, taught the names of every bone, nerve, artery and vein in the human body?'

'Yes, it was an important part of the syllabus.'

'Can you remember all that stuff now?'

I thought for a moment. 'No, I don't suppose I can. No, I definitely can't.'

'And you learned reams of stuff about physiology and chemistry and masses of information about pharmacology that was out of date before you qualified.'

I nodded.

'Most of this stuff we learn is taught to us simply so that we can be made to jump through hoops. We are taught stuff, we are tested to make sure we've learned what we've been taught and then we're allowed to forget it all. I doubt if five per cent of the stuff you were taught at medical school was of any practical value. It was a long memory test; an obstacle course for the brain. Am I not right?'

I was feeling rather uncomfortable. 'I think you probably are,' I agreed.

I remembered that the stress of learning all the information we were fed was debilitating. By the end of my second year at medical school, around a third of my student colleagues were receiving treatment from psychiatrists. Nervous breakdowns and suicides were common. I didn't mention this.

'The two important attributes for a doctor are a more than average dollop of common sense and a questing mind,' said Dr Eckersley. 'Students are taught to believe what they are told. This is wrong. They should be taught to question everything they are told. They should be taught to develop their common sense.'

'I don't imagine that way of thinking goes down too well with the rest of the faculty at the university.'

Dr Eckersley laughed and slapped his hand on my desk. 'No, no, it doesn't, doctor. Indeed it doesn't. Worse still, modern education has become wedded to technology. I am encouraged to use visual aids and computers in my teaching. If I don't make use of their latest gadgets, some nerdy fellow comes round to tell me off. Did they have computers when you were a toddler?'

118

'My education took place in a low technology era,' I told him. 'At my infant school I wrote on a slate with a slate pencil. I had a damp cloth constantly at the ready so that I could, litcrally, wipe my slate clean. At grammar school, we had real inkwells filled with real ink. We used the ink and blotting paper to make rubber band pellets and we wrote with wooden pens with interchangeable nibs which seemed to start life already crossed. The technological high point of my education was reached when I was in the sixth form and one of our teachers started writing on the blackboard with yellow chalk.'

Dr Eckersley beamed. 'And look at you!' he said. He grinned broadly. 'You worked out fine, didn't you?'

'I'm not sure about that,' I said, smiling back at him. 'There are a few people who would probably disagree with you.'

'Oh, I would hope so! And if so then that'll be because you don't fit into one of those nice, little cookie cutter shapes they like people to fit into these days.'

'Perhaps,' I agreed, though I suspected that he was right. I still didn't seem to be getting anywhere. 'But what can I do to help you?' I asked.

'I don't know,' he said. 'Probably bugger all. Probably just listen to me for a while. That's maybe all I need.' Dr Eckersley paused and took a deep breath. 'Do you know, I have suddenly realised that it irks me that no one ever asks me how I feel. No one cares about me. On Mondays to Fridays, I spend eight hours a day listening to enormously rich people whingeing about their lives when ninety nine per cent of the time they've got bugger all to complain about it. Some of them want a bottle of happiness pills, but I haven't got any magic happiness pills. Most of them have absolutely bugger all wrong with them apart from oversized egos.' He sighed wearily. 'They wouldn't last five minutes if they tried to live my life.' He looked at me. 'They probably wouldn't last five minutes if they tried to live your life, either.'

'My life is fine, thank you. What's so bad about your life?'

'Everything you can think of. My wife left me for a man who runs a carpet shop. He is a franion and a deipnosophist, he drives an Aston Martin, is vice-captain of his golf club and pays £90 once a fortnight to have his hair crimped and dyed.'

'What's a franion and a deipnosophist?' I asked.

'Don't you speak English?'

119

'I thought I did.'

'A franion is a licentious person and a deipnosophist is someone who is skilled at making dinner party conversation.'

'Right,' I said.

I made a mental note of the two words, hoping that I could perhaps squeeze them into a conversation of my own. I was beginning to think that if I spent much more time with Dr Eckersley, I'd need to buy myself a bigger dictionary.

'My daughter lives in America,' continued the runaway psychiatrist. 'She works for a drug company and when I heard from her last, she'd just helped invent a new drug that does nothing but is much admired because it has no side effects. They're apparently very excited about it because they can create all sorts of needs for it. I haven't heard from her for months, though I have no doubt that I will hear from her when she needs more money. She's paid well but, like my ex-wife, seems to regard money as something that should be unloaded as soon as possible. My son Edgar does something with computers. He's also in America, living in somewhere called Silicon Valley wherever that is. I told him that it sounds like a stripper's cleavage but he has no sense of humour. He always needs money too. He's got a job working for a company run by two fellows who are both called Steve. I think he said something about them selling apples. He says they're going to make a fortune and he's got a chance to get in on the ground floor. What a silly bugger. He wants me to put some money into the company. He says I'll get rich beyond my wildest dreams if I buy £1,000 worth of shares. How can you make a fortune out of apples? I know a cove in the country who inherited a fruit farm. He tells me it's a constant struggle to break even. I keep telling Edgar to get a proper job. He should sell carpets. That seems to me to be where the money is. I haven't got any money. My wife and my children have been spending more than I've been earning for decades. All I've got to show for 30 years of slavery is an overpriced house. I think I may own my car and the suit I'm wearing. And I've got rotten health. I've suffered from gastritis for years but now I've acquired gout and gall stones and I seem to be working my way through the 'G's' in the medical dictionary. Any minute now I expect to find that I've got a goitre and German measles. What else is there that begins with G?'

'Glomerulonephritis?' I suggested.

120

'Oh splendid, I'll have some of that,' said Dr Eckersley gloomily. 'I've probably got it already. I've got everything else beginning with 'G'. I'll probably get gangrene next. And gastroenteritis and gynaecomastia. And Gaucher's disease. Have you heard of that one?'

'Vaguely,' I said. 'I'd have to look it up.'

'Me too. Not my line of country. And then there's gingivitis and glossitis. And Gilbert's disease and Gilchrist's disease. Why do all these bloody people want diseases named after them? Goldenhar's syndrome. What the hell is that? I'm buggered if I can remember. Guillain-Barre syndrome. Was that two people or one bloke called Guillain-Barre? And why do some of them have a disease named after them and some have a syndrome? If there's an Eckersley's something, I'd want it to be a syndrome rather than just a mouldy old disease.'

'You seem depressed,' I said.

'Do I? Is that your diagnosis, doctor?'

'Maybe. You're the expert.' Actually, he seemed to have remarkable mood swings. I wondered if he was suffering from manic depression.

He sat for quite a while, staring at his knees, and then he once again took his pipe out of his left hand jacket pocket and a leather pouch out of his right hand jacket pocket. 'Do you mind?' he asked.

'Well,' I began, 'I'm afraid…'

'Of course you do. Everyone does. My wife would never let me smoke in the house.' He put the tobacco pouch away but kept hold of the pipe. He paused and thought for a moment. 'Mind you, she's gone now, hasn't she? Good riddance. I can go home smoke in bed if I like.' He thought for a moment. 'But I don't want to go home,' he added sadly.

'You can smoke in here,' I said suddenly, changing my mind. I felt sorry for him though I wondered how I would get rid of the smell of tobacco afterwards.

'May I? Really?' He seemed childishly delighted by this.

I nodded.

'Do you know, they even want to stop me smoking in the hospital? Some snotty little bastard administrators came waltzing into my consulting room and demanded that I put out my pipe. One of them was called Entwhistle and I think the other was called something else. They said someone had complained about the smell. Why do people have to complain about everything? It's not as if I was smoking in an operating theatre. I would never do that. Not with all those explosive gases around.' As he spoke, he packed the bowl of his pipe with tobacco from his pouch. 'I sometimes think that half the people who give up smoking end up taking tranquillisers to calm them down, and although it's heresy to say so, I'm not entirely sure that the cigarettes weren't doing them less harm than the drugs we give them. It wasn't a patient who complained about my smoking. I'm pretty sure about that. I think it was Doctor Bloody Phillips. He's a righteous do-gooder who strongly objects to anyone enjoying themselves. He complained about one of the nurses – said her skirt was too short and she was wearing seamed stockings. Apparently, they have rules about things like that. At Christmas, he insisted that we all drank fruit punch without any alcohol in case we upset any Muslims in attendance. The only Muslim working at the hospital is an anaesthetist and he drinks like a fish.'

'How long do you think you have been feeling depressed?'

'How long is a piece of string?'

'But you would agree that you seem depressed?'

'I'm a bit under the weather, maybe. But to be honest with you I would say I was confused and angry rather than depressed. Wouldn't you agree? It's a tricky diagnosis – depression. My problem is that I have no life. Oh yes, of course, I have a life. I have a job. I am paid intolerably well. I have a car with six galvanised iron buckets in the boot. But I don't feel that I am living my life. I'm not in control. I'm playing a part. I'm an actor playing this fellow Eckersley but as the actor I have no other life; no life of my own. I've given myself over completely to this creature. Does any of this make sense?'

'It does,' I said. 'Have you any history of depression or mental illness?'

'I'm a bloody psychiatrist! Have you ever known a sane psychiatrist?'

I smiled. I had to admit I couldn't think of one. I once knew a GP who worked as a part time psychiatrist. He went a bit potty and put a big bowl of drugs on his waiting room table. He then put a notice by it saying 'Help Yourself' and went out to play golf. Another psychiatrist I knew went very potty and refused to prescribe any drugs that didn't come in the form of red tablets or capsules. No one noticed anything odd about his prescribing habits for three months and then the hospital pharmacist noticed that he'd prescribed copious quantities of red iron tablets for 42 patients in a row. The psychiatrist's legal representative claimed that his client had prescribed the iron tablets because he'd believed his patients to be suffering from anaemia. This argument rather fell apart when it was shown that the doctor had done no blood tests on the patients he had diagnosed as suffering from anaemia. In mitigation, the psychiatrist claimed that the iron tablets he had prescribed had probably done less harm than the tranquillisers and antidepressants which any other psychiatrist might have prescribed. A third psychiatrist, who was a good friend of mine, once invited me to lunch at a smart hotel where he was staying. As we studied the menu, he was called to the telephone. He never came back to the table and I was left with a bill which pushed my credit card into dangerous territory. Four months later, the doctor who had disappeared suddenly remembered our luncheon and telephoned me from Dubai to apologise. I told him that if he hadn't been a psychiatrist, he would have probably been prescribed happy tablets and put into some sort of institution. He agreed with me.

'What made you come into my surgery today?' I asked Dr Eckersley.

'You're the only damned doctor in the village,' he replied with disarming honesty.

'That's true,' I agreed, though his blunt response didn't answer the question. 'But what I really meant to ask was, why did you come to see me? What did you want me to do for you?'

'Dunno, really. Funny you should ask that. I suppose I wanted someone to talk to – just to help get things straight in my own mind. That chap at the shop was all right for a while, though more of a talker than a listener, but he kept selling me things. I left him and his shop when he tried to sell me half a hundred weight of beetroot. What was I going to do with half a hundred weight of beetroot? The chap said they'd keep and I could use them in salads, but I told him that I doubted if I could eat enough salads to use up half a hundred weight of beetroot before they went off. He said I could pickle them and he could sell me six gallons of vinegar and two dozen pickling jars which would doubtless do the job very nicely. I think it was when he offered me the vinegar that I realised I had to get away.

Still, it was nice of him to offer them to me. He said that he was able to let me have them at half the normal retail price because I was such a valued customer. I didn't expect you to sort my life out and I don't want pills. That's the last thing I want. I wouldn't take anything so it would be a waste of time prescribing pills for me. The rubbish doctors prescribe for patients who are mentally ill is astonishing. You need to be bloody fit and healthy to survive the stuff that's handed out these days.' He stopped for a moment and then added: 'You should perhaps get down to that shop and stock up on some of that beetroot while it's still on offer.'

'Are you staying in the village?'

'No.' He pulled out a little silver tool and packed down the tobacco in the bowl of his pipe. 'Well not yet. I might though if I can find a room somewhere. Seems a pretty out of the way spot. Do you get much through traffic?'

'No, not really.'

'Just people like me who are lost?'

I laughed. 'How did you come to be here so early this morning? You said you'd been in the waiting room for a couple of hours.'

'I ran away last night and drove west. Isn't that what they used to say in America? 'Go west young man!'?'

'I think so,' I smiled. 'What time did you leave London?'

'Dunno. About midnight I think. I had a pizza and half a bottle of red wine in an Italian café near my house and then just got into the car and set off.' He finished packing down his tobacco and put away the silver tool.

'You didn't bother to pack anything?

'I didn't even have a toothbrush until the chap at your village shop sold me a few.'

'A few?'

'He only had them in packs of twelve. He said he wasn't allowed to split up the packs. Something to do with the Common Market.'

'And then, after the pizza, you just drove west?'

'Yes. I went to Bournemouth but it seemed shut so I didn't stop there for very long.'

'What time did you get to Bournemouth?'

'About three I suppose. It was all dark. Everyone seemed to be asleep. I found an all-night petrol station and bought some petrol and a cheese sandwich. I think it was supposed to be cheese. It smelt of

124

petrol and tasted of chipboard. Not that I've ever eaten chipboard. But it tasted as I suspect chipboard might taste. And then I decided to go to Lynmouth. I went there once when I was a boy. I remember I was happy there. It was a nice little village with a river and a beach.' He took out a box of matches. 'I expect it's changed a lot,' he added.

'Lynmouth hasn't changed at all,' I told him. 'And I doubt if it ever will. But Bilbury is quite a few miles away from Lynmouth. Did you lose your way or change your mind about Lynmouth?'

'What's Bilbury?'

'The name of the village where you are now.'

'Oh. Is it? I suppose I got lost. The lanes around here all look the same and there aren't many signposts. I parked in a gateway and slept in the car for a while. Then I woke up with backache and stopped at the little shop and bought a pie and a box of aspirin. Actually, I only wanted a pie, some aspirin and a cup of tea but the man in the shop managed to sell me a box of six pies and some other stuff. He hadn't got any tea but he sold me some tins of soup though I didn't have anything to heat them up with. I've never much liked cock-a-leekie soup but it was all he had. I must say he seemed a very good salesman. I do remember him telling me that the buckets were a once-in-a-lifetime bargain.'

'You bought a bucket?'

'Yes. No. Well, actually, I bought six buckets. All galvanised, whatever that means. Doesn't it mean they have zinc on them? To stop them going rusty I suppose. I have no idea what I'm going to do with six galvanised iron buckets. Would you like them? I can let you have them at a very reasonable price. They come with a five year guarantee. Nothing written down you understand but I expect it's a transferable guarantee. He seemed the sort of bloke you could trust with your life.'

'I think we're OK for buckets, thank you. And Mr Marshall directed you here?'

'Who's Mr Marshall?'

'He's the man who runs the local shop. His name is Peter Marshall.' I was still smiling inside at Dr Eckersley's description of Peter as 'the sort of bloke you could trust with your life'. I couldn't wait to tell Thumper, Patchy and Frank.

'Ah, you know him? Yes, I suppose you would; you both being local. He's a wonderful fellow that Marshall. He sold me the hat.' He pointed to the watch cap which he'd placed on my desk. 'Marvellous hats those are, you know. You should get yourself one. They're waterproof, windproof and everything else proof. If you stood underneath a nuclear bomb, the only thing left would be the hat. Mr Marshall told me that they're guaranteed not to blow off your head even in a hurricane. And he said they float if they land in water. I've always been keen on hats. When I was a boy, the other kids spent their pocket money on marbles, comics and sweets but I used to save my coins and then buy hats whenever I could afford them. By the age of 10, I had a fine collection of headgear: a bowler, a trilby, a flat cap or two, a sombrero, a ten gallon cowboy hat which was my pride and joy, a top hat which I found in a junk shop, a fedora and a deerstalker with flaps. I used to keep them all under my bed and try them on in my bedroom. I never wore them when I went out, of course.' He paused, apparently slightly embarrassed at how much he had told me about himself. He coughed and then continued. 'But I have to admit that these are pretty damned special, don't you think? You really ought to buy yourself one. One thing that has puzzled me though – if they never blow off, how would one ever land in water and float? I suppose if you were at a regatta and you took off your hat and threw it in the air while cheering, the thing might land in the water.'

'I've got one,' I told him. 'Everyone I know has got one of those hats.'

We'd all bought our watch caps from Peter when he'd brought them into the Duck and Puddle. I vividly remembered the day we'd bought our hats. In an attempt to prove that his headgear helped the body retain heat, Peter had stood outside wearing little else but one of his hats. When he'd come back into the pub he'd been blue with cold and shivering.

'Mr Marshall told me that they're called Chapeau Watch Caps and that they are thermally insulated,' continued Dr Eckersley. 'As far as I can remember 'chapeau' is French for hat but I suppose that's probably the name of the manufacturer, eh? French, I assume. Or they might as well call them Hat Watch Caps which would be a pretty damned stupid name. I can't stand the French – they're

humourless and nauseatingly self-important. Disorganised too –
most of them couldn't organise a piss up in a vineyard.'

I didn't tell Dr Eckersley but Peter had bought the hats from a
wholesaler who had, in turn, purchased the entire stock from a
Canadian manufacturer who had gone bankrupt. It was, I assumed,
the Canadian connection which explained the French name.

'Apparently these hats are wind proof and rain proof and they
absorb the sun's rays, thereby protecting the head in all weathers,'
said Dr Eckersley still enthusing about his new hat. 'They retain
more heat than any other hat ever made. I really think everyone
should have one. Apparently, they automatically adjust to fit the size
of the head of the wearer. I suppose it's something special to do with
the material. Mr Marshall said they were very reasonably priced too.
I bought three though, I'm not sure why since I've only got one head
and he said they are guaranteed never to wear out.'

'Are you taking any medication?' I asked him, trying to drag the
conversation away from hats.

'Never take anything,' he said. 'If I took pills I'd have to stop
drinking alcohol and I don't want to do that. Besides the pills they
make for treating loonies are all complete rubbish.'

'How much do you drink?' I asked.

'Alcohol, you mean?'

'Yes, alcohol.'

'I drink. Probably more than I should. I think I'd become an
inveterate worrier if I didn't drink occasionally. I wasn't always a
worrier but I think I could become one.'

'What would you worry about?'

'Everything. I would worry about everything. I would worry
about my patients. Bloody silly thing to do. None of them worries
about me. I pretend that I don't worry but I do. I try to give the
impression of being a 'devil take me to the hindmost' sort of rogue.
But I'm not. I'm a sham; an actor playing myself. I want to be a
rogue but I'm not.'

'So how much do you drink?'

'Ah, you're being a doctor again!'

'Yes. How much do you drink?'

'Not a lot. I never drink until the sun's over the yardarm.'

'When is that? I've never really understood what it means. It
sounds nautical.'

'It's about 11 a.m. in northern latitudes, so I'm told. That's the time when the sun rises up above the upper mast spars of a sailing ship floating around in the North Atlantic.' He struck a match and lit his pipe. It took him a couple of minutes to get it going. 'Mind you, I've never been on a sailing ship so it's all a bit moot, wouldn't you say?' Thick smoke curled from the bowl of his pipe. To my surprise, it smelt rather sweet and not at all unpleasant.

'I bought some dog food too,' he said suddenly. 'And a basket of radishes. And tins of custard. About 36 tins of the stuff, I think.

'From Peter Marshall?'

'It's the only shop round here. So it says on a notice outside. I don't think he'd lie about that, do you?'

'No. It is the only shop in the village. Do you have a dog?'

'No, not actually, no I don't have a dog per se. No, I don't have a dog. But you never know. I might get one. Or one might attach itself to me. Or I might find a hungry stray. Or if the economy falters we might all find ourselves bartering with dog food instead of money.'

'How much dog food did you buy?'

'I think there were 24 tins in a crate. Your Mr Marshall wanted me to take two crates but I was running a bit short on cash and he said he preferred cash. He said cash was better for the economy in some way. I didn't understand his argument but he seemed convinced by it and I didn't like to argue with him.'

'So, how much alcohol do you drink?'

'I have a glass of beer with my lunch in the pub – maybe two. To be honest, I need them to get me through the afternoon. And then in the evenings I drink martinis but I like them without any damned vermouth in them. And I certainly don't have damned fruit and vegetables floating on the top.' He stopped for a moment and then added, as though in explanation: 'No lemon and no olives.'

'How many very dry martinis do you drink in an evening?'

'Oh, no more than two or three,' said Dr Eckersley. 'But I like them in a tumbler not one of those fancy little lady's glasses.' He squinted at me. 'I wouldn't mind a drink now if you have one. A glass of beer would be nice if you're having one yourself.'

'I haven't got any alcohol with me,' I said. 'Seriously, how long have you been depressed?'

'Have we decided that I'm depressed? I must have missed that part of the conversation.'

128

'Well you do seem rather low.'

'Would you say so? I'd describe myself as euphoric to be honest. But then you don't know me from Adam so it's probably tricky for you to make a judgement. I think if I were making a diagnosis I'd probably be inclined to go for something along the lines of what I've always thought of as manic depression but which some of my younger colleagues now insist on calling it bipolar disorder.'

Dr Eckersley puffed at his pipe and thought for a while. 'But if we make the assumption that I am depressed then I'd say I've been that way for about 30 years,' he replied at last. 'I was happy enough in my 20s when I was working as a registrar in general medicine. But then I did an idiotic thing and decided to specialise in psychiatry.'

'And you've been depressed since then?' I asked, incredulously.

'I would say so,' he said firmly. He thought for a moment. 'I would definitely say so. It was my wife's idea, don't you know. She used to read the British Medical Journal – not the juicy bits but the job adverts at the back. She noticed that there were very few posts for consultant physicians but loads of jobs for consultant psychiatrists. If I'd stayed in general medicine, I'd have been a registrar until I was 40 or more. But as a psychiatrist, I got a job as a consultant when I was just 30. More money and status, you see. That's what the wife wanted. Her sister was married to a neurosurgeon. There were no consultant jobs for neurosurgeons so her husband was a registrar and I was a consultant. All the difference in the world. It meant that my Clarissa could lord it over her sister. Funny isn't it how our lives are influenced by the strangest things? I've always admired those people who plan their lives. Mine has just lurched from one crisis to another leaving me exhausted by experience, weary of a world of never ending confusion and bewildered by a litany of frustrations, disappointments and injustices. Do you know, when I was young, younger than you are now, I once believed that if I worked hard I would one day be able to clear away all the crap and concentrate on the important aspects of life: doing good work and having fun. Ha! Now I just feel twice as old as time itself.'

'Clarissa is your wife?'

'Huh? What?'

'I asked if Clarissa is your wife?'

129

'My ex-wife, thank the Good Lord. She's the wife of the carpet fellow now. She's Mrs Whateverhisnameis. He's welcome to her. I expect she gets all her shagpile carpets at a good discount. She went off me when her sister's husband finally became a consultant. She'd lost her edge then, you see. Socially a consultant neurosurgeon is a bit grander than a consultant psychiatrist. So she thought, anyway. I remember her saying that among the ladies at the golf club it was generally agreed that psychiatrists were only one rung above dermatologists and orthopaedic surgeons, so in her eyes I'd let her down. She blamed me for not hanging on and becoming a consultant physician. She had an affair with a barrister and then went off with a weather forecaster for a while. But although she thought he was famous because he was on the telly, he didn't have any money. They don't pay weather forecasters much, you know. Then she found the carpet guy at the golf club.'

'The one with the Aston Martin and the expensive hair?'

'You know him then? I wouldn't have thought you'd have known him. I don't think he comes round this neck of the woods.'

'No, I don't know him. But you mentioned him before.'

'Oh yes, I suppose I did. He's an obnoxious little runt. He has to sit on two cushions to see over the steering wheel in his Aston Martin. I'm not obsessed with him but I do think of him from time to time.'

'Wasn't your wife impressed by your status as the psychiatrist who looks after the celebrities?'

'Oh she was, indeed she was. But she left me seven years ago and it was only three years ago that I began to achieve my current notoriety. It began when an American movie star had a well-publicised nervous breakdown and came to see me because my consulting rooms happened to be close to his hotel. In fact, he hadn't had a nervous breakdown at all. He'd had a hissy fit and wasn't sure how to go back to work without losing face. I sat and listened to him whinge for three hours and he left my consulting room a healed man. The producers of the film he was making at Pinewood were so thrilled that they sung my praises to the media. It was generally assumed that I must have been able to offer some mystical words of wisdom. But the truth was that after the three hours of whingeing, I stood up and told him what a pathetic, self-obsessed, ungrateful little twat he was. I pointed out that millions of people envied his lifestyle, his wealth and the trail of starlets queuing at his dressing room door. I then told him to grow up, piss off and get back to work.'

'And that did the trick?'

'He congratulated me, paid me the biggest fee any psychiatrist in the world has ever received and told me that he would tell the world that I had restored him to perfect mental health. He explained that by healing him I had saved him from embarrassment since he could now explain that his unforgiveable behaviour on the film set had been a result of a mental illness. He told the world I had helped him conquer his problems by unveiling his inner demons, exposing them to the light and thereby exorcising them completely. It was all absolute bollocks, of course.'

'And after that other celebrities wanted to see you?'

'I became the fashionable psychiatrist who understood how celebrities worked, or did not work. My working hours were block booked by producers and agents and managers and lawyers who wanted their celebrity clients restoring to health and good working condition. I had, entirely by accident, invented a new medical speciality: healing people who had nothing wrong with them. They didn't need treatment. All they really needed was slapped legs and to be sent to bed without any supper.'

'And now you're fed up with it all?'

Dr Eckersley looked at me, 'Wouldn't you be? Wouldn't anyone be fed up? I am a fake doctor who sees fake patients. I earn more in a day than you probably earn in a year. Funny thing is that I always seem to be broke. I have an accountant who stuffs all the money into some sort of offshore scheme. At least he says he does. He pays my bills and gives me £500 a week in spending money. My wife, as you will have surmised, is now desperate to come back to me. She rings me five times a week to tell me that she misses me terribly.'

I stared at him in astonishment. How, I wondered but did not ask, could a doctor earn so much money that he received £500 a week in spending money. And with all the important bills paid for you how could anyone get through £500 a week? Dr Eckersley was clearly living in another world. Actually, he seemed to be living on a different planet. I was not envious in any degree but my surprise was simply engendered by the fact that I had never in my life been overcome with such riches. A country GP and author of books does not find gold raining down upon him in embarrassingly large quantities. I had known what I thought of at the time as real wealth only three times in my life. At the age of 14, I won £3 in a writing competition organised by the *Sunday Times* newspaper. (That was in the day when £3 to a 14-year-old boy seemed to offer an interminable supply of marbles, comics and bottles of dandelion and burdock.) At the age of 15, I had won £10 with a £1 premium bond an aunt had bought me for Christmas. I had not been thrilled by the gift of the premium bond but the £10 win was joyfully received. And at the age of 20 I had been so excited at passing an examination at medical school that I had rushed to the nearest bookies and put 10 shillings on a horse called 'Notachance' (I was a contrarian even in betting terms) which had romped home at 12 to 1 and left me wishing I could bottle the day and cart it around with me for the rest of my life, dipping into a minute here and an hour there whenever the need arose.

'Couldn't you just give up the celebrities and start seeing real people again?' I asked. 'Real people with real problems?'

Dr Eckersley laughed. 'Oh, I tried that,' he said. 'But it proved to be quite impossible. The hospital administrators had instructed the secretarial staff to book only rich and important people into my clinic. They like having the place littered with celebrities. Besides, the agents and managers and other hangers on made huge donations to the hospital and the administrators didn't want to give up all that lovely lolly. One of my patients paid for a new X-ray unit. It's all peanuts for them, of course, and they get yards of wonderful publicity. The amount of money slopping around looking for a good home is quite scary. None of that really matters because no ordinary doctor refers real patients to me anymore. They all assume I'm too busy, too important and too expensive to deal with any patient who doesn't have a stache of multi-million pound contracts in their Louis Vuitton briefcase.'

'So you're stuck with your life?'

'I was indeed, as you say, stuck with my life. And I didn't like it.' He puffed at his pipe and then smiled at me. It was a strange, rather appealing, lop sided smile. 'And so I ran away.' He puffed at his pipe again. Plumes of sweet smelling smoke drifted up towards the ceiling. 'Now do you think I'm just depressed?'

I thought for a while and then shook my head. 'No, I suppose not. But why did you come and see me?' I'd asked him this several times because I still wasn't sure what he wanted me to do.

'Needed to talk to someone,' he said bluntly. 'I'd have stayed and talked to that shopkeeper chum of yours but if I'd told him my problems he'd have just sold me more buckets and another crate of dog food. He'd have probably sold me the shop.'

'I'm not sure I know what to do to help you,' I told him.

'You've already done what I needed,' said Dr Eckersley. 'You've lent me your ears. It was what Caesar wanted and it was what I needed.' He stood up. 'You've given me good advice and I know what to do.'

'But I haven't given you any advice!' I protested.

'Exactly,' said Dr Eckersley. 'That's the best sort of advice there is. Is there a pub in the village? Somewhere I can stay for a few nights while I have a look around and decide what to do with the rest of my life?'

'You want to stay in Bilbury?'

'I have a feeling that no one will ever find me here,' said Dr Eckersley. 'So now that I've run away I'll stay run away for a while. Who knows I might run away permanently and stay around here. It seems a good place. And if I need to buy dog food or buckets I know where to go.'

'What about your celebrity patients? And your hospital committee? And your medical students?'

'Nuts to them all,' said Dr Eckersley. 'Nuts to them all with double knobs on.'

I picked up the telephone on my desk and rang the Duck and Puddle.

'Have you got a room free?' I asked Gilly, who answered the call. She said they had.

I told her that the room was now let and that the occupier would be with her in a few minutes.

'You've got a room at the Duck and Puddle,' I told Dr Eckersley. 'When I introduce you to Frank and Gilly I shall tell them your real name for these are my friends and there is no way I'm going to lie to them about you.' I assured him that if you told Frank and Gilly a secret then it remained a secret.

133

Dr Eckersley accepted this without a murmur of protest. 'Quite understand,' he said. 'You can't have a stranger sailing into harbour under false colours.'

'It's up to you whether or not you tell everyone else your real name. If you think people are really going to be looking for you...'

'I think I shall be Dr Crippen,' said Dr Eckersley. 'Dr Hawley Harvey Crippen from Michigan in the United States.'

'People may suspect you are travelling under an alias,' I said.

'If they ask, I shall tell them that the original Dr Crippen was my great uncle and that although I have spent my life trying to live down the connection, I steadfastly refuse to change my name simply to avoid the unwanted and associated notoriety. I shall add that my father was intensely proud of the family connection, that he believed my great uncle to be innocent of the crime for which he was hung, and that he gave me my great uncle's Christian names as a sign of respect for the only member of the family to be famous for anything other than hog stealing. If I am pressed I shall add that my great uncle on my mother's side was a notorious hog rustler who was hung for stealing three hogs and a bushel of fresh beetroot.'

'Isn't there a risk that people will then become curious about you, and take an interest in you because of your infamous relative?'

'Indeed there is,' agreed Dr Eckersley. 'But no one looking for Dr Eckersley would think him stupid enough to register as a guest in a pub under the name 'Dr Crippen', would they?'

I laughed.

'Anyone seeing the name will believe my story because it is too absurd not to believe.'

'I've got some house calls to do,' I told him. 'I've got to go past the pub so follow me in your car and you won't get lost.'

Dr Eckersley, soon to metamorphose into Dr Crippen, thought this was a splendid idea. He put on his Chapeau watch cap and we left.

Before we set off in our two car convoy, he opened his boot and insisted on giving me the six galvanised buckets which he had purchased from Peter Marshall. He refused my attempt to pay for them.

The Psychiatrist Who Ran Away (Part 2: The Metamorphosis)

Dr Eckersley settled in well at the Duck and Puddle.

Indeed, he settled in so well that when I called in at the pub a couple of days later, I found him standing behind the bar reading a copy of *The Times*, which was spread out on the counter in front of him, and clearly settled as comfortably and as confidently as if he had been stationed there for a decade or more. He was puffing happily at his pipe, which was stuck in the corner of his mouth as though it had been welded into position. We were the only people in the snug.

'You look well established,' I said.

'I am the new barman,' said Dr Eckersley. 'On Mondays, Wednesdays and Fridays I stand behind the bar and provide the world with refreshment. I am, I believe, on approval. I sound like a packet of stamps supplied through the mail but I feel as though I have come home. My only complaint is that the post of barman does not come with a uniform.'

'Why on earth do you want a uniform?

'It would help me establish my new position in my mind. As a psychiatrist, I was always conscious that whatever advice was likely to be followed. As a barman, I can offer advice with absolutely no sense of responsibility. A uniform would remind me that I can talk to people without having to feel any responsibility at all and it would help me remain aware that if I feel bored by a conversation, I can wander off and do something else saying something like 'Please excuse me, I have to go and rebore the limitation pipes connecting the spygot to the pump handle. If I don't do it regularly the spygot pipe gets crapsulated and Mr Parsons gets terribly upset.'

'Do people accept that sort of rubbish?'

'Of course they do! As long as you say it earnestly and with utter conviction then people will believe anything. It's jargon, do you see? People expect jargon and they respect it. These days everyone has

135

their own jargon. Social workers, policemen, lawyers, doctors – all have jargon. A uniform would help people accept the fact that I am, as a barman, a person with jargon at his disposal.'

'What sort of uniform would you like?'

'Oh, I don't know, something simple but at the same time distinguished. The barmen at the best London establishments are all togged out in snazzy waistcoats, usually in some bright colour, with matching bowties. They're not as smartly done out as the doormen, of course, for the fellows burdened with the responsibility of opening and closing the door are invariably dressed in the sort of ceremonial uniform usually worn by the Commanders in Chief of the Ruritarian Army Forces. But a bright waistcoat would be acceptable and would give my position the gravitas it deserves.'

'Have a word with Gilly,' I suggested. 'I'm sure she could run you up something from a nice piece of old curtain material.'

Dr Eckersley sniffed at my comment and then leant forward and lowered his voice to a sotto voce stage whisper. 'I must say,' he said, 'that my work has been made easier by the fact that my predecessor was, I gather, an unmitigated frample. As a barman, I find that I am free to offer simple words of advice and comfort without expectations or responsibility. I like to argue the bad side of an argument; to put forward and then sustain the illogical, apparently indefensible and perverse point of view.'

I laughed at this.

'You may laugh! You may sneer. But I spent a very pleasant hour yesterday evening arguing that the Government should give everyone daily coupons for free cake. I managed to persuade a couple in matching puce anoraks that it is cake not bread which is the staff of life. I knew I'd got them when one of the pair, I think it is was a woman but it was difficult to tell, asked me what sort of cake I thought was most beneficial. I told her a triple layer sponge cake with cream and raspberry jam filling had been proven to be nutritious and to contain elements proven to combat a wide range of mental health disorders.'

I stared at him in astonishment. Just a day or so earlier, this man had been a Professor of Psychiatry and an eminent Harley Street consultant.

'In my previous life I had to attempt to be rational and sensible but I have now realised that these are not my natural inclinations.

136

You cannot begin to imagine the sense of freedom which I now feel.' He blew out a great cloud of smoke and leant across the bar towards me. 'I was born to be a barman,' he confided.

'I know what unmitigated is, but what's a framble?'

'A frample, you ignoramus, not a framble! A frample is a sour or peevish person.' Suddenly he stood upright and hit himself on the forehead with the palm of his hand. 'My apologies, doctor. I am forgetting my duty as the on approval bartender in this establishment. What can I get you to drink?'

'Nothing at the moment, thank you. I just popped in to see that you'd settled in well. And I'm delighted to see that you have.'

'I love it here!' he said. 'My host and hostess are good people. The food is excellent, the accommodations are a little cramped but satisfactory and there is ample room to store my radishes, my custard, my dog food and my new hats. The work is convivial to say the least. I have, as they say, landed on my feet. There are things which are vital to our lives; absolutely crucial things which we could not easily live without. In this category I put breathing, fresh drinking water and sewage pipes. All these are essential. We could not live without them. But they are not things which give our lives excitement; these things are not important to us personally. Oxygen and sewage pipes are vital but they aren't important to me as an individual.'

'So what is important to you?'

'Peace, honesty and a chance to live a simple life,' he said. 'I needed to get away from the hypocrisy and superficiality of metropolitan life.'

I leant across so that I could whisper to him. 'By the way, are you now Dr Eckersley or Dr Crippen?'

'Neither,' he replied in what I think he thought was a sotto voce comment but would, I believe, have more accurately been described as a stage whisper. 'My name is now Gengolphus Stottle. I am reborn. With age comes cynicism and weariness and the old Dr Eckersley was as cynical and as weary as you can get. However, the newly born Gengolphus Stottle is alive and full of enthusiasm. I have changed my name, my mind and my life.'

'Gengolphus Stottle?'

'But you can call me Harry.'

'Harry?'

'Do you have to behave like an echo chamber? Or is this annoying habit of yours a ploy?'

'A ploy?'

'There you go again!'

'No, I'm curious. What sort of ploy?'

'It's a ploy favoured by those of my patients who were in politics. They repeat whatever you say so that they have time to catch up with the conversation, look for any loopholes or swampy bits, assess the risks and then think up a suitable lie in response.'

'No, no, it wasn't a ploy. I just didn't understand.'

'If you're going to question everything I say, we won't get anywhere very quickly.'

'No, I can see that. But why are you called Harry if your name is Gengolphus?'

'Harry' is a name which was given to me by Mr Parsons.'

'Mr Parsons?'

'Mr Parsons is the landlord of this esteemed establishment and, of course, my employer.'

'Ah, you mean Frank.'

'As a mere employee, and a junior one at that, in terms of employment if not of years, I do not feel it behoves me to refer to my employer by his Christian name.'

'No one will know who you mean if you call him Mr Parsons. He's Frank. Everyone calls him Frank. And try not to talk like that. You sound like a Professor of Psychiatry who's run away to the country to escape from himself.'

The new barman looked concerned. 'Do you really think so? I thought I sounded like a friendly man of the people; a man born to turn on the taps which release the elixir of life. By the way, the beer sold in this pub is like nothing I've ever tasted. They don't sell stuff like this in London, you know. We sell a beer called 'Old Restoration' which must have a higher alcoholic content than vodka.'

'Yes, I know about 'Old Restoration' and I'm afraid I do think you still sound a tad like a Professor of Psychiatry. And I don't understand why Frank calls you 'Harry' when you told him your name was Gengolphus? And where on earth did you get the name Gengolphus Stottle anwyay?'

138

'Mr Parsons seemed to think it a good jape to call me Harry. I think he liked the name 'Harry Stottle'. If you think about it, I'm sure you'll see why. Try saying it loud. I rather like it myself. Besides, the name Harry has for centuries been a good, solid English name though it is, of course, of German origin. I may change my name by deed poll. Get rid of Gengolphus and replace it with Harry.'

'Can you do that? Change your name?'

'Oh yes! I had a patient who did it. You go and see a solicitor, fill in some forms and change your name,' explained Harry. 'Once you've changed your name you can get a new passport and driving licence in your new name. You can do this as often as you like. And if you keep your old passport and driving licence but tell the authorities that you've lost them, you can have several identities. As far as the world at large is concerned, there is nothing to link the various names. You can open new bank accounts with your new name and keep your old bank accounts under your original name. You can then write yourself a cheque in your old name and put the money into an account in your new name. You can open an account abroad and then go back to the UK and change your name yet again. As soon as you have a new name and bank account, you rent a property and acquire some utility bills. Bingo! You've got brand new identities.'

'How on earth do you know all this?' I asked him.

'Patient of mine did it all the time,' said Harry. 'In books and films the characters who want a new identity always go rooting around graveyards. They find the name and birth date of a child who died early in life, someone who would now be approximately their age, and they get hold of a copy of the birth certificate. They can then use the information they've got to apply for a passport and so on. It's all very complicated and risky. Simply changing your name by deed poll is much easier.'

'But there's no need to change your name by deed poll because Gengolphus isn't your name!' I pointed out.

'No, but I could change my name from Eckersley to Stottle,' said Harry. He thought for a moment. 'I think I might do that.'

'Why did you call yourself Gengolphus Stottle in the first place?' I asked him. I was clinging to the edge of the conversation by my fingertips. 'Where the devil did you get that name?'

'Oh, that's easy. I once had a patient called Gengolphus Stottle. He was a film star; a most interesting fellow with an endless series of hang-ups. They were for me very profitable hang-ups. He was very famous and whenever he was in my consulting rooms, there would be a crowd of screaming girls gathered outside. For months, I assumed the girls had somehow managed to follow him to my rooms but he confessed one day that the girls were all unemployed actresses who had been hired by his management team. The girls were paid film extras' day rate to stand around, shout the star's name, demand autographs and hurl items of underwear in his direction. At the start of each day, they were all issued with three assorted items of underwear which the management team obtained wholesale from a store in the East End of London. All this nonsense worked and everyone assumed that my patient was hugely popular. You would recognise the stage name by which everyone knew him but his real name was Gengolphus Stottle. I find that Americans in show business often have very strange real names. That is probably why so many of them adopt a nom de guerre when they are working. You can't imagine the name Gengolphus Stottle lit up on a cinema marquee, can you? It's difficult to picture a crowd of screaming girls shouting out 'Gengolphus, I love you Gengolphus. I want you to have my baby, Gengolphus!' However, I always rather liked the name so I appropriated it. He won't mind because he's dead. One of his many peccadilloes was that he liked to spend his evenings dressed as a baby and he always slept with a dummy in his mouth. Unfortunately, the rubber nipple came off the pacifier and he choked on it. His managers told the fans that he'd died of a broken heart after his pet dog had been run over. A medical colleague of mine signed the appropriate certificate and arranged for a speedy cremation. His management agreed that was the only way to ensure that his back catalogue continued to churn out decent profits.'

'How awful! Had his pet dog really been run over?'

'Whose pet dog?'

'Gengolphus's.'

'Oh, Gengolphus didn't have a dog. He couldn't stand animals of any kind. He hated anything on four legs. There were wild rabbits on his land in Arizona and he used to mow them down with a souped-up Uzi. He was a terrible shot and wounded two assistants, though he did once put a very neat line of bullet holes in a Buick which was

140

driving past. His managers had to buy the family a new car and pay all the little girl's hospital expenses. The family were very nice about it. Gengolphus sent them all signed photographs and tickets for the premier of his next movie. The little girl couldn't make it but the parents were taken there in a stretch limousine and they were thrilled. I think the appropriate phrase is that they were 'over the moon'.'

I stared at him uncomprehending.

'It's a different world,' he explained with a shrug.

I just nodded. I was actually quite shocked. I suppose I was naïve in those days. 'It all sounds very manipulative and deceitful,' I said at last.

Harry laughed. 'Film stars are no more dishonest than politicians or company bosses. The world I see is full of spin and misdirection; corruption is endemic and democracy is just a word that used to mean something.' He sighed. 'I just got tired of it all. I want to find an oasis of peace; somewhere as yet untouched by the 1970s. I'd like to go back 50 years but I'll settle for a lifestyle stuck in the 1950s.' He waved a hand around. 'And so here I am happy. I have found contentment.'

It was my turn to laugh. 'Are you suggesting that Bilbury is stuck in the 1950s?'

'Are you suggesting it isn't?'

'Peter Marshall has acquired a new set of weighing scales that measure in grams and kilograms,' I pointed out. 'And the local garage mechanics are now happily servicing post-war cars. Well, some of them.'

'And you drive around in a Rolls Royce that should be in a museum!'

'Touché!'

'This is the 1970s but you are living in a community which is naturally isolated and therefore self-reliant. Living here is more like living in a village in the Middle Ages than living in a village in the middle of the 20th century. I hope it never changes. Mr Marshall, the fellow who runs the village shop, told me yesterday that all the fruits and vegetables he sells are grown locally. What happens in a snow storm? I wager you cope very well.'

'We do,' I agreed. 'Nothing much changes. Peter runs out of something after a few days, usually beetroot or spinach, but we never run out of bread because people make their own and we never run out of milk because we have cows. The pub might run low on one type of beer but there is always something else to take its place. If all else failed we could drink home-made wine.'

'There you are, you see! In the city, everything comes to a halt when the first flake of snow hits the ground. The buses and the trains stop running. The drivers of motor vehicles panic. Shops run out of food and schools close. Everywhere you look, people are panicking. City life has much to recommend it. There are theatres, museums and opera houses. But I never had time to visit any of them. If I wasn't working I was threading my way through the traffic.'

I thought about it and knew he was right. Most of the people I knew who lived in London never visited any of the cultural centres which were supposed to be the reason they wanted to live in London in the first place.

'A little earlier we were talking about animals,' continued Harry.

'Were we?'

'The film star's imaginary dog.'

'Oh yes.'

'Is it true that you keep a pig? Is that really so?'

'Oh yes. Patsy and I have a pig called Cedric.'

'A pet pig?'

'Yes.'

'And you have no intention of turning him into the filling for a mountain of bacon sandwiches?'

'None whatsoever.'

'Delighted to hear it! People usually do things with their pets. They fuss over them, stroke them, teach them tricks and exhibit them. What do you do with your pig? Why do you keep him?'

'Does there have to be a reason?'

'Of course! In London no one does anything without at least one very good reason.'

'Well, we feed him. And we admire him a great deal. He's a very fine specimen. And like all pigs, he's a very intelligent animal. He actually belongs to a very lovely American couple. I like Americans. My father was on destroyers during the Second World War. He was torpedoed three times and on the last two occasions he was rescued by American ships.'

'How did an American couple find themselves the owners of a pig?'

'They won him in a Bowling for the Pig competition at the Duck and Puddle. I think they were a little surprised. Normally people win a big silver cup if they win a competition but the winner of the skittles competition at the pub always collects a pig. Cedric was a bit smaller when they won him but he just keeps growing.'

'I take it they didn't want to take him back home with them.'

'They'd have liked to but...'

'...they worried he wouldn't fit into the overhead luggage lockers.'

'Or onto an aeroplane seat. Even when he was young he was still quite a size.'

'So you and your wife are in loco parentis?'

'Exactly. We've adopted him and we send his real owners pictures of him.'

'But what do you do with him apart from feed him? Do you take him to shows and then pin up rosettes on the wall of his sty?'

'We talk to him and we take him for walks. He's got a lovely personality. But, no, we don't exhibit him. We don't think he'd appreciate being prodded and poked by strangers with stout sticks. He's a very sensitive pig.'

'You take him for walks?' Harry, the former Dr Eckersley, seemed surprised by this, as though I had said something odd.

'Oh yes, he loves going for a walk. I suppose it's the opportunity to sniff some strange smells and nibble at a few bits of unusual hedgerow.'

'On a lead?'

'Well, we tie a piece of string around his neck. But it's not really a lead. It isn't like taking a dog for a walk. You can't pull him back or make him go where you want him to go.'

'I didn't know people took pigs for walks.'

'Oh yes, as long as the pig is properly registered with the Government. And as long as the owner has a licence.'

'What sort of licence?'

'You need an annual licence if you want to take a pig for a walk.'

143

Harry laughed. 'Now you're pulling my leg. You think I'm a silly city fellow and you're laughing at me!'

'No, no, I'm not. Honestly, you need a licence if you want to take a pig for a walk in England. I think it's probably the same everywhere in Britain. And you have to carry the licence with you at all times.'

'You're serious?'

'I am. Moreover, an inspector must approve the route that the pig is going to take. And the pig has to have a tattoo or a tag or a mark of some kind.'

'In case he gets lost?'

'Presumably.'

'Is your pig tattooed?'

'No. He's not the sort of pig to have a tattoo. He has a collar.'

'A dog collar?'

'Well, it's much bigger than a dog collar. But it's like a dog collar. A chap in the village made it for him out of a leather belt. It's got his name on a little, metal disk and there's a hook on the belt to which I can attach his lead.'

'And how much does he weigh?'

'About 700 pounds, give or take a turnip or two.'

'How the devil do you weigh him? Not on the bathroom scales I assume.'

'My wife's father is a farmer. He's got a weighing machine for farm animals. We walk Cedric round there occasionally.'

'Has he ever escaped?'

'Who, Cedric?'

'Yes. I don't mean your father-in-law. I assume he is safely settled in captivity.'

'Cedric got away from me once, early on in our relationship. We were in the lane and he just sort of bolted and I lost him. I couldn't keep up with him. He was missing for nearly two hours. Patsy and I were in quite a state. We had just about everyone in the village looking for him.'

'But there's a happy ending?'

'Oh yes. He'd wandered off to the Duck and Puddle where there was a coach parked outside. The passengers weren't staying there – there aren't enough rooms for a coach party – but they'd stopped for Devon cream teas. Gilly makes a splendid cream tea, by the way.

The coach driver had opened the luggage compartment so that he could reorganise some of the luggage. Apparently, he'd heard some of the cases moving around as he drove round the lanes. When he'd finished doing the rearranging, he'd gone into the pub for his cup of tea and had left the door to the luggage compartment open.'

'And that's where they found Cedric?'

'The coach driver had a fit when he came out of the pub and found a pig comfortably settled among the suitcases.'

'I hope none of them was pigskin.'

'Hmm. I hadn't thought of that. Anyway, the coach driver fetched Frank who recognised Cedric. And ten minutes later, I coaxed him out of the luggage compartment with an apple.'

I looked at my watch. 'I must go,' I said. 'I've got several home visits to do before lunch.' We said our goodbyes and I hurried off.

It was good to see Dr Eckersley/ Dr Crippen/Gongolphus Stottle/Harry so comfortably established at the Duck and Puddle.

During his first month in the village, Harry Stottle became a regular visitor to Bilbury Grange.

Although he was happy to be away from London, and was enjoying his new, less stressful existence, Harry was not a natural loner. It is, I suppose, rather difficult to switch from being a busy and important psychiatrist, fawned over by celebrities of all kinds, to being a part-time barman living in a pub. The Duck and Puddle can sometimes be very busy but it can also be deserted for hours at a time.

On the days when he wasn't working at the Duck and Puddle, Harry would often wander around the village. He liked to chat to anyone and everyone and as I drove around on my visits, I would often see him leaning up against a farm gate chatting to a farm labourer. When he wasn't working behind the bar, Harry became a Duck and Puddle stalwart.

'Do you know the food here tastes better than anything I've ever eaten in my life! The air is like wine. I stand outside, drink it in and feel alive. The gardens and hedgerows are full of wild flowers. Nature is unconfined and spreads herself around with an easy grace. Do you have butterflies in the summer?'

'Yes, loads of them.'

'What sort? Not just the white ones which are reputed to be so fond of cabbages?'

I reeled off the names of a few that sprang to mine. 'Red admirals, skippers, orange tips, peacocks, brimstones, small coppers, fritillaries – all sorts, including the white ones which are reputed to be so fond of cabbages!'

'I haven't seen a butterfly since I was a boy! What about conkers. Do you see conkers?'

'Of course! In late September we're up to our knees in them.'

'In the street where I live the council has pollarded all the trees. Residents complained that the fruits of the horse chestnut trees, the conkers, fell onto their motor cars. There was talk of bonnets being dented and lawsuits being initiated. Have you ever heard such nonsense? So the trees were pollarded and there are no more conkers. Now, the hapless trees stand naked and pointless, as decorative as telegraph poles.'

A few days after arriving in Bilbury, the erstwhile Dr Eckersley decided that he didn't want to go back to London at all. He decided that part of his life was over for ever. He sent letters resigning from his consultancy post and his teaching position and telephoned the firm of accountants which looked after his financial affairs and instructed them to sell his house and offshore holdings and put the proceeds into his bank account. I don't know how much money was involved but I rather suspect it was a considerable sum. The house apparently sold in days to a Greek shipping millionaire.

And, as he had discussed, he went to a solicitor in Barnstaple and had his name legally changed to Gengolphus Harry Stottle.

As soon as the name change had been completed, he used a cheque book for his old account to move all his money into an account in the name of Gengolphus Harry Stottle.

Moreover, the newly minted Harry Stottle opened a Post Office Box in Barnstaple to ensure that no one from his past would be able to find him. All his correspondence went there.

It would not, I suppose, have been impossible for anyone to find him if they'd been really determined but, after the first week or so (and a few headlines such as 'Celebrity Psychiatrist Goes Missing' and 'Psychiatrist Goes Potty?') the world had pretty much lost interest in his disappearance.

Before the first month was over, Harry decided that he wanted to use some of his money to buy himself a cottage.

'I want somewhere small, cosy and unpretentious,' he said. 'It must be detached and it must have some land because I want to keep animals. And it must be close to a river because I intend to take up fishing.'

I asked around and telephoned a few relatively reputable estate agents and managed to find him a couple of possibilities. And so it was that just a few weeks after leaving London, and running away from all his responsibilities, the newly minted Harry moved out of his room at the Duck and Puddle and into a traditional, detached residence called Bread Cottage which was just a quarter of a mile from the pub and which he bought for cash with a chunk of the money his accountant had sent him.

Bread Cottage had acquired its name as a result of the fact that it had, back in the 17th century, been the village bakery. In those days, home owners who ran small businesses from what are now rather stuffily known as residential premises, didn't give their homes unoriginal names such as 'Chez Nous', 'Wee Nook', 'The Willows' or 'Honeysuckle Cottage'. Indeed, they didn't give their homes names at all. Why should they? There was no postal service and no delivery drivers with parcels to deliver. Cottages and houses were given names according to the occupation of the person living there. So, in an ordinary sort of village, there would be a Mill House, a Vicarage, a Smithy and, of course, a Bread Cottage or a Bakery Cottage.

Harry had become a resident of Bilbury and although I was delighted, for he was good company, I was rather surprised.

I had suspected that after a few days, a week or ten days at the most, he would tire of country life, hanker after the bright lights and excitement of London, and return to his old life, his professorship, his consultancy and his lucrative private practice.

But he didn't.

Indeed, he got on so well at the Duck and Puddle that Frank and Gilly told him that his period of approval could be considered at an end. His working hours were increased and he became the resident barman during daytime hours throughout the week. Gilly still did the cooking, of course, and Frank could be found behind the bar during the evenings and at weekends but having a reliable barman on weekdays made life much easier for them both.

Harry was absolutely fascinated by our animals and whenever he came to Bilbury Grange, he insisted on saying hello to all our creatures. We introduced him to Ben (our dog), Emily, Sophie and Jeremy (our cats), Lizzie, Petula, Cynthia, Sarah-Louise and Miss Houdini (our sheep) and Cedric (the pig we were looking after for Edgar and Delphinium Rathbone). Harry was particularly taken by Cedric and told me that his ambition was to have a pig of his own.

'When I lived in London, I longed to have a dog,' he said. 'But that pig of yours is wonderfully intelligent and I swear he understands me when I talk to him. Once I've settled in and got my new place sorted out, I'll have a sty built and find myself a decent sized pig to put in it.

'Just remember that you have to check on the site if you're building a pig sty,' I told him.

'There are rules about that?'

'Oh yes. Keeping a pig near a street 'so as to be a common nuisance' is illegal, under the town Police Clauses Act of 1847.'

'There seem to be a lot of laws about pigs.'

'There are.'

And inevitably, Harry wanted to take Cedric for a walk.

Before I even considered letting him take Cedric out by himself, I insisted that he came out with Cedric and me on a couple of occasions. I tried to give him some simple lessons in 'How to Take a Pig for a Walk'. This may sound rather silly but in practice, the human walker has to remember that taking a pig for a walk is entirely different to taking a dog for a walk.

'The first thing to remember,' I told him, 'is that the lead is there purely as a formality. It's partly psychological and partly for appearance's sake. It's not so much a lead as a sort of friendly reminder to which Cedric responds as a courtesy. With a good strong lead, even a big dog can be pulled back or pulled along if he's misbehaving. But you can't use the lead to control Cedric. If you get into a battle with a pig then either the lead will break or your arm will come out of its socket – probably the latter. Always remember that a pig tends to go where a pig wants to go. All we can do is try to make him want to follow us and encourage him to want to go where we want him to go.'

'And you say he weighs 700 pounds?'

'That was a month or so ago when we last weighed him. He's probably put on a bit of weight since then. Whatever the precise figure might be, there's no doubt that he weighs four or five times as much as you or me and so even if we both tried to control him, we'd fail. If he really wants to go to the left, he will go to the left, and if he wants to go right, he will go right.'

'Right!'

'The second thing to remember is that pigs like to trot occasionally. And they can keep up the trotting for a long time. Cedric managed to get away from me once and I couldn't keep up with him. I eventually found him eating the flowers in Mrs Winchcombe's front garden. I think it's fair to say that Cedric was considerably happier than Mrs Winchcombe.'

'How fast can a pig run?'

'About 11 miles an hour is pretty good for a pig. But they have surprising stamina and can keep up that speed for a long way. At 11 miles an hour, Cedric could run a marathon in just over 2 hours – which is as fast as the fastest human athlete could run it and probably faster than you or I could manage it.'

'Ah! So if Cedric makes a break for it I'll have a job to keep up with him?'

'You will.'

'So how do you keep him under control?'

'Apples,' I replied. 'Cedric knows our voices and he'll usually come when we call him but as a backup, I stuff my pockets with apples and use them to keep him on the straight and narrow if he gets tempted to stray too far.'

'You can use them for steering?'

'Absolutely! But if he's stopped because he's admiring the view or has found something tasty to eat on the roadside, it's probably best to leave him be for a while.'

'Use the apple as an incentive. Like carrots and donkeys?'

'Exactly?'

'Any particular brand? Does he prefer Granny Smiths or Red Delicious?'

'I don't think Cedric much minds what the variety is. Just hold the apple where he can smell it. And then let him eat it. Hold the apple on the flat of your hand so that he doesn't accidentally munch his way through your fingers. He probably won't notice but you might.'

'That sounds like good advice.'

'It is.'

'Does he respond to his name?'

'He does when Patsy or I call him. But that's probably partly because he recognises our voices. He won't know your voice yet so you'll have to rely on the apples.'

And so one Saturday, about six weeks after he'd arrived in the village, Harry turned up at Bilbury Grange to take Cedric for a walk. I gave him the pig walking licence and several pounds of apples in a shopping bag and warned him to dole them out sparingly. 'The first time I took Cedric for a walk, I used up all my apples before we'd covered 200 yards. So be a bit mean with them to make them last.'

And off they went.

Patsy and I stood in the driveway and watched them go with beating hearts.

'I feel as though I'm watching my teenage daughter go off on her first date,' I said.

'I think Cedric will be fine,' said Patsy.

'It's not Cedric I'm worried about,' I said.

Two hours later, when the pair of them had not returned, I started to worry. After two and a half hours, I climbed onto my old bicycle and started riding along the lanes, looking for them. Eventually, I wondered if Harry had taken Cedric along to the cottage he had just bought and so I pedalled off in that direction.

The guess paid off.

They were both there, in the rather overgrown orchard that was part of the property. Cedric was flat out on the grass. He looked asleep. Harry was standing next to him, calling to him, telling him to get up and occasionally poking him with what looked like a branch broken off an apple tree.

'What on earth's happened?' I asked.

'I thought Cedric would like to come and see my place,' explained Harry. 'The orchard is full of windfalls and knowing how much he likes apples, I thought he could have a little party all by himself – a sort of apple crunching feast.'

I looked down into the long grass and kicked at one of the apples. 'These are rotting!' I said.

'Yes, I suppose some of them are,' agreed Harry. 'But they're obviously still edible. He ate quite a few and seemed to enjoy them. Do you think he's upset his tummy by eating too many?'

'I don't think pigs get upset tummies,' I told him. 'Cedric certainly doesn't.'

'Good. That's a relief!'

'But they do get drunk.' I bent down beside Cedric. He was breathing perfectly well but his breath was a giveaway. 'He's been drunk before. I don't let him into our orchard at Bilbury Grange.'

'Drunk? He can't be. I haven't given him any booze. Honestly! Not a drop.'

'You didn't need to. He's eaten half a bushel of fermenting apples. What do you think happens when apples start to ferment?'

'They turn into alcohol?' said Harry, very quietly. 'Oh, whoops. I'm so sorry.'

'Oh whoops indeed. Poor Cedric is as drunk as a lord.'

'Oh damn. I really am sorry. Now what do we do? Can we move him back to your place? Maybe we could get a truck and take him back home.'

'How do you suggest we get him into the back of a truck?'

'Lift him?'

'We'd need a forklift truck to do that. And it's Saturday. And the ground in your orchard is so rough and overgrown that I doubt if we'd get a forklift truck through to where he is lying.' I looked up at the sky. 'The trouble is that it's clearly going to rain.'

'And Cedric doesn't like rain?'

'He absolutely hates rain.'

'Do you think he might get a cold?'

'I don't want to risk it.'

'So what do we do?'

'We need to cover him up with something.'

'A tarpaulin? There are some old sheets of corrugated iron at the bottom of the orchard. Maybe we could put up some sort of shelter.'

'No.'

'No, I suppose not. Rotten idea. So what do we do?'

I thought for a while. 'We borrow a tent from Frank.'

'Does Mr Parsons have a tent?' Harry seemed surprised. 'I really don't see him as a camper.'

'I doubt if Frank has ever been camping in his life. But he and Gilly have a couple of tents which they use for weddings and so on. I think they're more small marquees than tents. They put them up on their back lawn to provide overflow accommodation.'

I walked round to the Duck and Puddle and half an hour later Frank, Harry and I had erected the Duck and Puddle's smallest and second best marquee over and around Cedric who was sleeping off his fermented apple binge. We took the marquee round to Bread Cottage in an old-fashioned hand-cart of Frank's. Cedric never budged as we worked, though he did keep on snoring and snuffling. There is something surprisingly soothing about a snuffling pig. God timed things well and the rain only started about ten minutes after we had finished putting up the marquee.

'Phew!' said a relieved Harry. He turned to Frank. 'You saved my bacon, Mr Parsons!'

'If you keep addressing me as Mr Parsons I'll sack you,' said Frank sternly.

Once Cedric was safely settled, and safe from the rain, Harry invited us back to his cottage for a drink and a packet of crisps. Bread Cottage was a good walk from the orchard. Before we left the orchard, I made sure that the entrance gate to the field was firmly shut. If Cedric woke up and started wandering, I didn't want him wandering too far. A quick check confirmed that there was a good, solid post and rail fence around the rest of the orchard.

'This is all I've got,' Harry said, apologetically, when we were comfortably settled in the lounge at Bread Cottage.

He had produced a crate of Old Restoration and a large box full of packets of crisps.

'I've not had time to do any proper shopping yet so it's either a packet of salt and vinegar crisps or a tin of dog food.'

Once he'd produced the beer and the crisps, he lit a fire in the cottage's huge log burner. The fire had already been laid when we'd entered Bread Cottage and there was a fire burning in the log burner in the other main downstairs room. There was no central heating in the cottage and without the two stoves, the place would have been terribly cold.

'I didn't know you'd got a dog,' said Frank.

'I haven't,' replied his new barman.

Frank looked puzzled. 'But you said you'd got dog food.'

'Harry visited Peter's shop when he first arrived in Bilbury,' I explained. 'When he was still Dr Eckersley.'

'Ah,' nodded Frank, understanding.

'I called in at the shop because I wanted to buy a bar of chocolate and a drink,' explained Harry.

'Did Peter sell you anything else interesting?' asked Frank. 'Apart from the dog food for the dog you don't have.'

Harry, obviously embarrassed, looked at me.

'One of his watch caps and a few galvanised buckets,' I interspersed. The fire was by now burning very brightly.

'Golly, you got away lightly,' said Frank. 'One of the purple caps made in Canada? Guaranteed waterproof, windproof and safe from nuclear explosion?'

'Yes, that's right. An absolutely brilliant hat.'

'They shrink. The material tightens up if it gets wet but don't worry because it stretches if it gets hot. Mine fits me like a vice in the wet but comes down over my eyes if it's sunny. How much dog food did he sell you?'

'A tray full of cans.'

'And nothing else?'

Harry looked more embarrassed.

'Go on,' said Frank. 'You can tell me. Peter does it to everyone.'

'A rather embarrassingly large quantity of radishes and rather more custard than I'm ever likely to eat. And, of course, the galvanised buckets.'

'Not bad,' said Frank. 'Everyone ends up with the custard and the buckets. But I have to confess that the radishes are a bit unusual.'

We each drank a bottle of Old Restoration and ate a packet of crisps. The beer was fine but the crisps were soggier than is usually considered preferable in snacks of that nature. Peter tends to buy his crisps from a wholesaler who specialises in vintage stock – usually obtained from retailers who've gone bankrupt. The result is that the crisps tend to lose some of those qualities such as taste, crunchiness and freshness which are traditionally regarded as integral.

'Another bottle?' asked Harry. 'Another packet of crisps?'

Both Frank and I thanked him and said that since it was getting late, we thought we'd better be getting home.

'I'll pop round early in the morning and collect Cedric,' I told Harry. 'He should have sobered up by then. If you could possibly keep him in the marquee, and away from the fermenting apples, that would be splendid.'

'I've got some radishes I could give him if he fancies a snack,' said Harry.

'That would be marvellous,' I agreed. 'Just keep him off the fermenting apples.'

'I'll just have another couple of bottles of this Old Restoration, then before I bed down for the night, I'll totter along to the orchard and check that he's OK,' promised Harry.

Frank and I looked at each other. Old Restoration is a potent brew and the only local beer I know of which is capable of stripping paint. The local church of Saint Dymphna (named after the patron saint of various degrees of insanity) once had a curate called Murgatroyd who was the politest, neatest, most cautious man I ever met. He was a dedicated belt and braces man who rode around Bilbury on an ancient sit up and beg bicycle which had once belonged to the wife of a previous vicar. In order to prevent his flapping trouser legs from catching in the chain, he wore bicycle clips and tucked his trousers into his socks. After one pint of Old Restoration, I saw him throw a soft boiled egg, a packet of pork scratchings and a large portion of spotted dick (complete with custard) into an electric fan and then laugh merrily at the mayhem which ensued. I always thought it was a pity that he took the incident to heart and left the village so shortly afterwards.

'Don't worry about me!' said Harry, with city-born confidence that was a couple of hundred miles misplaced. 'I can handle a couple of pints of beer!'

And so Frank pushed his empty hand cart back to the Duck and Puddle and I climbed aboard my rusty but trusty old bicycle and pedalled my rather weary way back to Bilbury Grange.

It was at exactly twenty seven minutes past one in the morning, that the telephone went.

I know the time because I looked at the clock and wrote down the time the minute I had the telephone receiver tucked between shoulder and ear. It was my habit to keep a record of the time when emergency calls came in. I also used to write down where the call had come from so that Patsy would know where I had gone. She always woke when the telephone rang but she wasn't always completely awake if you know what I mean.

154

It was Frank on the telephone and he sounded only slightly short of hysterical.

'Bread Cottage is ablaze!' he shouted. 'I closed up ten minutes ago and Thumper passed that way on his way back home. He just came racing back to tell me he'd seen flames licking out of the thatched roof. I've rung the fire brigade but they won't be here for half an hour. Gilly suggested I should ring you in case we get Harry out and he has any burns.'

Patsy, alarmed by Frank's voice, was now as awake as I was.

I told her where I was going, pulled on my trousers, a shirt and a jumper and was in the car on the way to Bread Cottage less than five minutes later. I stopped only to put my black bag into the boot.

I could see the flames almost as soon as I left Bilbury Grange.

The roof, of Bread Cottage was, of course, a thatch and thatched roofs may look very pretty, and make wonderful photographic images for tourists, but they tend to burn with great ferocity. A thatched roof will be fully ablaze in a fraction of the time that a slate or tiled roof will take to catch fire. And the result is too often that the entire building is destroyed.

I parked the car as close to the cottage as I could and ran to the small crowd of people who had gathered to do what they could to help. Thumper was there and so were Frank and Gilly.

The trouble was that there was absolutely nothing that anyone could do.

We all tried. Heaven knows, we tried.

Frank had brought three buckets with him and since there was a stream near to Bread Cottage, we thought we could organise a human chain, taking water from the stream and throwing it onto the flames.

But there was no way we could make a difference.

Not even a fire engine would have been able to dowse those flames.

We threw buckets of water over the blazing cottage but the water turned immediately into steam. We tried to get into the cottage but we were beaten back by the flames while we were still yards away from the front door.

Few things are more terrifying than a blazing house fire – apart from a blazing house fire when there is someone inside it.

'He'd be drunk and dead to the world by now,' muttered Frank to me. 'If he had three bottles of Old Restoration he'd be unconscious.'

I nodded agreement.

Old Restoration is sold as beer but those who know it well and who love it drink it more like a spirit than a low alcohol beverage.

'It was those damned log burners,' said Thumper Robinson glumly. 'I begged Archie not to put in a log burner at all. But the old fellow ignored me and put in two! He did promise me that he'd only light one at a time but I bet Harry didn't realise the danger. And I never thought to warn him.'

Thumper, bless his heart, likes to give the impression that he is a hard man, and in truth he can be when required, but at heart he is a kind and gentle soul who cares enormously about those around him. He was, I could tell, seriously upset.

Archie Jarvis had been the previous owner of Bread Cottage. He had died six months earlier in a nursing home in Barnstaple. Archie had been 97-years-old when eight decades of heavy smoking and drinking had finally killed him. For at least two decades, he had drunk a full bottle of whisky a day and he had been smoking 60 unfiltered cigarettes a day for much of his life. He had been the only person I knew who wore a monocle. He told me that his father, who had begun life as a police constable in London, had worn a monocle all his life even though his eyesight had been perfect. A police constable with a monocle must have been quite a sight. Unusual eyewear was not unusual in Bilbury. Several elderly, female residents favoured lorgnettes, and the pince nez could be seen regularly throughout the village and the environs.

Archie had run an ironmongery shop in Barnstaple. It was one of those gloriously old-fashioned shops which sold screws singly, rather than in plastic blister packs. The counter staff used to put every item purchased into its own suitably proportioned brown, paper bag. Archie retired at the age of 80 and his son, who was 58 at the time, took over. The business, which had been called Jarvis and Son was then officially renamed Jarvis and Father. I rather liked that. I remember Archie telling me, with a cackle of laughter, that the doctor who looked after him at the nursing home, and who had diagnosed heart failure and severe bronchitis, had told him sternly that he was now, at the age of 96, paying the price for a dissolute lifestyle.

I've always taken an interest in the houses in the village of Bilbury and so I already knew that Bread Cottage had, back in the 17th century, been half of a pair of matching, attached cottages. When the bakery started to do very well, and provide bread to the citizens of surrounding villages, the baker and his wife bought the cottage next door and knocked the two houses together. The upwardly mobile couple also took advantage of the need to expand to knock the two properties into one to combine the two chimneys into one in order to reduce their liability to the chimney or hearth tax. This much hated tax had been introduced in 1652 and it meant that property owners had to pay a tax for every chimney their property contained. Knocking two chimneys into one obviously reduced the liability to the chimney tax by half. The snag was, of course, that it meant that all the heat from two fireplaces, the fireplace in what had been the bakery and the fireplace in their living room, went into a single chimney. Knocking through the wall between the two chimneys had been done very crudely and was, it seemed, a very early example of what was later to become fairly widely known as the Bilbury Bodge.

And then, as Thumper had pointed out, the problem had been exacerbated when the owner before Harry had installed not one but two wood burning stoves into the two hearths.

Combining the two chimneys into one had been the first step towards disaster for it meant that the one chimney got twice as hot as it should have. Putting in two log burning stoves had been the second, and final, step towards disaster. Wood burning stoves dramatically increase the heat in a chimney. Having two wood burning stoves both using a single chimney was an accident waiting to happen, though the cottage might have survived if it had not been for the thatched roof.

And so, since there was nothing, absolutely nothing, we could do to stop what was happening, we stood there and we watched.

I could not believe that the unfortunate Dr Eckersley had found peace and happiness only to have it snatched away from him after so short a time. It seemed so cruel.

As Professor Eckersley, the teaching hospital professor and the consultant psychiatrist, he had spent all his working life in London;

living and working in a world populated almost exclusively by poltroons, galliards, gangrels and myrmidons.

Reborn as Gangolfphus 'Harry' Stottle he had been about to begin a new life and was already settling comfortably into the quiet, respectable community of Bilbury.

I stood there dreading the moment when I would have to go into the burnt out wreck of a house and identify Dr Eckersley's remains as being all that was left of a human being. I would, I supposed, have to tell the police the real identity of the burnt cadaver.

The police and the fire brigade always need a doctor to certify a body as dead. Even when it is painfully obvious to the most inexperienced eye that someone is dead, the authorities must have confirmation from a doctor before they can move the body. Officially, the police would need a police surgeon to confirm that the burnt out carcass was that of a human being. The nearest police surgeon was in Barnstaple but I suspected that he would ask me to stand in for him.

I had, only once before, been required to view the remains of someone burnt in a fire. And it had been an awful, awful business. The body I had seen had been a tramp who had died in a barn fire. The coroner ruled that he had probably lit a cigarette and gone to sleep without extinguishing the nub end properly. He had been burnt so badly that it had been impossible to identify him.

There wouldn't be any difficulty in identifying the corpse in Bread Cottage. We knew who was in there.

Authors who write books in which bodies are burned, usually describe the awful sight of a charred body but forget to mention the smell. If they had ever been within a quarter of a mile of a burnt human body they would know that the acrid, sharp smell of burning flesh can be smelt a long, long way away and will stick in the nostrils for days afterwards.

The fire engine arrived less than half an hour after I had driven up to Bread Cottage. The driver had done well. I am always impressed at how quickly the drivers of ambulances and fire engines can take their huge vehicles through the North Devon lanes. It is always much quicker at night, of course, when there is not much oncoming traffic and that which there is can see, and be seen, a mile or so away.

Bread Cottage was still blazing when the fire engine arrived and the firemen dowsed the flames surprisingly quickly. Frank, Gilly,

Thumper and the others wandered off because there was nothing else to be done. The fire chief told me that it would be hours before it would be safe for me to go into the remains of the cottage and identify the owner.

Before I drove off home, I decided to walk around to the orchard to see how Cedric was doing. I was feeling very depressed. I was devastated that Dr Eckersley was dead. He was a fascinating character and I had been looking forward to getting to know him better and to learning more about him and his life in London.

It would, I thought, be impossible to make up an individual like Pelham Ronald Eckersley. He had enough personality for a regiment. There had hardly been time for me to get to know him but I knew that I would miss him. I was so sad that he should find some peace and then have his life snatched away from him. It was yet another cruel reminder that not all dreams come true and not all dogs have their day. There were tears in my eyes and on my cheeks.

I unfastened the ties on the doors of the marquee. I wasn't quite sure why we had bothered to knot them together. If he had wanted to leave the marquee, Cedric could have walked through the side of the canvas tenting as if it hadn't been there, pulling out the tent pegs we had driven into the ground as though they were nothing more than dressmaker's pins.

But Cedric was still fast asleep, snoring and snuffling and still sleeping off the fermented apples he had eaten.

I was relieved to see that he was fine; absolutely fine.

And I was startled but relieved to see that sharing the marquee with him, curled up inside a thick blanket and wearing his purple Chapeau watch cap, lay Gengolphus 'Harry' Stottle.

I stared for a moment at the sleeping barman and then bent down and shook the erstwhile Professor Eckersley.

'What is it?' he demanded. His eyes were red and he was still sleepy and clearly fairly drunk. 'What the hell are you doing here?'

'I came to see Cedric. What are you doing here?' I asked him.

He sat up, rubbed his fists into his eyes and looked around. 'I felt so bad about letting Cedric get drunk that I decided to sleep with him in here so that I'd know when he woke up,' replied Harry.

'He could have rolled on top of you!' I told him.

'I never thought of that,' said Harry. 'But I thought I might be able to stop him eating more fermenting apples.'

'We thought you were dead!' I cried, suddenly angry in the way that mothers are when they discover that the child they thought was lost was in truth merely asleep in the airing cupboard. 'We thought you were done to a crisp!'

Harry sat up, suddenly awake. 'What do you mean? Why should I have been done to a crisp? What the devil are you talking about?'

I bent down and put a hand on his shoulder. 'I am so pleased to see you,' I said softly. 'You'd better come with me. I'll take you to the Duck and Puddle. I think they'll be able to find you a bed.'

'I can go to my cottage,' said Harry. 'I've got a very nice second-hand bed there. I bought it from a pal of yours, a lovely fellow called Patchy Fogg. I got the bed at a bargain price. It was apparently the only bed in Stratford-upon-Avon that the bard did not sleep in so he let me have it cheap. '

'I'm afraid you don't have a cottage or a lovely bed,' I told him. 'I'm sorry to have to tell you this but your cottage burnt down.'

'Has it?' he said. He slowly hauled himself to his feet. 'Oh, that's a bit of a bugger,' he said.

Cedric snuffled and snorted, lifted one trotter and then put it back where it had been. He seemed to be dreaming but was definitely happy enough. I found myself wondering, for a moment, if pigs do dream. And if they do dream, of what do they dream?

I drove Harry to the Duck and Puddle where Gilly and Frank were absolutely delighted to see him alive and well. Frank rang Thumper to give him the good news. I went to Bread Cottage to tell the firemen that there were no charred bodies in the house.

I picked up Cedric the next morning and Frank and I took down the marquee which was no longer needed.

I honestly expected that the burning down of his cottage would result in Harry going back to London.

But I was surprised, and delighted, when the Duck and Puddle's new barman announced that he still intended to stay in Bilbury. He said he intended to rebuild the cottage and that he would instruct the architect to try to stick to the original design – except that there would be two separate chimneys and a slate roof.

Harry said that until the cottage was rebuilt he would be living at the Duck and Puddle and he was thrilled when Gilly presented him with two maroon and gold brocade waistcoats which she had fashioned from a spare piece of curtain material. She'd also made him a matching bow tie.

'It isn't far to go to work,' Harry told me. 'I just totter down the stairs. And my cottage is only a short walk away so I can keep an eye on the builders.'

As the builders recreated the burnt down cottage, Harry told me that since the place had been called 'Bread Cottage' for three centuries he thought it was about time for a change. After toying with various names, including 'Bacon's End', Harry decided to call his rebuilt cottage 'Cedric's Cottage'; in a permanent tribute to the pig who had unwittingly saved his life.

'Thank God I was sleeping with the doctor's pig! I would have fried if I hadn't been tucked up with Cedric in Frank's second best marquee,' the elegantly costumed barman explained to anyone who would listen.

I couldn't help wondering what a certain Dr Eckersley, psychiatrist to the stars, would have had to say if one of his celebrity patients had made a similar confession.

A Hectic Day in Bilbury

Bank holidays were usually an especially busy time for me in Bilbury and it was not unknown for the morning surgery to last so long that it pretty well ran into the evening surgery. On not a few occasions, I found myself doing my non-urgent home visits in the evening. When I had seen the last of the patients in the waiting room, I would usually grab some supper (having missed luncheon completely) and then set off around the village to see those village residents who needed to be seen in their homes. Sometimes I would wait for my supper until I'd completed the visits.

These days, most GPs do very few home visits. But back in the 1970s, I saw many of my patients in their homes. Indeed, I don't think there was a patient on my list whose home I had not entered on business on at least one occasion, either to see them or to visit a relative. I found that by visiting my patients in their own homes I learnt a good deal more about them. It is so much easier to know how to treat a patient when you know a little about them, their lives and how they live. Sadly, home visits seem to be rare and getting rarer. Many doctors seem to be too busy filling in forms and attending meetings to make house calls.

The popular North Devon holiday resorts of Ilfracombe and Combe Martin are not far away from Bilbury and the famous twin villages of Lynton and Lynmouth are also relatively close by. There are numerous hotels and boarding houses in these resorts, and a variety of caravan sites and campsites cater for many thousands of additional holidaymakers.

Cheap flights and ridiculously cheap hotel accommodation meant that in the 1970s, it was often cheaper to take a holiday in Spain, France or some other destination than to have a holiday in Britain but there were still millions of Britons who preferred to have their holidays nearer home – and a holiday in England invariably meant a holiday by the seaside. Young parents, with happy childhood memories, wanted to recreate the joy of their own family holidays.

And they were perhaps a little nervous of taking their small children abroad. Many did not enjoy the prospect of having to travel to a suitable airport, deal with customs officials and then sit for a few hours in a cramped, budget aeroplane packed with hundreds of other tourists and harassed airline staff. And, of course, many genuinely enjoyed and preferred the traditional North Devon holiday experience: fishing for shrimp in rock pools, huddling under a sun umbrella on one of the inevitably rainy days, shivering while making sand castles, surfing on the vast sandy beaches at Croyde and Woolacombe, enjoying fish and chips on the sand, taking a boat trip out to Lundy Island and sipping warm beer at a traditional Devon pub with a thatched roof and a wasp infested garden. And then, of course, there were the joys of pasties and scones covered in Devon cream. As a visitor once said to me: 'You can't buy a decent cream tea in Torremolinos'.

It is true that the lanes in North Devon tend to be on the restricted side of narrow and they tend to wind and wriggle rather a lot too, and are as a result sometimes rather daunting to motorists who are accustomed to driving on roads where there is, at the very least, room for a line of traffic going this way and a line of traffic going that way.

The result of the nervousness created by the narrowness of the roads, means that the traffic queues can be exhausting – particularly if a car towing a caravan comes radiator to radiator up against a tractor towing a trailer loaded with half a hundred bales of hay.

But North Devon was still a popular destination for holidaymakers; particularly those who came from the English Midlands; from the urban sprawls of Birmingham, Wolverhampton, Walsall and so on.

It is true that not many visitors chose to stay in the village of Bilbury itself (there were, in any case, only a few cottages which were rented out to visitors and the only residential accommodation was in Bilbury's only pub, the Duck and Puddle, an inn which has only a few bedrooms for guests) but a good many tourists passed through the village on their travels through North Devon or chose to visit for the day. And, of course, holidaymakers staying on campsites, under canvas or in caravans, were often as close to Bilbury as to anywhere else. It was also not unusual for holidaymakers to get lost and find themselves in Bilbury by mistake.

163

The result is that at the height of the holiday season, I often saw quite a number of strangers.

I vividly remember one August bank holiday that seemed to go on and on forever.

It possibly wasn't the busiest day I've ever had but it was certainly the strangest and by the end of the day, when I eventually settled down to enjoy two slices of buttered toast and a glass of Bunnahabein malt whisky, served in a tea glass with a little hot water, I was pretty well drained.

There are, incidentally, few English delicacies in quite the same league as hot, buttered toast.

I usually prefer making toast for Patsy and myself on a long handled, brass toasting fork held in front of a log fire, and I still feel disappointed if we have to make our toast under the grill in the kitchen because the weather is too warm to light a fire.

I remember that at the end of that particular day, Patsy and I listened to 'At the Drop of a Hat', a long playing recording of a comedy duet called Flanders and Swann. Michael Flanders and Donald Swann were the two halves of a popular musical comedy act and they had been at their most popular in the 1950s and 1960s. They were responsible for a number of comic songs such as 'The Gasman Cometh', 'The Hippotamus' (with its wonderful chorus of 'mud, mud, glorious mud') and 'The Gnu'.

By the time side one of the record had finished playing, I was beginning to feel relaxed and I poured myself a second glass of Bunnahabein malt whisky to complete the relaxation process. Patsy, who has never liked whisky, had a cup of hot chocolate. By the time side two of the album was finished, we were both ready for bed.

But that was later, much later.

Before we got to the buttered toast and to the joys of Flanders and Swann, there was quite a good deal of the day to get through.

And it really was one of those days that I'd like to forget but which sticks in my memory and probably won't ever fade away. It was, without doubt, an unusual day.

The first outsider I saw was a boy of about fourteen. I can't remember his exact age but I'll call him Phillip Nixon for the very good reason that his name was something quite different and if I were to tell you what it was you would probably recognise it.

164

(I saw 'Phillip' again a couple of decades later. We met in a rather gloomy, unprepossessing BBC radio studio in Leeds. I didn't remember him since he had grown up considerably, of course. But he remembered me and introduced himself. I was in the studio to talk about a book I'd written. He was there because he was a Junior Minister in the Government of the day.)

Phillip had come to the surgery with his father but he came into the consulting room by himself. Ostensibly, he came because he had fallen playing cricket on the beach and had bruised his leg on a half-hidden rock. The skin had not been broken and neither had the bone. I knew the moment I saw him that he had come to see me for some other reason. No healthy 14-year-old visits a doctor to complain about a bruise.

'Is there anything else worrying you?' I asked, when I'd taken a look at the bruise, offered the usual expression of sympathy and told him what he already knew – that there was no need to do anything about it since it would doubtless go through the usual variety of colours and then disappear.

'Well there is, actually, sir,' he replied, apparently surprised that I had seen through his stratagem.

I waited.

It was clear from the 'sir' he had added on to the end of the sentence that he was a pupil at a fairly posh school. I remember it occurred to me that I could not remember the identity of the last person who had called me 'sir'. It may have been a tailor, selling me a made-for-measure ill-fitting, ill-made jacket. Or perhaps it was a traffic warden, slipping a parking ticket under one of my windscreen wipers. If it had been the latter then it was doubtless said with more than its fair share of irony.

'At school I play in the second eleven at cricket,' he told me. 'I'm very young for the second eleven and the cricket master is pretty confident that one day I'll play for the firsts.'

(The cricket master's prediction was modest. Young Phillip eventually played cricket for his university. The word was, he told me decades later when we met in that BBC radio station in Leeds, that if politics hadn't taken over his life he could have made a career as a professional cricketer.)

I nodded, said nothing and waited again.

165

'The thing is,' he confessed, 'that I did something pretty dreadful during the last match of the term.'

I sat still and waited.

'I'd scored 49, which was a pretty decent effort on that pitch, and then I hit a slow ball into the air over mid-on. I thought it was going for four but the fellow at mid-on ran backwards and it was pretty clear that he stood a good chance of catching it. I really wanted that 50 because boys who score a 50 or take five wickets have their names read out at morning assembly. Besides, I knew that a 50 would push me up to second in the batting averages.'

He paused and I said nothing. I wondered what on earth he was going to tell me.

'And then,' he said, 'I did a pretty caddish thing. A very caddish thing actually.'

I raised an eyebrow and leant forward an inch or two, as though emphasising that whatever he told me would go no further. In those days, doctors were allowed to keep patients' secrets. These days there is really no such thing as patient confidentiality. But back then, the doctor's consulting room was like the priest's confessional.

'I prayed that the fellow at mid-on would drop the catch,' he said, his voice now not much more than a whisper. 'The other batsman and I had run the single and so I would get my 50 if the fielder didn't hold the catch. If he held onto it, of course, I'd be out for 49 and I'd miss my half century.'

'You prayed that the fielder wouldn't hold onto the catch?'

'I know,' said Phillip, now blushing bright red. 'I know it's an awful thing to say, sir. But I really wanted that half century.'

'What happened?' I asked.

The boy looked puzzled.

'Did he hold onto the catch?'

'Oh, of course. No, he didn't.'

'And now you feel guilty that you prayed for something so selfish and relatively trivial?'

Phillip paused and swallowed. 'Well, it wasn't actually trivial, sir,' he said. 'It was pretty important. But it was totally selfish. I realised immediately afterwards.'

'Have you told anyone else about this? Your father? A teacher at school? The cricket master? The school chaplain?'

'No, sir. I'm afraid I haven't.'

166

'You told me because you needed to tell someone, the bruise was a good excuse to see someone in some sort of authority and you knew that you'd probably never see me again and so it doesn't really matter what I think?'

He looked embarrassed.

I waited.

'I suppose I did, sir. Yes, that's about the size of it.'

I looked at him. It was a trivial thing but it was clearly important to him. I was impressed that he had worried about the praying. But less impressed that he had chosen to confess to a stranger, someone he had never seen before and would probably never see again, rather than to someone whose authority and opinion he would doubtless respect more deeply. It is sometimes easier to confess to someone you don't know than to confess to someone you do know.

'Would you describe yourself as fairly religious?' I asked him.

'Fairly,' he said. 'About average, I would say, sir.'

'Do you really think that the praying had any effect on the fielder's ability to catch the ball?'

'I don't know, sir. I can't really say. That's the thing, isn't it? If I knew that it had no effect then I wouldn't worry about it. But, you know...' His voice trailed off.

'Your school cricket is over for the year, I suppose?'

'Oh yes, sir. We'll be playing rugger in the autumn.'

'Do you play for any other teams? Do you have any other cricket matches this summer? Apart from beach cricket, of course.'

'They've asked me to turn out for the village side,' said Phillip. 'My father plays for them.'

'And obviously you'd like to do well?'

I couldn't give him Hail Marys or extra homework or lines or keep him in after school but a thought had occurred to me. I clearly needed to punish him in some way or the boy would nurse this guilt for the rest of his life.

'Oh yes, sir. Very much so.'

'It was a pretty caddish thing to do,' I told him. 'Praying for the other chap to drop the catch.'

'Yes, sir. I've been worrying about it quite a bit.'

'When you bat for the village you can score 20 runs,' I told him. 'But when you've got 20 you must give away your wicket.'

Phillip swallowed hard. 'Just 20, sir?'

167

'You can score 20 runs. If you score less, then that's fine. The praying is cancelled out. But if you score 20 then you give away your wicket. Doesn't matter how you do it. Let a straight ball hit your wicket or your pad. Or scoop a return catch to the bowler.'

'And you think that would do it? That would be a just penance, sir?'

'Definitely,' I told him, as though I were an expert on religious punishments.

'Thank you, sir,' he said. He looked glum but strangely relieved. He stood up.

'And don't worry about it anymore.'

'No. Thank you, sir.' He headed for the door and then stopped and turned. 'You won't say anything to my father, will you, sir?'

'Not a word,' I assured him.

When he'd gone, I sat for a few moments trying to think how else I could have handled a problem that was more theological than medical. Eventually, I gave up. I couldn't think of anything better. And although I suspect that you can probably think of a more suitable way to handle it, I still cannot think of anything more appropriate or effective.

It was, to say the very least, a unique problem and a tailor made solution. And a pretty good example of the sort of non-medical problem that country doctors sometimes find themselves facing.

My second patient of the day had also fallen down.

But instead of a simple bruise, Edna Biddulph had a small cut on her hand. The cut, more of a graze to be honest, was on the thenar eminence, the part of the hand at the base of the thumb. It was the sort of injury that most people would be happy to deal with by running it under the cold tap for a few minutes, to wash away any dirt, and then slapping on a sticking plaster. I doubt if the cut was as much as half an inch long. The cut had bled a little and the blood had long ago dried. It appeared that she had made no effort to wash it.

'How did you do this?' I asked, as I cleaned the small wound as gently as I could. I was, I thought, merely making polite conversation. It was a question along the lines of 'Where did you go on your holidays this year?'

But if I had been expecting a simple 'Oh, I tripped over the dog' or 'I fell while playing with my youngest' I was sadly mistaken.

Ms Biddulph (when she introduced herself, she was most insistent that I should refer to her as 'Ms' Biddulph – a form of address which was quite unusual at the time in my part of the world) was a neat woman in her early thirties; there wasn't much of her but you could tell she was pleased with what there was and regarded herself as having been hewn by a sculptor of talent using materials of the very best quality. The term Ms has been in use since the 17th century but it was the first time I'd ever heard anyone use it.

Sadly for the world, she was, I think, a woman who lived to complain.

You know how some people eat to live and others live to eat, well there are some people who complain to make their lives better and there are some people who complain because they like doing it. She was definitely one of the latter group.

'I fell on your cliff path,' she said accusingly.

'I'm afraid I don't have a cliff path,' I said, perhaps rather defensively. She had said it as though she were about to announce that she was planning to take legal action against me. Some people can turn a simple statement into the beginnings of a tort.

'Where did you fall?' I asked her.

'Just outside Padstow,' she replied.

'That's in Cornwall,' I pointed out. 'It must be nearly 100 miles from here!'

'That's as maybe,' she said. 'It's all the same thing.'

'Why didn't you go and see a doctor in Padstow?'

'My partner and I were out for the day,' she said. 'We took the children down to Cornwall. I didn't have time to go looking for doctors. But we're staying in Combe Martin.'

'When did you fall?'

'Yesterday,' she said. 'You should insist that they have all the loose stones removed from the path,' she told me as I finished cleaning the small wound. She examined her injury critically. 'Does that need any stitches?'

'No, I don't think so,' I said. 'A sticking plaster should suffice.'

'I think it might heal better with a few stitches,' she said. 'Stitches would bring the edges closer together and there might be less chance of a scar.'

So I put in a stitch. The customer is always right. The cut was so small that I could only manage to put in one stitch.

'I don't need a tetanus injection,' she told me. 'So don't think you're giving me one of those. I had a series of tetanus jabs last month. And I'm not taking antibiotics either. I always get thrush and diarrhoea if I take antibiotics.'

'You'll need to see a doctor in five days to have that stitch removed,' I told her. I didn't think she needed antibiotics.

'I won't be able to get an appointment see my doctor for a week or so,' said Ms Biddulph. 'He's a very busy doctor.'

'Well, you must explain to the receptionist that you need to see him urgently,' I said.

'I could have easily fallen off the cliff. If I had fallen off the edge I would have gone down onto the rocks,' complained the woman. 'You should put a fence along the edge of the path.'

'But there are miles of footpath along the cliffs,' I pointed out. 'It would cost a fortune to put up fencing along the whole coast.'

'Well, it doesn't matter what it would cost, you should put up some fencing,' said the woman. 'You should insist that it's done.' She still seemed to be holding me responsible for the abscnce of fencing.

'Don't you think that having fencing all along the cliff path would rather spoil the view?' I asked.

'You'll wish you'd put up fencing when someone falls,' she insisted.

'I think there are already some warning signs on the cliff path,' I said. 'There are signs asking people to be careful and to keep away from the edge.'

'Well, that's not good enough,' said the woman. 'What's your name?'

I told her.

'I shall be writing to the authorities to complain,' said the woman. 'I don't think you have a very good attitude. It's your responsibility to protect members of the public. And I will also complain about the fact that I had to sit in your waiting room for forty minutes before you would see me.'

With a weary heart, I explained that I had been seeing other patients and that I did not have an appointment system.

The only complaints I ever received about not having an appointment system came from visitors who had never been to Bilbury before and would probably never visit again.

Ms Biddulph wasn't the first visitor to complain about the fact that I ran open surgeries where patients were seen on a first come first served basis, and she probably wouldn't be the last.

'My GP has an appointment system,' she said tartly.

'Many GPs do,' I agreed. 'And in fact I lose money by not having an appointment system. If I had one I would be paid more because the National Health Service pays a bonus to GPs who have them.'

I then pointed out that I had conducted an informal survey among my patients to see what they wanted me to do. I had, I explained, told them that the choice was simple. If I organised an appointment system they would have to visit or telephone Bilbury Grange to make an appointment to see me. Because of the way these things always work there would, I pointed out, probably end up being a waiting time of a few days before they could be seen. And I pointed out that even the best run appointment system tends to run late occasionally. If I had a patient with a complicated problem, or I had to go out to see a patient with an emergency, then the patient with a 10.00 a.m. appointment could still have to wait an hour or more to be seen. On the other hand, if we stayed as we were then anyone could walk into Bilbury Grange during the hours of any weekday morning or evening surgery and be seen without making an appointment. They would probably have to wait a while for other patients to be seen but they would be seen on the day they wanted to be seen and, with some delay, at roughly the time of day they wanted to be seen. Complications and emergencies would still delay things, of course, but patients would have the choice of coming back to the next surgery – a choice probably not available if we had an appointment system.

I told her that my regular patients had made it pretty clear that they felt that they were better off without having to make an appointment. Patients turned up at my surgery, sat in the waiting room and waited. If there was a long queue they would pop out, do some shopping at Peter Marshall's shop, and come back half an hour later. I explained that the system worked well and that because everything was fairly simple to run, Miss Johnson my secretary and receptionist managed quite well by herself. All she really had to do was to take each arrival's medical records out of the filing cabinet and give the records to me as patients turned up. I pointed out that GPs who ran appointment systems usually ended up with teams of receptionists and that patients often had to wait three weeks to see a doctor. In addition, the telephone line was usually blocked with callers making appointments and so patients needing a home visit would have to ring several times to get through.

I didn't tell Ms Biddulph but I had long suspected that appointment systems were introduced not to please doctors or patients but to please bureaucrats and to give a sense of order to a service that could never be ordered because there are too many variables. I also did not point out to her, though perhaps I should have done, that if I had run my practice with an appointment system then she would have probably not been able to see me for two, three days or more days – and she would have probably been back home by then. And I really didn't want the argument to continue so I didn't mention to her that she had told me that she would have difficulty in seeing her own doctor in less than a week – because he ran an appointment system!

Ms Biddulph then left.

For the record, over the next three months I received letters from the local council, the local administrators for the National Health Service, the General Medical Council and several other organisations. Ms Biddulph's complaint to the GMC was that I hadn't wanted to put a stitch in her wound until she had demanded that I did so. All of these organisations wrote to let me know that they had received complaints about me. And eventually all told me that I had done nothing wrong. The bit of the NHS that administers general practice told me what I already knew, which was that they would have liked me to have an appointment system but that I didn't have to have one. The General Medical Council took six months to decide that I had not done anything wrong. These things are worrying even when you know that you haven't done anything wrong.

After Ms Biddulph had left, I saw half a dozen Bilbury residents. None of them was difficult to deal with. There were a couple of patients who needed to have their blood pressures taken. One or two required repeat prescriptions. And Mrs Walthamstow simply came to

172

be weighed and to be encouraged. She was trying to lose weight and had managed to reduce her weight by half a stone in two months.

When Mrs Walthamstow had left, duly encouraged and, hopefully, inspired to cutting down her consumption of cream buns still further, I had to pop into the hallway to deal with a King Charles Spaniel which was choking on a tennis ball.

The dog's owner, not a Bilbury resident, had thrown the ball and the dog, being over-enthusiastic in its effort to retrieve it, had half swallowed it. Since the nearest vet was some miles away in Combe Martin, the owner of the dog had brought it to the surgery in the hope that I could help.

The good news was that the ball was still visible and although it was clearly stuck, and causing the dog a great deal of discomfort and distress, I didn't think there was any immediate risk that it was going to go any further down the animal's throat. A King Charles Spaniel has a fairly small mouth and throat. A bigger dog would have doubtless posed a bigger problem.

I contemplated trying the canine equivalent of the Heimlich manoeuvre and was trying to decide whether this would work when Patsy, who had heard the commotion and knew what was happening, appeared clutching a large adjustable pipe wrench which she had found in the shed where I keep my tools.

I knew immediately what she had in mind and while the owner of the dog held the animal still, I took hold of the ball with the wrench and pulled it out of the dog's throat. The dog gasped and coughed and shook himself but within a moment he was fine.

I tossed the wrench and the ball on the floor and beamed at the owner thinking that he would be pleased. It was my first operation on a dog and it had been entirely successful.

'You've ruined this ball,' said the owner, who had picked up the ball I'd removed from the dog's throat. He seemed uninterested in the dog, now that it was no longer in danger, and showed the ball to me.

When I'd applied the wrench to the ball, I'd tightened it as much as I could to make sure that I had a good grip. I was frightened of pushing the ball further down the dog's throat. And the wrench I'd used had punctured the ball.

'This won't bounce,' complained the man. He tried to bounce the ball on the hall floor but the puncture meant it had no bounce left in it at all.

I apologised.

'You owe me for a new ball,' said the man.

I opened the cupboard where we keep our croquet set, some old tennis racquets and a variety of old balls. I selected a tennis ball which looked to be about the same age and condition as the ruined one and handed it to the man. He looked at it and sniffed. 'I suppose this will do,' he said. He had clearly been expecting me to give him the money to buy a new ball. Or perhaps he had been expecting me to give him a box of new balls.

He and the dog then left without so much as a bark or a grunt of thanks. I didn't even know his name. The only thing notable about him was that he wore a tie which had clearly been bought for him by a female relative; possibly one with poor eyesight. The fact that he wore it suggested that his filial duty was more powerful than his taste in neckwear.

'Some people are so ungrateful!' said Patsy who was still standing in the hallway.

'I think it's going to be one of those days,' I muttered wearily.

It was still only morning but I had an awful feeling that the day had not yet got into its stride. Some days in general practice are like that.

The next patient was a girl of 16. She too was a visitor to the area. She had come with her mother who was, she told me, sitting in the waiting room. The girl, I noticed, had what is sometimes called a monobrow but is known in medicine as synophrys; a condition in which the two eyebrows are joined in the middle and which can be associated with a variety of genetic faults. Some of these produce noticeable abnormalities – such as a shortage of fingers or toes, a malformed limb or a facial abnormality. But most commonly, the monobrow is just what it is. Some people shave the middle bit. Some are proud of having a single eyebrow. I understand that like hairstyles and skirt lengths, single eyebrows go in and out of fashion.

'Would you squeeze my pimples please,' she asked.

I looked at her, not quite believing my ears. The girl had terrible acne and her face and neck were covered in spots.

'You want me to squeeze your pimples?' I asked, slightly stunned by the request.

'Yes, please,' said the girl.

The girl had at least 50 visible pimples. I thought it a pretty safe bet that if she undressed I would fine another 100 or so on her back.

'I don't think that would be a good idea,' I told her. 'Squeezing pimples can be dangerous and can cause the infection to go into the body.'

The girl began to cry.

She didn't wail or scream or sob. She just began to cry; quite noiselessly. They were the tears of someone who is overcome by hopelessness and despair. I felt desperately sorry for her.

'Where do you live?' I asked.

She told me. I had heard of the town. It was in the English Midlands, not far from where my friend Will had his practice.

'Have you seen your own GP?' I asked her.

She nodded.

'What has he done?'

'He won't do anything,' she said. 'He says that they'll go as I get older.'

'He hasn't prescribed anything?'

'No. He says he won't give me anything because they're just teenage spots and I will grow out of them.'

To describe the girl's acne spots as 'just teenage spots' was, I thought, a bit like describing Mount Everest as 'a bit of a hill'. I had never seen such bad acne. It seemed to me that for a doctor to refuse to treat the girl's condition just because it was almost certainly age and hormone related was as close to professional neglect as it is possible to get.

'Your doctor hasn't referred you to anyone else? He hasn't arranged for you to see a skin specialist?'

'No. My mother asked him to arrange an appointment for me to see a skin doctor but he refused. He said he wasn't going to waste a specialist's time with some teenage spots.'

I closed my eyes and counted to ten to stop myself saying something wildly uncomplimentary about my unseen colleague.

'How far do you live from Birmingham?' I asked.

'Not far,' said the girl. 'My dad works in Birmingham.'

I then asked the girl to wait for a few moments while I rang my pal Will. He too was in the middle of his morning surgery but I was lucky enough to catch him between patients. Will and I studied medicine together at Birmingham University.

'What was the name of that dermatologist we studied under at the Birmingham General?' I asked him. 'The slightly dotty one who admitted that he'd only become a dermatologist because dermatologists never had to attend emergency night calls!'

'Oh, yes, I remember,' said Will laughing. 'He is the best skins guy I know. I send patients to him occasionally if they've got difficult problems.'

I explained that I had a girl in my consulting room who had terrible acne and that her own doctor wouldn't treat her or refer her to a specialist.

'Do you think he'd see her if I referred her to him?' I asked.

'Of course he would.'

Will gave me the specialist's phone number. I asked him when he was bringing his family down to Bilbury for a weekend, and he promised it would be soon.

I then asked the girl to pop into the waiting room to fetch her mother.

While she was gone, I telephoned the skin specialist's secretary at the General Hospital in Birmingham. A moment later, the girl and her mother both returned. I noticed that the mother also had a monobrow and couldn't help wondering if anyone else in the family had the same condition. Synophrys is sometimes inherited but it can also just happen. Indeed, it is so common that it was perfectly possible that it was merely a coincidence that both the girl and her mother had the condition. It clearly wasn't relevant to the problem with the spots so I said nothing about it.

I pointed to the two chairs near my desk and while they sat, I asked the secretary at the Birmingham hospital how soon the specialist could see a patient with very bad teenage acne. The secretary gave me a date just a week ahead. I told the girl's mother the date and asked if she could take her daughter to Birmingham on that day. The girl's mother, who looked rather surprised, said she could. I confirmed the appointment and then wrote a letter of introduction which I gave to the teenager.

'Go to the hospital and take this letter with you,' I told her. 'The doctor you'll see is one of the best skin specialists in England. He'll help you.'

The girl took the letter from me and thanked me. The mother thanked me. The girl thanked me again. They were now both crying.

'Do we have to tell our GP about the appointment?' asked the mother.

'You can if you like,' I said. 'But you don't have to. The specialist will write to him and he'll simply explain that your daughter was seen by another doctor when she was on holiday in Devon.'

'Will he make trouble over it?' asked the mother.

'I don't think so,' I said. 'Not for you.'

I thought their doctor might well complain that I had interfered with his treatment of his patient. But I really didn't care about that. I was tempted to tell the mother that they might like to consider finding another GP but I thought that would probably be pushing my luck. The GMC did not take kindly to doctors criticising other practitioners, however indirectly and however much the criticism might be deserved.

The girl and her mother were effusive in their thanks. I was rather embarrassed. The truth was that I had done absolutely nothing that any decent doctor wouldn't have done.

Miss Johnson, taking pity on me then popped in before the next patient to bring me in a cup of lemon tea and two digestive biscuits.

I thanked her and took a bite from one of the digestives. I told her that if she'd known what I had been through already that morning she would have brought me two custard creams. Or maybe even a couple of bourbon biscuits. (I had given up eating chocolate covered biscuits in the surgery after an unfortunate incident involving a chocolate biscuit which had melted and covered my hand, my pen and my tie in an unfortunate looking brown stain.)

Miss Johnson looked at me over her spectacles. She's still never sure about my sense of humour. 'You've got a busy day ahead of you, doctor,' she said. 'The waiting room is still crowded. There are quite a lot of holidaymakers here today.'

She then hurried out.

I remember I found myself wishing I could follow her and hide in the filing cabinet where we keep the medical records.

For me one of the joys of a quiet rural practice was always the fact that I had time to talk to my patients, understand their problems and deal with them as people rather than as symptoms and diseases. Doctors working in busy hospitals or city practices are forever rushed; never having enough time to listen properly. Now I was beginning to feel as though I were working in a busy inner city practice. I almost wished I had an appointment system so that I could at least control the number of patients attending a single surgery.

The next half a dozen patients were all fairly straightforward. There were three with summer colds, one with blistered feet and I can't remember what the others had wrong with them.

And then came a woman in her forties called Madge Compton. She complained that she was suffering from nausea and frequent stomach cramps. She was definitely an unhealthy colour and my first thought was that she might be slightly jaundiced.

'I'm feeling very weak and tired,' she said.

She also told me that she needed to urinate more often than usual and that she was suffering from occasional attacks of palpitations.

Her condition sounded complex and since she was only in the area for another two days (she was staying with her husband in a guest house in Ifracombe) I didn't think I would be able to solve her problem. I would, I thought, need to have some blood tests done and it was unlikely that I would get back the results before she left.

'How long have you had all these problems?' I asked.

'About two months,' she told me.

And for the umpteenth time that summer, I wondered why on earth she had chosen to come and tell me about her problem.

'What made you come to my surgery?' I asked her.

'It's difficult to see my own doctor,' she said. 'He has an appointment system and he's very busy. I have to wait two or three weeks to see him.'

I couldn't help wishing that Ms Biddulph were sitting in a corner of my surgery.

'Have you lost any weight?' I asked her.

'Oh yes,' Mrs Compton replied. 'I've been on a diet. I go to a slimming club and they've been advising me.'

'How long have you been dieting?'

'Around six months.'

'And how much weight have you lost?'

'A stone,' replied Mrs Compton. 'I was fifteen stone but I'm down to nearly fourteen. My slimming adviser has put me on a strict diet. I eat lettuce and tomato on brown bread with plenty of fruit juices.'

That was, I remembered, the diet originated by a 19th century music hall chorus singer called Florrie Forde. She used to sing songs like 'Down at the Old Bull and Bush', 'Pack Up Your Troubles in Your Old Kit-Bag' and 'It's A Long Way to Tipperary'. Miss Forde started her career at 8 stone but built her way up to 15 stone and decided she needed to lose weight if her career wasn't going to founder. So she found or created a diet which consisted of tomatoes, lettuce, brown bread and orange juice. She stuck to it and lost weight. Amazingly, the diet still had its enthusiastic supporters three quarters of a century later.

I remember reading that she was so pleased with the diet that Miss Forde had copies of it printed and sold them. This was, in effect, the first commercial diet book. I also remember that the book was very successful but that one woman failed to lose weight and turned up at the theatre to complain.

'Did you follow the diet I gave you?' asked Florrie.

'Oh yes, I followed it to the letter.

'You ate the lettuce and the tomatoes and the brown bread and you drank the orange juice?'

'Yes, but I haven't lost any weight.'

'Did you eat anything else?'

'Well, only my ordinary meals, of course.'

And that is where the gag came from.

'Have you tried taking anything for your symptoms?' I asked, hoping this question might produce a clue, but not honestly expecting that the answer would provide all the information I required.

'Oh yes,' said Mrs Compton. 'I've been taking some tablets that my slimming adviser recommended.'

'What sort of tablets?'

'Supplements,' said Mrs Compton. 'They contain ingredients which are essential for the human body – vitamins and minerals and so forth.'

'Have you got the bottle with you?'

She had. She took it out of her handbag and handed it to me.

She was, I saw, taking a vitamin and mineral capsule that contained enough vitamins and minerals to satisfy the body's entire daily requirements.

'Marvellous,' I said, handing back the bottle. 'How often do you take them?'

'I take 40 a day,' she replied.

I thought I had misheard.

'Sorry,' I said, 'how many did you say you took each day?'

'I take 40 a day,' she said again.

I pointed to the bottle she was still holding. 'You take 40 a day of those capsules?'

'Yes,' she said proudly.

'Did your slimming adviser tell you to take that many?'

'Oh no, she said to take one a day. But I thought that if one a day was going to be good for me than 40 a day would make me super fit!'

It took me ten minutes to persuade her that the tablets would kill her if she kept taking them in such huge quantities. 'Vitamins and minerals are essential for the body to function,' I explained. 'But they can be toxic if you take them in excessive quantities.'

I told her that all the symptoms she had described to me were probably a result of her body being poisoned by the pills she was taking. I took her blood pressure, listened to her heart and did all the other tests I could easily conduct in the surgery. I even thought about having her admitted to the hospital in Barnstaple so that she could be properly investigated but I eventually decided that she didn't seem to be in immediate danger. I did, however, make her promise to stop taking the capsules and to see her doctor as soon as she got home. I told her that he would probably want to have some tests done.

Mrs Compton wasn't the first patient I'd seen who had been poisoning herself by overdosing on vitamin and mineral tablets. I suspected this was going to be a big problem in the years ahead.

The next patient was also a visitor to the area and she was staying in what sounded as if it was a very overcrowded caravan on a site near Combe Martin. I wasn't sure why she ended up in my consulting room. A doctor in Combe Martin, who had some sort of contract with the proprietor, usually looked after people staying at the caravan park.

The patient, who introduced herself as Miss Jennifer May, was in in her late twenties and she came into my consulting room with an entourage of two very small children and three adult males. Miss May looked very pregnant. She was short, plump and had sideburns and a nicely developing moustache. She wasn't wearing very much and what she was wearing had either been bought when she was a stone lighter, or had been bought for someone about six sizes smaller. There wasn't enough spare room inside what she was wearing for her to be able to fit a goose pimple. Looking at her, I thought it safe to assume that she would be as easy to embarrass as a fan dancer with twenty years' experience.

I asked the three men if they would mind going back into the waiting room or, if it was crowded in there, if they would perhaps be kind enough to wait outside.

'I want them to stay with me,' said Miss May firmly.

'Why's that?' I asked.

'Because I'm pregnant and I think I'm about to go into labour,' said Miss May.

'I don't understand,' I said. I looked at the three men. 'Are any of you medically qualified?'

'Oh no,' said Miss May with a laugh. 'They're not doctors – they are the fathers.'

It took me a moment to realise what she meant but when I finally understood it was immediately clear that a more appropriate name for Miss Jennifer May would have probably been Miss Jennifer Does.

This was one woman whose eyes had probably never been full of maybe and this was, I confess, a situation I had not come across before.

I had, of course, known mothers who weren't sure of the identity of the father. But I had never before had a mother walk into my surgery with three putative fathers. Moreover, the three men all seemed quite relaxed about the situation. One of them was very short and rather stout. He was considerably older than the rest. He was balding and had a fringe of red hair. The second was tall, black and powerful looking. The third was no more than a youth. He looked to be twenty at the most. He was of middle-eastern origin and had acne and long, straggly, black hair. It occurred to me that there was a chance that when the baby was born we might not have too much

181

difficulty in uncovering the identity of the real father. We might, at the very least, be able to exclude one of the men from the final shortlist.

'You'd better climb up onto the examination couch,' I told her. 'Are the two children yours?'

'Oh no!' replied Miss May, laughing again. She stood up and walked over to the couch. One of the men, the big, black fellow, helped her up onto the couch. Actually, he just lifted her up and put her down, very gently. 'They're my sister's kids. She's got another four with her but I said I'd look after these for her. I didn't know then that I'd be going into labour today.'

'If one of you men would stand on the other side of the couch, one on this side and one at the head that would be useful,' I said. 'That way you can make sure Miss May doesn't roll off and onto the floor. The examination couch is a little on the narrow side for giving birth.'

I didn't really think it was too narrow, and to be honest I didn't really think Miss May was about to give birth, but I wanted to do something with the trio of expectant fathers because they were rather cluttering up the surgery.

Out of the corner of my eye, I could see that the two small children Miss May had brought with her were trying to open a glass-fronted bookcase wherein my collection of medical textbooks were stored.

'It'll be a relief to get my body back,' said Miss May. 'I feel like I've loaned it to this monster inside me.' She paused. 'I hope I get my figure back,' she said, rather plaintively. She caressed her swollen abdomen. 'This little fellow is a guest who's outstayed his welcome!'

'Or a little girl!' said the short, stout father.

Miss May looked at him.

'It might be a girl,' he pointed out.

'Oh I don't think so,' said the mother-to-be. She turned her attention back to me. 'You know, it's funny. I never really thought about having children. I spent a lot of time considering whether or not to keep a goldfish. I spent hours thinking about that and eventually decided that I didn't want the responsibility. But I didn't spend a minute thinking about whether or not I wanted children. It just happened.' She laughed again. The two small children were still trying to open the bookcase. Fortunately, they hadn't yet realised that there was a key. And they weren't tall enough to be able to reach it.

Despite my instinctive scepticism I was, at this point, still taking Miss May at her word that she was pregnant. She looked pregnant and I assumed that a woman of her age would probably know whether or not she was going to have a baby.

But it is easy to make sloppy assumptions when you're busy.

There are lots of reasons why a woman might appear to be pregnant when she isn't – and probably even more reasons why she might falsely believe that she's pregnant.

For example, idiopathic pseudo-cyesis (a fake pregnancy of unknown origin) is far more common than most people might imagine.

'If there's any stitching to do when the baby's out will you make me nice and tight,' said Miss May. She looked at the three fathers-to-be. Two of them blushed and looked at the ceiling. The third, the one who looked Middle Eastern, grinned at her. 'But don't sew her up completely!' he said. She giggled.

'How many months are you?' I asked, as I slipped on a pair of rubber gloves.

'I'm not really sure,' said Miss May.

'When was your last period?'

'Oh, a while ago,' she replied. 'I can't really remember.'

'How long have you been putting on weight?'

'Oh, for about a year, I think.'

It was at that point that I knew that Miss May's swollen abdomen wasn't big because she had a baby in her uterus. I should have realised earlier. The sideburns and moustache were pretty good clues.

'Have you been to your own doctor?'

'No, I haven't had the time. My sister never goes to antenatal classes. She says that with her it's like shelling peas.'

'But she's had a lot of children?'

'Oh yes, loads.'

'So you haven't been seen by your doctor or at the hospital?'

'No. I just thought I'd wait until something happened and then find a doctor.'

'And what has happened today to make you think that you're in labour?'

'Oh, you know, I had a bit of pain when George and I were doing it this morning.'

I wasn't going to ask which one was George. It didn't really seem important. By now I was no longer thinking of any of the men as fathers-to-be. Indeed, I was wondering how I was going to tell the four of them that they didn't need to be working out a babysitting rota or deciding which one of them was going to knit the bootees.

Examining a woman with her three lovers standing inches away was a peculiar experience though I think the three lovers probably found it even stranger than I did.

The stout fellow went bright red and started to sweat profusely. The Arabian chap giggled a lot and didn't know where to look. The black lover, who was standing on the far side of the couch, stood to attention as though on parade. He didn't move a muscle and as far as I could tell he didn't even blink.

Out of the corner of my eye, I could see that the two small children were now trying to open the bookcase with a wooden tongue depressor they'd taken out of a box they'd found. Since their hands looked none too clean, I made a mental note to throw away the box of tongue depressors when they'd gone.

When I had finished my examination, I removed my rubber gloves and threw them into the bin where I put disposables that needed to be burnt.

And then I told Miss May the truth.

Since she had insisted on having her entourage with her, I told them too.

'I'm afraid you're not in labour,' I told her. 'In fact, you're not pregnant.'

'I'm not expecting?'

'No.'

'Then how do you explain this?' she demanded, indicating her swollen abdomen.

'There are several possible explanations,' I said. 'I suspect that you may possibly have a condition called polycystic ovary syndrome. It's fairly common among women in their 20s and 30s.'

I really should have made the diagnosis earlier.

184

When I was at medical school, I saw a woman who was the bearded lady in a travelling fair. The initial diagnosis had been that the woman was suffering from hyperandrogenemia, a condition in which the androgen levels are raised and the patient acquires hair growth in a male pattern. However, tests showed that her hirsute condition was a result of the fact that she had polycystic ovaries. I remember the consultant who was looking after her telling her that he could cure her and that her beard would disappear after an operation. The woman had refused surgery, pointing out that without her beard she wouldn't have a job.

I remember that she was married to a man who had been a hairdresser working in a salon in the suburbs of Reading in Berkshire. They had met when she visited the salon to have her hair and beard permed. 'Just because I have a beard it doesn't mean that I don't like to look well presented,' she told him. He had given up his job at the salon and they had married. He had become her travelling hair and beard dresser and, I think, her manager too. The woman had not come to the hospital because of her beard but because she had gallstones. And so instead of dealing with her polycystic ovaries, the surgeons had removed her gall bladder and sent her and her beard on their way.

So Miss May's moustache and sideburns really should have been all the clues I needed.

'How common is it?' asked the black former father-to-be.

'Some studies suggest it affects one in ten women.'

'Is it cancer?' asked the stout man, rather bluntly and tactlessly I thought. 'It's cancer, isn't it?'

'No, no,' I said, as emphatically as possible. 'It isn't cancer.'

I was actually grateful that he'd asked the question, rather than merely kept the thought to himself and then, perhaps, shared it later with Miss May.

I have found that most patients can be put into one of two categories: the optimists and the pessimists.

The optimists always assume that even the most serious symptoms are a sign of nothing that cannot be put right with a packet of pills or a tube of ointment and, maybe, a week of some sort of abstinence – giving up alcohol or chocolate perhaps.

The pessimists, on the other hand, assume that any trivial sign or symptom, a hangnail or a slightly sore throat, must be a precursor of some deadly disease; an early warning sign of impending doom.

Clearly relieved, the pessimist sighed and blew out a few cubic yards of air.

'You need to have some tests done,' I told Miss May. 'Your own doctor can organise them when you get back home.'

'Well, I think that's all nonsense,' said Miss May. She swung herself off the couch, moving much easier now that she was no longer in labour. 'I still think I'm pregnant. And I should know. Anyway we did it often enough.'

I didn't like to point out that infertility is quite common in women suffering from polycystic ovaries.

'I'm going to see my own doctor when we get back home,' said Miss May. She said this as though it were a threat. 'I'll tell him to fix me an appointment with the antenatal clinic.'

'That's fine,' I said. I was happy enough that she was at least going to see her doctor.

She took the two children by the hand and stormed out of the consulting room. One of the children was clutching the wooden tongue depressor. The other child was clutching the box complete with all the wooden tongue depressors it still contained. At least I wouldn't have to bother throwing the box away. I glanced over at the bookcase. It remained firmly shut and locked.

Two of her lovers went with Miss May. The third fellow, the stout one, stopped behind for a moment. 'She's really not pregnant?'

I shook my head.

'But you don't think its cancer?'

'No,' I said. 'There's absolutely no reason to think it's cancer.'

'Good,' he said. He thought for a moment. 'That's good.'

And then he left too.

I looked at my watch. It was now lunchtime. I used my internal telephone to ask Miss Johnson how many more patients there were in the waiting room.

'A few, doctor,' she replied tactfully.

I knew her well enough to know that she meant that there were still too many for her to count.

'You'd better warn Patsy that I'll be very late for lunch,' I told her. I pressed the buzzer for the next patient.

The next four patients were all locals.

None of them had complicated problems.

One needed her blood pressure checking (it was fine).

One needed to have a repeat prescription for diabetes medication.

Bevan Jeffrey, who had pernicious anaemia, came for his B12 injection.

And the other had stitches which were ready to be removed.

None of them took very long. And although I would have probably chatted more if things had been different, all realised that it was a busy day and that it wasn't a time to talk about the weather or the forthcoming vegetable show.

The next non-resident I saw was in a bad mood when she came into the consulting room.

'I've been waiting for over an hour,' she snapped.

I had no idea how old she was but I thought she looked very business-like for a holidaymaker. This was perhaps not surprising since she turned out not to be a holidaymaker but a cosmetics representative who was travelling through the area. Her name was Mrs Winifred Wendell. She was wearing a grey trouser suit and had on more make-up than Patsy uses in a year. She told me that she lived in Newbury in Berkshire, and worked for a company which had its offices near Reading. She was the West Country representative and had to cover every county south of Bristol and west of Reading. She reeked of tobacco smoke.

I thought she was about to complain about the absence of an appointment system but that wasn't her problem.

'I telephoned and spoke to your receptionist,' she said. 'But she refused to put me through to you. I could have saved myself an hour if you'd been prepared to talk to me on the phone. I really just wanted a prescription.'

'I don't like to do consultations over the telephone,' I said. 'Especially not for patients I don't know.'

When I first started in general practice my mentor, Dr Brownlow, taught me that although it is often tempting to make a diagnosis on the telephone, it is often dangerous to do so. He told me that a good family doctor will make diagnoses by feel, by sight, by touch, by smell and by instinct – and the telephone excludes all those senses.

'What did you want a prescription for?'

'I don't know! You're supposed to be the doctor aren't you?'

I looked at her and then looked down at my blotter and waited a moment while I bit my tongue. Most of the patients I saw were thoughtful and polite. But I seemed to be having all my rude and aggressive patients in one day. Still, I thought, maybe it's better to get them all over and done with at once.

'Do you want a prescription for a medicine you already take?' I asked, thinking that perhaps she had run out of a medicine she usually took for some chronic condition of which I was not aware.

'No, of course I don't!' she snapped. 'If I already took it then I wouldn't need a prescription for it, would I?'

'So, what symptoms do you have?'

'I have very dry eyes and a dry mouth,' she said. 'I've tried drinking lots of water and sucking peppermints but nothing helps. My eyes and mouth are always very dry.'

'How long have you had these problems?'

'Oh, for months and months; I can't remember for how long precisely. But the symptoms seem to be getting worse. And I feel so tired all the time. I don't know why that should be.'

She suddenly started to cough. I fetched a glass of water which seemed to help.

'Does anything make your symptoms worse?'

'Stress!' said the woman instantly and pointedly, as though I were the cause of all her stress and all her problems. 'Can't you just give me a prescription so that I can get on my way? I have to be in Taunton this afternoon. I have three important appointments.'

I don't know why but I got the feeling that all her appointments were important ones.

'I'm a bit old-fashioned,' I said. 'And I like to make a diagnosis before I recommend a treatment.' I didn't mean to say something quite so sarcastic. It just sort of came out that way. And the sentiment was, at least, an honest one.

And then she burst into tears.

Three paper tissues later I asked her why she'd come to see me, instead of waiting to see her own doctor when she got back home.

Before she could answer, she started coughing again. It was a strange, nervous sort of cough: the sort of cough you get with an uncomfortably dry throat. It certainly didn't suggest that she had a chest infection. And although she was clearly a smoker, it definitely wasn't a smoker's cough.

'I just felt I needed to speak to someone about it today,' she confessed. 'I'm hardly ever at home so I never get much chance to see my own GP.'

'But these problems have been getting you down? Worrying you?'

She nodded.

'How many cigarettes do you smoke?'

'Oh, not many,' she said far too quickly. 'Ten a day I suppose.'

I said nothing but looked at her and waited.

'Thirty to forty,' she admitted at last.

I still didn't say anything. It is, perhaps, surprising but it is true that patients will often conceal the truth when talking to a doctor – maybe in the hope that the lie will, in some way, protect them from the consequences of the truth.

'Sometimes more I suppose.'

'How old are you?'

'I'll be 50 on my next birthday.'

'You don't look it,' I said, because she didn't.

'You wouldn't say that if you saw me without my war paint.'

'Do you have any other symptoms?' I asked her.

A redness appeared on her neck and spread to her face. 'I've noticed that sex is rather uncomfortable,' she confessed, clearly embarrassed.

'Because your vagina is dry?'

She nodded.

I examined her eyes and looked into her mouth and down her throat. I checked her blood pressure and auscultated her heart and lungs. I could find absolutely nothing wrong with her except that her salivary glands seemed slightly swollen. Her eyes and throat were fine.

But, despite this relative absence of physical signs, I thought I knew what was wrong with her.

'I think you've got a condition called Sjogren's syndrome,' I told her. 'It's pronounced just like that – 'showgrin'. It's an autoimmune disease which causes all the symptoms you've got.'

'What on earth is 'showgrin'?' she asked. 'Why has it got such a funny name?

'The doctor who first wrote about it was a Swede called Sjogren, though another doctor called Mikulicz had written about something similar in the 19th century so it really ought to be called Mikulicz's syndrome.'

I don't know why I remember these titbits of fairly useless information. And I'm not entirely sure that patients are much interested. Still, I think some patients like to know as much about their condition as they can find out.

'Is it fatal?' she asked immediately.

'No, no!' I said quickly.

'Is there a cure?'

'Not a specific cure, no, but there are lots of things you can do to ease the symptoms. You must go and see your GP. I'll write you a note explaining the things you've told me and telling him what I've told you.'

I reached for a piece of notepaper and started to write out a letter to her doctor, explaining my findings.

'OK,' she said. She seemed calmer now that she knew what was wrong.

People are often like that. Once they have a label they can put on their symptoms then things become easier to accept and manage. 'What causes it?'

'Your immune system is working against your body,' I told her. 'No one knows why it happens. It affects those parts of the body which produce fluids – tears, saliva and vaginal secretions for example. What's the name of your doctor?'

She told me her doctor's name and address. I wrote it at the start of my letter and then put the name and address onto an envelope.

'But there are things I can do?' she asked.

'The first thing is that you must stop smoking. The cigarette smoke is making your mouth and throat worse – and it's responsible for that cough of yours.'

She nodded and sighed. 'I know,' she said.

'This is important,' I told her. 'The cigarette smoke will also irritate your eyes. Your body doesn't produce enough tears so the smoke just irritates your eyes and makes things worse. You can also help by buying some artificial tears from a pharmacy. Drop the artificial tears in when you need them. And also ask about sprays that might help keep your throat moist.'

I put the letter into the envelope and handed the envelope to her, unsealed.

'I haven't stuck down the envelope,' I told her. 'You can read what I wrote and then seal it afterwards.'

She looked at me, slightly puzzled.

'That way you'll know that I've told you the truth; and that I haven't held anything back from you.'

She smiled and I guessed I had probably read her mind.

'Thank you.' She put the envelope into her handbag.

When she'd gone, I glanced at the clock. It was now well after lunchtime. I rang through to Miss Johnson to ask her how many patients I had left.

'Just the two,' she said. 'Are you ready for the next one?'

I tried to stifle a weary sigh.

'It's a boy of seven,' said Miss Johnson. 'His name is Bismore Thrupp and he's here with his mother and father.'

I told her to send them all in.

'And Mrs Thrupp has got four other children with her,' said Miss Johnson.

It seemed to be a morning for large families.

I closed my eyes for a moment.

'Send them all in!' I said, after a pause. I couldn't help hoping that these would be better behaved than the previous two.

Seconds later the door burst open and I was invaded by a band of marauding, mini-Visigoths.

Well, that is what it sounded like, looked like and definitely felt like from my vulnerable position by my desk.

For a few moments, I began to wish that I were armoured, armed and able to defend myself. A lance, a pike and a broadsword would have made me feel a little more comfortable.

These were not, to put it as politely as I am able, well-behaved children.

And since it seemed unlikely that they were all suffering from hyperactivity (a diagnosis which was very common in the 1970s and, I seem to remember, blamed largely on the red additive commonly used to dye sweets sold to children) it seemed not unreasonable to assume that they were, perhaps, simply badly behaved.

They came in at such a speed, and attacked my furniture and belongings with such ferocity, such wild enthusiasm, that I could not, at first, decide how many of them there were. I did, however, wonder how much of the waiting room remained intact now that they'd finished with it.

Patsy always tried to keep the waiting room clean, tidy and well equipped with comfortable chairs. I hated to think what damage this marauding tribe must have done.

The parents who had accompanied them seemed quite oblivious to the mayhem they were causing.

I looked around as the children rampaged from one corner of the room to the other. Doctors' surgeries are not the best places for rampaging children. There are drugs, syringes, instruments, 'dirty' bins and many other potential hazards and it is difficult to keep an eye on four uncontrolled children while also trying to listen to a patient's history and make a diagnosis.

It is impossible to keep everything which could be dangerous locked up and out of reach. Instruments such as auriscopes (aka otoscopes) and ophthalmoscopes are as delicate as they are expensive to replace.

I am sure that there are many, many parents who go on holiday with well-behaved children. Indeed, I have seen many such children myself. But Miss May's sister's pair of children, and this small crowd of young Thrupps, definitely did not fit into the 'well-behaved' category.

'How can I help you?' I asked the couple who had accompanied the children. It seemed a fair assumption that these were Mr and Mrs Thrupp.

'Bismore's got very sore skin,' said the woman. She looked around the room, clearly trying to spot Bismore. I followed her eyes. Bismore was, it appeared, crawling underneath the examination couch. He was the only child who had red hair. The other children all had jet black hair, as did Mrs Thrupp and Mr Thrupp.

'Come here, Bismore!' she shouted.

I must admit that she had a powerful pair of lungs.

This surprised me somewhat since she was a weedy-looking little woman who looked as if she would run a mile if she'd spotted a spider. She was, I suppose, no more than an inch over five feet tall and I doubt if she weighed more than eight stone after a big meal. Nevertheless, her voice was so powerful that I'd have been able to hear her if I had been at the bottom of our garden. Damnit, I'd have been able to hear her if I'd been sitting in the snug at the Duck and Puddle.

Mr Thrupp seemed accustomed to his wife's enthusiastic manner. Looking at him, I suspected that the people who had built King Kong for the movies had kept the plans and persuaded God to build a human with the same dimensions.

It was, I thought, a good job that the child in question was not called something like 'John' or 'David'.

If she'd called out 'John' or 'David' with that sort of volume and enthusiasm the surgery would, I suspect, have been inundated with visits from boys and men of that name responding urgently to the call from all over Devon. Most would have doubtless brought with them guilty faces and sheepish looks because when a boy or a man is called in such a way, and with such volume, he invariably knows that he has done something he should not have done.

Bismore arrived at my side.

He had jam on his face, on the fingers of both hands, on his short-sleeved shirt and in his hair. You didn't need to be Sherlock Holmes to deduce that he had recently been eating something with jam in it. I glanced around. The other children who had accompanied him into the surgery were similarly decorated with jam. I had no doubt that everything in the surgery would by now also be covered in jam. Experience tells me that jam shares with blood the ability to spread itself over an unreasonably large area. A tablespoonful of jam or blood is enough to smear twenty square yards of human, upholstery or carpet.

'Take your shirt off!' commanded his mother.

It seemed that everything she said was produced at the same ear-shattering volume. I wondered if her loving blandishments to her husband were issued with the same complete absence of decibel control. 'I love it when you nibble my ear, darling,' must lose something when it is issued as loudly as that.

Young Bismore had by now removed his shirt. He had simply grabbed it by the collar at the back of his neck and yanked it upwards. He threw the now jammy shirt onto the floor. I couldn't help wondering what the Thrupp household looked like at bedtime.

The poor child's chest and back were burnt bright red. I could see that underneath the burns lay a large number of freckles. The burns looked sore. There were several blisters.

'He looks as if he's been playing in the sun,' I suggested. 'Without a shirt.'

Mrs Thrupp looked at me rather pityingly. 'Ten out of ten for the diagnosis, doctor,' she said drily. Or, rather, she shouted drily.

Mr Thrupp, who had still said absolutely nothing, just sat quietly and listened. He might have been a stranger who'd come into the surgery by mistake.

I felt embarrassed. 'Are they all sunburnt?' I asked, trying to recover my dignity. I waved a hand to indicate the other children.

'Oh no,' said Mrs Thrupp. She had a stentorian voice and gave loud instructions for the other children to remove their tops. After she had repeated the instructions three times they obeyed. These were clearly not children who believed in hierarchical government. The funny thing was that although she spoke loudly, her voice was curiously indistinct. I could hear her well enough but I wasn't entirely sure what she was saying. This wasn't due to any speech impediment but, rather, due to the fact that she spoke quickly and carelessly and never bothered to finish her words or sentences. The end result was that it was like listening to a Tannoy announcement in a railway station. You know you can hear something, you know that something has been said, but you're not quite sure what it was that you heard.

The other children were sunburnt. But they were brown and looked healthy. They looked like children who had been playing in the sunshine for several days. They were not burnt in the way that Bismore was burnt. Bismore looked as if he'd be ready to eat if you gave him another five minutes and then added a little mustard.

'This one always burns,' said Mrs Thrupp. 'The others don't.'

'You don't put any sunscreen on him?'

'The others don't need it.'

'Bismore is red-headed and pale skinned,' I pointed out.

'Do they teach you this observational stuff at medical school or were you born this way?' asked Mrs Thrupp. 'Have you got any suggestions as to what I might do about it? Put on something creamy and soothing, perhaps?'

I found myself blushing. 'I can prescribe some lotion that will ease the soreness,' I told her. 'But you should keep him covered up when he goes out in the sun. Keep him indoors for a few days. And if he doesn't have a hat then you should get him one.' As I spoke, I

194

wrote out a prescription for a soothing lotion. 'Actually, they should all wear hats if they're playing in the sun.'

'Well, if he has a hat they'll all want one. Have you any idea how much children's hats cost these days?'

'The village shop sells hats,' I pointed out. I knew that Peter was selling a new line in floppy, broad brimmed summer hats made out of white cotton. 'They aren't made in Jermyn Street but they have broad brims and they'll keep the sun off.'

'Why does Bismore suffer in the sun?' demanded Mrs Thrupp. 'His brothers and sisters can stay out all day without burning.'

'Bismore is red-headed,' I pointed out. 'Red heads are always more liable to burn than brunettes.'

'My husband thinks I had an affair with the man who delivers our nutty slack,' said Mrs Thrupp.

I looked at her. This wasn't a joke or a light aside. She was deadly serious.

'Nutty slack?'

'Cheap coal. Tiny bits of coal mixed in with coal dust. It's cheap. It's all I can afford.' I noticed that she said 'I' and not 'We'. It seemed clear that Mrs Thrupp was in charge of everything including children, housekeeping and the purchase of nutty slack.

'And am I right in thinking that the man who delivers your nutty slack has got red hair?'

'He looks like a carrot. But he's ugly, he smells and I don't fancy him. I've never been unfaithful but Ernie thinks I had it off with Kelvin and that's why Bismore is red-headed.'

'Ernie is your husband?'

'Of course.'

'And Kelvin is the man who delivers the nutty slack?'

'Well, it's not the milkman is it? He's as bald as a coot,' said Mrs Thrupp. She looked at her husband. 'And I don't fancy him either,' she said, with all the emphasis on the word 'him'.

'You always smile at Kelvin when he delivers,' said Mr Thrupp. It was the first time he'd opened his mouth since he'd entered the room. He said this rather defensively.

I realised that this was why they had come to see me. Bismore's sunburn was merely an excuse. They both knew damned well why Bismore burnt so easily. I had an awful feeling that they had deliberately allowed him to burn so that they'd have an excuse to come to the surgery. They were in my surgery because they wanted me to adjudicate on a long simmering family dispute. I suspect it was something they didn't want to discuss in front of their own family doctor.

'If I'd had it off with him I'd have been scrubbing coal dust off my skin for a week!' said Mrs Thrupp. 'His hands are as black as the ace of spades!'

'He always looks at you like he's already had you,' complained Mr Thrupp. 'He leers.'

'He doesn't leer. He's a bit stupid and he's got a wall eye. He can only see out of one eye. He told me that. Otherwise he'd have been a pilot. That's what he wanted to be. He wanted to join the RAF but they wouldn't have him.'

'You know a lot about him!' said Mr Thrupp.

'We talk for a minute or two when I pay the bill!' said Mrs Thrupp.

'Are there any red-heads in either of your families?' I asked, tired of the family dispute.

'What's that got to do with it?' demanded Mr Thrupp, suddenly surprisingly belligcrent. 'I haven't got red hair and neither has she.' He nodded towards his wife.

'We all have two genes which decide our hair colour,' I explained. 'We get one gene from our mother and one from our father. Red hair is a recessive gene – it is always dominated and overruled by any other hair colour gene. That means that a child needs to have two red-hair genes to have red hair. If both of you have only one red-hair gene, then your children will probably have black or blond hair unless you each pass on your red-hair gene to a child.'

'You mean that we could have made a red headed baby – like Bismore?'

'Yes.'

'Even though we've both got black hair?'

'Yes. If you both carry the red-hair gene but neither of you has red hair then there still is a one in four chance that you'll have a child with red hair.'

'My uncle Douglas had red hair,' said Mrs Thrupp very quickly.

'I didn't know you had an uncle called Douglas,' said Mr Thrupp.

196

'He died before we met,' said Mrs Thrupp. 'But you've got red hair in your family, haven't you?'

'My grandmother had reddish hair,' admitted Mr Thrupp.

'Ah, there you are then, so there's a good chance you both carry the red-hair gene,' I told them.

'But I think she might have dyed it,' added Mr Thrupp.

'Don't be daft,' said Mrs Thrupp. 'She had red hair. She just put a bit of henna on it to liven it up.'

'So we could have produced a red headed baby?' asked Mr Thrupp. There was incredulousness and hope in his voice.

'Of course we did,' said Mrs Thrupp. She folded her arms across her chest and stared at her husband defiantly. 'You can apologise now.'

'I'm sorry, love,' said Mr Thrupp. 'I'm very sorry.'

I suspected that he did a lot of apologising.

The Thrupp parents stood up and collected their jam-covered offspring.

I handed over the prescription for the lotion for the unfortunate Bismore. They then headed for the door. When the others had disappeared into the waiting room, Mrs Thrupp turned back and walked across to me. 'Thanks very much for that, doctor,' she whispered. 'He's been going on about Kelvin for years. I only did it with him the once and I didn't enjoy it. He was very small and not very good at it. I should have known – he had small feet. It was all over in two minutes and it took me an hour to scrub off the coal dust. What sort of bad luck was that, eh? Me catching for Bismore after that one time!'

Having made this strange confession she then hurried off.

I looked around.

Everywhere I looked there was jam.

There was jam on my desk, jam on my sphygmomanometer, jam on the examination couch – there was jam absolutely everywhere. Judging by the seeds, I could see it had probably been raspberry jam.

Wearily, and with a rather annoyed feeling that Mrs Thrupp had played us all rather well, I rang the buzzer. The morning surgery had by now lasted through the day and had become the evening surgery.

My next patient was a nine-year-old boy called Thomas Gaskin who was complaining of stomach ache. He and his parents were staying in the caravan park just outside Combe Martin. The boy was in so much pain that his father had to carry him into the surgery. I told the father to lay his son down on my examination couch so that I could examine him.

'Do you think he needs his appendix taking out,' asked his mother. She and her husband were clearly and understandably very worried. They were, I suppose, both in their early thirties.

'How long has he been ill?' I asked.

'It started a couple of hours ago,' replied the mother.

'It's gradually got worse during the day,' added the father.

I palpated the boy's abdomen. There was no sign of any tenderness or stiffness and although he was clearly in pain, I could find absolutely no signs of any serious pathology. However, I already knew what was wrong.

'Has he eaten anything that might have upset him?' I asked.

'No, I don't think so,' said the mother. 'We had fish paste sandwiches for lunch. We'd been blackberry picking this morning and I was going to make a blackberry pie this afternoon.' She looked at her watch. 'It's too late to do it now.'

'Did you have any pudding?'

'Thomas had a chocolate biscuit. One called a 'Wagon Wheel'.'

I looked at the boy. 'Did you eat any other sweets today?'

He shook his head.

'Blackberries?'

Another shake of the head.

'You didn't eat any when you were out picking blackberries?'

'Only a couple.'

'Just a couple?'

This time I got a nod of the head.

'What about breakfast? What did he have for breakfast?'

'Just a bowl of cornflakes with milk and sugar,' said his mother.

'And to drink?'

'A glass of milk.'

I turned back to Thomas. 'And you ate no more than a couple of the blackberries you picked this morning?'

Thomas nodded but as he nodded he suddenly sat up, made a strange noise, looked at me with horror in his eyes, half moved off the examination couch and then, unable to stop himself, vomited enthusiastically over me and my desk.

Everything on my desk was covered with purple vomit.

Some of the second-hand blackberries were half digested and some of them were hardly digested at all. It looked as though he had eaten half a pound of fruit. It was hardly surprising that he had stomach ache.

Within minutes, Thomas was feeling a little better.

He then managed to bring up another couple of mouthfuls of half-digested blackberries.

And then the excitement was over.

And he was feeling pretty fine.

His parents were very apologetic and the mother insisted on helping me start to clean up the surgery. There were second-hand blackberries almost everywhere.

I decided that used blackberries share the bizarre quality enjoyed by jam and blood: a little goes a long, long way.

'So you ate just one or two blackberries, did you?' said Thomas's father. He managed to sound cross but it was obvious he was really just relieved.

'I thought I'd only eaten one or two,' said Thomas.

Despite the mess, I couldn't help smiling to myself when they'd gone. It hadn't been a difficult diagnosis to make. The clues had been the blackberry stains around his mouth and the stains down the front of his shirt. You don't get stains like that from eating just one or two blackberries.

Finally, there was just one patient left; an elderly clergyman called Canon Gatling.

'You seem to have had a busy day, young man,' said Canon Gatling.

'It has been rather busy,' I agreed.

'I'm not a patient of yours,' said the clergyman. 'I'm staying down here on holiday with some friends.'

'What can I do for you?' I asked. 'What symptoms do you have?'

'Oh, I don't have much in the way of symptoms,' said Canon Gatling. 'I just thought I should have a check-up. My friends pushed me along and said I should have a medical. I'm 89-years-old.'

'You look good for 89,' I told him.

And he did. If you'd seen him in the street you would not have thought him a day over 88. Of course, I didn't know if he was a man of 90 who had to date lived a hard life or a man of 87 who had lived a bland, blameless life. Or, indeed, the other way round. The fact that he wore his collar turned round the wrong way strongly suggested that his had not been a life devoted entirely to the pleasures of the flesh.

'I thought maybe if you checked out my heart and other essential bits and pieces, that would put my friends at peace.'

I tried not to sigh. 'Is there any reason why you haven't been to see your own doctor for a check-up?'

'Well, he's a very busy man,' said Canon Gatling. 'And I'm rather busy too when I'm back at home. I have a busy social life, you know. So my friends thought it would be easier all round if I came to see you.'

You can't snarl at an elderly clergyman, can you?

I asked him if he could climb onto the examination couch. He said he thought he could. I told him to slip off his jacket, shirt and trousers and to lie down so that I could take a look at him.

I then gave him a pretty thorough examination.

'How am I?' he asked when I'd finished. 'Did you find anything wrong?'

'Well, there are one or two signs of wear and tear,' I explained.

'So tell me what you've found, doctor! Please don't be coy.'

'Would you not prefer me to write to your doctor with my findings?'

'No, no! I want you to tell me what you've found. I insist.'

'Are you sure?'

'Of course!'

And so I told him.

'You have a heart murmur,' I said. 'And your blood pressure is raised. There's a little fluid in your lungs and your liver is enlarged. Your spleen is enlarged too. You have cataracts in both eyes and your hearing is severely diminished on the left side – though that may be a result of the wax in that ear. You seem to have osteoarthritis in both hips and knees and rheumatoid arthritis in your hands. You have signs of gout, your prostate is enlarged quite considerably, though I am happy to say that the enlargement appears benign, you have inguinal hernias on both sides and your left testicle appears to be slightly swollen and tender. You have the beginnings of an umbilical hernia and you have quite severe prolapsed haemorrhoids and what appears to be a small anal fissure. You have a severe fungal infection of your toenails and you have psoriasis on both elbows and your left knee. You appear to have some sinus trouble and you have quite severe gingivitis. You have bunions on both big toes and on the left side you appear to have housemaid's knee.'

'That's it?'

'I think so.'

'You didn't find anything serious then?'

'Just the things I outlined. I will write to your own doctor and you and he can decide whether you want to treat any of the problems I've described.' It took me nearly a quarter of an hour to write the letter for him to give to his own GP.

'Well, that's all quite a relief,' said Canon Gatling, when I had handed him the letter. 'My friends will be comforted, I'm sure.' He stood up, shook hands with me and left.

I watched him go and found myself smiling and shaking my head in wonderment.

A man of 60 would have been horrified if I'd recited such a lengthy list of ailments. But to Canon Gatling, a man of nearly 90, my list of faults and failings were virtually a clean bill of health. After the Canon had disappeared, Patsy came in to tell me that there were no more patients. It was after seven o'clock. I'd been in the consulting room for over ten hours. Miss Johnson had gone home.

'Do you want something to eat now?' she asked.

'How many visits need to be done?'

'Three.'

She told me what they were. They were all patients who were locals and the locals were very local in that they all lived nearby. I said I'd have a quick wash and then do the calls immediately so that when I'd finished I could, hopefully, sit down and relax for a while.

By eight o'clock, I was kneeling by the fire making toast while listening to the delightful comic songs of Flanders and Swann. I was feeling hungry and had sliced up a whole loaf of fresh bread.

As I made the toast, so Patsy buttered it.

Ben, our rather ancient and loyal dog was sharing the hearth rug with me and the cats. When I sat down, Ben would insist on settling on my lap.

'I bet these fellows were excellent deipnosophists,' I said suddenly.

Patsy looked at me querulously.

'Flanders and Swann,' I said. 'I bet they were excellent deipnosophists.'

'Deipnowhats?'

'Deipnosophists,' I said.

'What the devil is a deipnosophist?'

'Oh, someone who is skilled at making dinner party conversation,' I explained. 'I'm expanding my vocabulary.'

'Why? When can you possibly use a word like that?'

'I just used it,' I said, trying not to sound too pleased with myself. I didn't mention that it had taken me ten minutes to think of a way of easing it into the conversation.

'How long did it take you to work out a way to wriggle it into the conversation?' asked Patsy, who knows me rather too well.

'Wriggle what into the conversation?' I asked. I knew I was blushing and it wasn't the heat of the fire.

'That word deipnowhats.'

'It just seemed to be the whatchamacallit,' I said. 'Fitted in rather nicely, I thought.'

Patsy laughed. 'How long?'

'No more than ten minutes,' I said.

When I'm talking with Patsy it is as though I have a little glass window in my skull. She knows what I'm going to say before I say it, what I mean to say when I'm struggling to say it and what I meant to say when I've almost said what I wanted to say.

'Well, maybe you ought to put the big words away and concentrate on the toast,' said Patsy. 'The piece you're making is black and burnt to a crisp.'

I looked at the end of my toasting fork. She was right, of course. I tossed the piece of charcoal I'd created onto the fire and replaced it with a fresh piece of bread.

I have to confess that Patsy and I didn't really need to have lit an open fire for it was still late summer and the weather wasn't cold at all. In fact, it was quite warm.

But I do find that when I am really exhausted, a log fire is an essential part of the relaxing process.

Besides, if I hadn't lit a fire, we would have had to put the bread into the toaster. And where on earth is the fun in that? Toast which has been made by putting a slice of bread in between two electrically heated wires does not taste anywhere near as good as toast which has been made in front of the naked flames of a log fire. And it doesn't smell as wonderful either.

Who cares that you're almost certain to burn some of the bread and that it is nigh on impossible to avoid ending up with a very hot hand. No one ever said that the really good things in life came without just a little pain.

By any standards it had, I think, been a busy day.

But it ended well.

I know there are people who believe it is impossible to have a good evening unless you hand over hundreds of pounds for a meal out in a posh restaurant where a self-important chef and a band of scurrying acolytes fuss over the food and the waiters fawn over the diners. Many people seem to drool over the prospect of dressing up, driving 50 miles and handing over a fistful of bank notes for a meal consisting of stuff which they probably cannot pronounce and which is almost certain to give them indigestion afterwards. I wonder how many of them would rather have a packet of fish and chips from their local chip shop? 'Generous with the vinegar and plenty of salt, please!'

I realise that Patsy and I probably stand alone in this but in our view, a dinner out in a posh restaurant is no way to enjoy an evening.

We prefer the simple life.

And how can you possibly beat sitting in front of a crackling log fire, nursing a glass of something agreeable and sharing a plateful of hot buttered toast with the one you love?

You Won't Let Him Die, Will You, Doctor?

Looking back, the whole thing began with a fairly innocuous visit to an evening surgery in late August.

Abigail Barnes was 10-years-old and had, like her parents, been born in Bilbury.

I could see from her medical records that my predecessor, Dr Brownlow, had delivered her at home.

Unless there were very exceptional circumstances, Dr Brownlow always delivered babies at home. He thought it was better and safer for both the mother and the baby if the birth could be managed in the mother's own bedroom. He insisted that the risks were much lower if a baby could be delivered away from the variety of dangerous infections which are inevitable in hospitals. And he once told me that one of the great joys of his life was watching the children he had delivered grow up and start families of their own.

'We have to be with our patients when their time on earth is ended,' I remember him saying to me one evening. 'And that's a sad, sad time. So it's good to be able to balance those melancholic moments with the enjoyment of the glorious moments when new faces are brought into the world.' At that time, none of the babies I'd delivered was old enough to have even thought about starting their own families but I had always followed Dr Brownlow's example and looked after my pregnant patients in their own homes. It seems to me, that a family doctor who delivers the babies in his practice has a much stronger bond with his patients and the community he serves.

'I think Abigail's got the flu starting,' said Mrs Barnes. 'I wouldn't have bothered you but she's got a terrible cough.'

I asked Abigail when her symptoms had started.

'This morning,' answered Abigail. She did look poorly.

It seemed odd that a patient who was developing the flu should have started a cough so quickly. The cough that is so often a symptom of influenza usually develops later on in the illness.

'What other symptoms have you got?'

'I ache a lot,' said Abigail.

'Whereabouts?'

'My chest and my arms and my legs.'

I touched her forehead with the back of my hand. She was hot.
'Have you got a headache?'

'Yes. It started with the headache.'

'This morning?'

'Yes.'

I took out a thermometer and took her temperature. It was up a couple of degrees. I listened to Abigail's chest and palpated her abdomen, just to make sure I wasn't missing anything else. In children, diseases can develop quite quickly and they don't always follow the pattern the text books describe. But I could find nothing odd or worrying. Abigail's tummy was soft and there was no pain when I examined her. I had been worried for a few moments that she might be developing appendicitis. It isn't unknown for young patients to present with really unusual symptoms and signs.

'Well it seems like the flu,' I agreed, talking now to Mrs Barnes. I explained that there wasn't anything I could do other than tell her to keep her daughter warm and well hydrated. 'Make sure she drinks lots,' I told her. And I gave Mrs Barnes a suitable painkiller from our pharmacy.

I honestly didn't think I'd have to see Abigail again for this problem. I thought her mother was right and that she had the flu. It was a slightly odd presentation and it had come on very quickly but these things happen and common things do happen commonly. You can make an awful fool of yourself, and, more important, worry your patients unnecessarily, if you are forever assuming that every ache is a sign of some deadly, rare muscular disease or that every cough suggests the start of tuberculosis.

The second patient with similar symptoms arrived in my surgery a day and a half later. His name was Barnaby Fothergill and his mother, who brought him to a morning surgery, reported that he had been up all night complaining of pains in his chest and a stubborn headache that just wouldn't go away.

I remembered that Abigail Barnes had complained of similar symptoms and asked Barnaby if he knew her.

'Oh yes,' replied Mrs Fothergill, answering for him. 'They're both members of a little gang. There are five of them in the gang and they call themselves the Bilbury Five.

I thought the name made them sound like the defendants in an important trial of some kind but I was told that they had named themselves after a series of books by children's author Enid Blyton. The books described the adventures of a group of children known as the Famous Five.

Mrs Fothergill mentioned the names of the three other children who also lived in the village and who were members of the same gang: Amber Lane, Judith Barker and George Dickson.

All five children were much the same age, though George Dickson was probably a couple of years younger and was, I remembered, much smaller than the others. He might have been smaller but he was no less lively. He once broke his leg falling out of a tree down near the pond on the edge of Softly's Bottom.

I told Mrs Fothergill what I'd told Mrs Barnes and assumed that the two children had caught the same infection. I wondered if the other three in the gang would develop similar symptoms.

I was right about the two children having the same infection.

And I was right to wonder if the other three would develop the same sort of symptoms.

But I was completely, woefully, dangerously wrong about the nature of the infection.

The third child I saw was Judith Barker.

At eleven and a half, she was the oldest of the gang and she was undoubtedly the leader. I knew her and her parents, of course. All the five members of the gang were long-term residents of the village and I was well acquainted with all the families.

I saw Judith at home rather than at Bilbury Grange and she was rather more seriously ill than the first two. She was in bed when I arrived. She had been one of the children who had been ill after using Giant Hogweed stems as peashooters at a children's party organised by Mr and Mrs Pinchbeck. Judith was coughing and complaining of pains in her chest and in her shoulders.

'How long has she been coughing?'

'Only since this morning.'

'Has the cough been very bad?' I asked.

Mrs Barker thought for a moment. 'I wouldn't say so,' she said. 'It is the pains in her chest that seem to trouble her most. That's why I asked you to visit rather than taking her along to the surgery.'

'Was there any warning?' I asked.

'None at all. She was absolutely fine last night when she went to bed. But she woke up this morning looking and feeling awful. Do you think she has the flu that the others have got?'

I said I thought it was the most likely explanation but asked her mother to telephone me at once if there was any change.

My next visit that same day was to Abigail Barnes, the girl I'd first seen at Bilbury Grange a couple of days earlier.

Her mother had telephoned the surgery and asked me to visit because she was worried about her daughter.

'She seems to be getting worse,' said Mrs Barnes. 'And she's now developed red eyes. It looks like conjunctivitis but she insists that her eyes weren't sticky when she awoke this morning.'

The conjunctivae of Abigail's eyes were clearly both red. Abigail looked very miserable and she had quite a fever.

'The aches seem to be getting worse,' said Mrs Barnes. 'And she's complained of some soreness in her tummy.'

I examined Abigail and there was some tenderness in the area of her spleen. I thought it was slightly enlarged. I was now beginning to suspect that my original diagnosis was wrong. It seemed that something else was going on but I didn't have the foggiest idea what it could be. The reddening of the conjunctivae wasn't normal. But how did it fit in with the enlarged spleen?

George Dickson was the last patient I saw that morning.

Once again, he had the same symptoms as his friends. He was coughing and he had aches and pains in his chest and in his shoulders and his arms. His legs were aching too. And he had one symptom that the other's had not exhibited: a symptom which rang very loud alarm bells. He had coughed up some blood.

I had never before seen a child coughing up blood and this startled and rather frightened me.

'How many times has he coughed up blood?' I asked Mrs Dickson, trying to sound calmer than I felt.

'Twice,' she said. She moved out of George's bedroom and onto the landing. She lowered her voice to a whisper I could hardly hear.

'My grandfather used to cough up blood. But he was a heavy smoker and he died of lung cancer.' There were tears and fears in her eyes.

'George hasn't got lung cancer,' I told her firmly.

'You won't let him die, will you doctor?' she said.

There was a fierce desperation in her voice.

George was her only child. She and her husband had been to an infertility clinic for three years before she had conceived.

No child is, or should be, any more special than any other child. But when George had broken his leg Mrs Dickson had, I remembered, been hysterical and inconsolable. Patsy had stayed with her until her husband had managed to get back from work.

I confess I had not always seen eye to eye with Mr Dickson.

I once had a patient called Jack Driver who was an alcoholic and was struggling to deal with his addiction. Mr Driver drove a removal van and was, inevitably, known to one and all as 'Laurie'. He and his wife were separated and he knew that as a result of his drinking problem he was in danger of losing his job.

After being dry for four months, he had received a setback when his wife had told him that she was leaving him permanently.

Broken hearted, Mr Driver had bought a bottle of wine at a supermarket in Barnstaple and had been arrested for drunk driving while on his way home.

I remember that it was a strange case. He hadn't been in an accident but the police had stopped him because they'd noticed that he was driving too slowly and too carefully.

Mr Driver came to see me at the time to ask if I could request the *Bugle*, the local newspaper, not to print his name when his case went to court. He wasn't worried about his job (he knew that he would lose his licence and therefore his job so that was a lost cause) but he didn't want his children to read about his disgrace, or for their friends at school to have ammunition to fire at them. I did ask the editor, Mr Dickson, not to print the report but he said that Mr Driver should have thought of the consequences of his actions before he'd drunk the wine. It was the second time in my life I'd asked for the same favour and on both occasions my request had been rejected.

And so the court case was duly reported in the local paper and for the sake of an inch and a half of fairly dull newsprint, what was left of Mr Driver's life was ruined. Twelve months later, Mr Driver was found dead in a shop doorway in Exeter. He had died of alcohol poisoning. When I'd heard the news, I'd telephoned Mr Dickson at his office. I don't know what I expected. I think I was probably just angry.

'I was just doing my job,' said Mr Dickson rather gruffly. 'We all have our jobs to do. You do your job, doctor and I'll do mine.'

I hadn't seen or spoken to Mr Dickson since then, though he and his family were all still patients of mine. And now his son, George, was ill.

'I won't let him die,' I promised Mrs Dickson. And I meant it. There was no way, no way on earth, that any of these small children, so full of life, were going to die if I could do anything to prevent it. I didn't know what the hell was going on but I would find out. My brain was buzzing with ideas, thoughts, diagnoses, prognostications and fears.

I knew that coughing up blood used to be horribly common, of course.

When consumption (aka tuberculosis) was endemic, children often coughed up blood.

But long before the 1970s came, tuberculosis had become rare; it was not something which was often seen in children.

Coughing up blood happens in bronchitis and it occurs among heavy smokers. It can be a sign of lung cancer, a lung abscess or pneumonia. There are dozens of possible causes.

But I couldn't get away from the knowledge that it isn't something that occurs often with children.

I began to wish that I were working in a large hospital where I could call upon expert help from consultant paediatricians. A general practitioner works alone and a country doctor, who works in a fairly isolated village, must work more on his own than any other doctor.

It was obvious now that these children didn't have influenza. It was also pretty clear that all five of them had the same thing wrong with them. But what the devil was it? I thought for a moment of simply sending all five of them to the hospital in Barnstaple. I even considered sending them to a larger hospital, maybe the one in Exeter. But sending children to hospital is traumatic for the children themselves and for their parents. I decided I could wait an hour or two while I tried to work out what was going on.

I carefully moved some children's comics and half a dozen toy soldiers out of the way and sat down on George's bed. 'What have your gang been doing this summer?' I asked him.

I remembered the time when I had seen him and the other children who had been using Giant Hogweed stems as peashooters. I wondered if they had perhaps all eaten berries that had poisoned them. It could certainly explain their symptoms.

'Just playing,' said George, defensively.

'Did you eat anything you picked?' I asked.

'Just blackberries,' said George. 'And some wild strawberries.'

'That's all?'

George nodded.

'It's important,' I said quietly. 'You won't get into trouble but I need to know if you ate anything else? Something that all of you ate?'

'There wasn't anything else,' said George. There were tears in his eyes.

'Honest injun?' said his mother. She was sitting on the other side of his bed and holding his hand.

'Honest injun,' whispered George, with a nod.

'He's telling the truth,' his mother said quietly.

'We built a swing,' said George. 'Barnaby's dad put a rope over a big branch on a tree over the pond. He tested it and said it was safe.'

'The pond by Softly's Bottom?'

George nodded.

I knew that pond. It was actually quite large as ponds go. It was fed by a small stream so the water wasn't entirely stagnant. It was also believed to be quite deep. Villagers sometimes fished there and it was rumoured that there was a large pike living in the pond. I always took this story with a pinch of salt for in every village in England there is a pond which is said to have a large pike living in it.

'What did he do with the bottom of the rope? Knot it or tie on an old tyre?'

'He tied on an old tyre,' said George.

Barnaby's father, Ted Fothergill, works at a garage in Combe Martin. He wouldn't have any difficulty finding an old tyre.

'And you swung across the pond on the tyre?'

'Sometimes,' said George. 'Sometimes we let go when we were over the pond.'

'And landed in the water?'

George nodded.

'Did you swim in the water?'

Another nod.

'All of you?'

'Amber can't properly swim but we always helped her and she did the dog paddle. We didn't let her fall into the water if one of us wasn't already in the pond. Judith said we had to do that to make sure she didn't drown.'

'So you probably swallowed some of the pond water?'

George nodded. 'But we all spat it out again.'

'What's wrong with him?' asked Mrs Dickson, as I prepared to leave.

'I don't know yet,' I told her. 'But if I don't have a good idea by his evening then I'll arrange for George to go into hospital. Have a bag ready for him. I'll speak to you later.'

'You won't let anything happen to him, will you?'

'I won't,' I told her.

How the devil could I know that nothing would happen to him? I didn't even know what was wrong with him.

But what good would it do her, or George, for me to tell her the truth?

I drove from their house to a lane which leads down to the area where Softly's Bottom can be found. I managed to park the Rolls in a field gateway, climbed over the fence and walked down the hill to the pond. In truth, I didn't have the faintest idea why I was there or what I hoped to discover. Maybe I would see some plants that might have caused the children's symptoms. Maybe there would be some berries growing on a bush. George's mother had been convinced he was telling the truth. But maybe he was frightened and had told a white lie.

I sat down on the trunk of an old tree and stared at the pond. It was quite an idyllic spot. I could see why the children loved playing there. The rope that Barnaby's father had slung over the tree was there; the old tyre hanging down over the water. Mr Fothergill or one of the children had tied another, thinner rope to the tyre and then tied the thinner rope to the tree. The thinner rope enabled them to pull back the tyre so that they could climb onto it, or into it, and swing over the water. It was, I could see, an old tractor tyre. There was a small, rough shelter made in one of the bushes. It was, I guessed, where they hid when it rained or if they heard pirates coming. They doubtless had picnics there. I looked around. There were no old cartons or tins or paper litter. They were good kids. They had taken their rubbish home with them. They would close gates, respect crops and do no damage to fences. They were country born and bred with good country manners.

And then I heard it.

Splash.

I didn't see anything but I definitely heard a splash.

I sat stock still for a while longer.

And then I saw it.

A rat.

It was swimming in the water.

I watched it swim around the edge of the pond and then disappear into a hole in the bank.

I don't like rats.

I love all animals but I have never been able to like rats. They always seem to me to be dirty, sneaky, cruel creatures. And, of course, they spread diseases to humans.

And now I knew what the problem was.

I knew, damnit.

I was certain I had the diagnosis I needed.

I raced back up the hill to where I had parked the car, climbed in and drove back to Bilbury Grange as quickly as I could. I slid to a halt in front of the house, leapt out of the car and raced into my consulting room where I plucked a copy of a standard medical textbook off the shelves. I knew exactly what I was looking for.

Leptospirosis.

I checked the symptoms and the signs and the incubation period. They all matched.

I had five small children with leptospirosis.

'Leptospirosis,' I read, 'is a biphasic disease. In the first phase of the disease, sufferers will have acute febrile episodes. Headache, chest pains and severe muscular aches are common. Conjunctival bleeds sometimes develop and haemoptysis may occur in some patients.'

Haemoptysis is the coughing up of blood.

The bug that causes leptospirosis usually originates with an animal, typically a wild animal and most commonly a rat, and can get in to the patient's body through the skin or mucous membranes, through the eyes, nose or mouth and through cuts and grazes. You don't have to drink infected water. It is not a terribly difficult disease to catch – which explained why all five of the children who had swum in the infected pond had become ill – all you have to do is be in contact with water contaminated with leptospira bacteria. Sewage workers sometimes catch the disease even though they are wearing protective clothing.

I read on.

'In the second phase of the disease there may be hepatic, renal and meningeal involvement. The second phase usually develops between one and two weeks after the first.'

I closed my eyes and uttered a prayer of thanks to God. The children were all in the first phase of the disease. They had the preliminary symptoms. The potentially deadly involvement of the liver, the kidneys and the brain would come later unless I stopped it happening.

I looked through the book to find out what tests I needed to do to confirm the diagnosis. But in my heart I didn't really need the tests. I was certain they had leptospirosis. How the hell did I treat it? I had never seen a case of leptospirosis before. Most doctors never see one. Now I had five.

'Antibiotic therapy is most effective,' said the book. It gave the recommended type of antibiotic and the recommended dosage. 'Patient isolation is not necessary but urine must be handled and disposed of carefully.'

And that was the beginning of the end of a truly scary day.

I took blood samples from all five children and sent them off to the laboratory in Barnstaple with a request that they telephone me with the results.

And even before I got the results back I started all the children on powerful doses of penicillin.

I told all the parents how to look after their children and warned them about the danger of their children's urine.

Thanks be to God, it was the right diagnosis. The children all made a full recovery.

And afterwards, Mr Fothergill took down the rope and the tyre so that no one would play over the pond again. And the farmer who owned the pond put a stout fence around it with several, large, red-lettered signs attached to the posts.

I went down to the pond before the fence went up and, after saying a quiet prayer to God for guiding me to the right diagnosis, I added a quiet 'thank you' to the rat whose splash had led me to the diagnosis.

Author's Note
I hope you have enjoyed this book about Bilbury and the people who live in and visit the village. If you did so then I would be very grateful if you would spare a moment to write a short review. This is the 13th book in the series entitled 'The Young Country Doctor'. I hope you will also enjoy the appendices which follow.
Thank you
Vernon Coleman

Appendix: 1
Wind: Official Types.

Here are the types of wind as classified on the Beaufort scale.
Different types of wind are given different names and since there are
still people around who do not carry wind meters with them all the
time, there needs to be a system that depends on less scientific
measurements. Here is my version:

Calm: smoke from chimneys, bonfires and pipes rises vertically
in nice, little twirly patterns

Light air: chimney and bonfire smoke drifts a little but flags and
weather vanes are pretty well immobile

Slight breeze: leaves rustle and flags start to flutter

Gentle breeze (around 10 mph): a smallish, light flag will be
extended and leaves (whether still on the tree or not) will be in
constant motion; most hat wearers are still confident although those
wearing wide brimmed confections and delicate fascinators may feel
some concern

Moderate breeze (around 15 mph): this amount of wind will mean
that small branches move around; all hat wearers may feel nervous

Fresh breeze (around 20 mph): small trees which are in leaf will
sway a little and wavelets can be seen on lakes, ponds and
swimming pools; hats which are blown off can be caught even by
those whose mobility is limited to gentle lumbering; wide brimmed
hats and hats which are light and flouncy should be nailed on or
taken indoors

Strong breeze (around 25 mph): large branches will be moving, it
will difficult to control an umbrella and people wearing hats should
take them off and put them somewhere safe because a hat blown in a
strong breeze will only be caught by a well-trained athlete capable of
changing speed and direction very quickly

High wind (around 35 mph): even quite large trees will now be
moving and pedestrians will find it difficult to walk; umbrellas will
fly away, most golfers will probably give up and loose slates, and

tiles will start flying around; hats will blow off and will probably never be seen again

Gale (around 40 mph): twigs and small branches will be broken off trees and car drivers will feel their vehicles being moved about; toupee wearers should prepare for embarrassment

Strong gale (around 50 mph): there is likely to be slight structural damage with chimney pots and slates flying through the air with the greatest of ease; summerhouses and greenhouses may suffer

Whole gale (around 60 mph): whole trees may be uprooted, garden benches will be blown about and there is likely to be serious structural damage to even sturdy buildings

Storm (around 70 mph): widespread damage is likely with cars being blown over; seaside promenades are likely to be deluged with sea water and eager amateur photographers risk being swept out to sea

Hurricane (above 75 mph): if there is a basement or cellar handy this is probably the time to be in it

Appendix 2
Flat Pack Castles

Patchy's tale of how the Normans who landed in England in 1066 brought with them flat pack ready to build castles is absolutely true. Patchy obtained his information from a book entitled *Fifteen Decisive Battles of the World* written by Sir Edward Creasy and first published in 1851. Creasy's book is widely regarded as the definitive history of war prior to the 20th century.

I purchased a copy of Creasy's book from a bookseller in Hay-on-Wye. As a single handed GP, I found it difficult (for which read 'impossible') to leave the village and so I bought my books from catalogues which arrived through the post.

Sir Edward describes the arrival of the Normans in his account of the Battle of Hastings – using the accounts put together by Norman chroniclers. He explains that the first ship to arrive belonged to Duke William. The ship was called the Mora and had been given to him by his duchess, Matilda. On the prow of the ship, according to the Normans, 'there was a brazen child bearing an arrow with a bended bow. His face was turned towards England, and thither he looked, as though he was about to shoot.'

And here is how Sir Edward quotes from the old Norman chroniclers describing the landing from the Mora:

'After the archers had thus gone forth, the knights landed all armed, with their hauberks on, their shields slung at their necks, and their helmets laced. They formed together on the shore, each armed, and mounted on his war-horse: all had their swords girded on, and rode forward into the country with their lances raised. Then the carpenters landed, who had great axes in their hands, and planes and adzes hung at their sides. They took counsel together, and sought for a good spot to place a castle on. They had brought with them from Normandy, in pieces, all ready for framing together, and they took the materials of one of these out of the ships, all shaped and pierced to receive the pins which they had brought cut and ready in large barrels; and before evening had set in, they had finished a good fort on the English ground, and there they placed their stores. And then ate and drank enough, and were right glad that they were ashore.'

Appendix 3
How Fast Can They Go?

In 'The Psychiatrist Who Ran Away: (Part 2: The Metamorphosis)' I explained how Cedric (the pig Patsy and I were looking after for our friends in America) had managed to put on an impressive turn of speed while being taken for a walk around the village.

Although a good human middle distance runner could eventually probably catch a pig in full flight, I doubt if many ordinary humans could catch a fleeing pig.

The odd thing about pigs is that they have tremendous acceleration and can reach their top speed within a couple of strides of a standing start. And their four trotter drive propulsion means that they can dodge and swerve far more skilfully than most humans – particularly when the ground is soft or slippery.

The table below gives the speeds of a few arbitrarily chosen animals and insects. These speeds were measured over fairly short distances by scientists with nothing better to do and although it is undoubtedly possible that even faster speeds might be attained for a second or two (or when travelling downhill or with a following wind) it would appear that these are pretty well the limit for the species listed. It should be noted that although some animals may appear to have a limited top speed, they may nevertheless have other qualities which make up for this shortcoming. So, for example, sheep, like pigs, may appear to be relatively slow moving creatures but their ability to change direction suddenly is unsurpassed and is a vital asset when they are attempting to avoid capture.

Cheetah 75 mph
Racehorse 50 mph
Hare 45 mph
Kangaroo 43 mph
Fox 42 mph
Hyena 40 mph
Deer 40 mph

Greyhound 35 mph
Rabbit 35 mph
Dragonfly 30 mph
Horsefly 30 mph
Bee 25 mph
Hippopotamus 25 mph
Man 24 mph
Cow 20 mph
Sheep 15 mph
Grey squirrel 12 mph
Wasp 12 mph
Pig 11 mph
Bluebottle 6 mph
Snail 0.07 m

Appendix 4:
Imperial Weights and Measures

Imperial weights and measures were introduced in Great Britain in 1824 and the systems of weights and measures used in the United States is derived from the Imperial system.

After 1965, the European Union forced Britain to adopt the metric system used on the Continent of Europe and it became illegal to use Imperial measurements when selling packaged or loose goods.

Nevertheless, Imperial measurements were still used in some Commonwealth countries and some Imperial measurements, notably the inch, were still used in Europe, particularly in France.

In Bilbury, however, Imperial measurements were still widely used in the 1970s and the villagers preferred their traditional measurements to the new-fangled type of measurement which was popular elsewhere. Throughout the 1970s, Peter Marshall was still using Imperial measurements when weighing out vegetables, etc.

I confess I have always found the descriptions and idiosyncrasies used in the Imperial system far more attractive than the bald, cold and very scientific metric system.

Imperial length measurements
4 inches = 1 hand (for measuring horses)
12 inches = 1 foot
3 feet = 1 yard
22 yards = 1 chain
10 chains = 1 furlong
8 furlongs = 1 mile
3 miles = 1 league

Imperial length measurements at sea
2.02667 yards = 1 fathom
100 fathoms = 1 cable
10 cables = 1 nautical mile

Imperial measurements for surveying
7.92 inches = 1 link
25 links = 1 rod

Imperial measurements for area
1 perch = 1 rod x 1 rod
1 rood = 1 furlong x 1 rod
1 acre = 1 furlong x 1 chain

Imperial weights
7000 grains = 1 pound
256 drachm = 1 pound
16 ounce = 1 pound
14 pound = 1 stone
28 pound = 1 quarter
112 pound = 1 hundredweight (cwt)
2240 pound = 1 ton

Appendix 5:
Mad Taxes

In 'The Psychiatrist Who Ran Away (Part 2: The Metamorphosis) I described how a cottage had been turned into a death trap when, in the 17th century, a baker had responded to the introduction of the chimney tax by merging her own chimney with the chimney of the adjacent property. This was not an uncommon practice at that time but it frequently caused problems – sometimes leading to multiple deaths as well as the destruction of property. Dr Eckersley's experience was by no means unusual.

British governments have, over the centuries, introduced some pretty bizarre taxes and the chimney tax (or hearth tax) was only one of many dotty ways of raising money.

One of Britain's first taxes was the scutage tax which was introduced by King Henry I in the 12th century. This allowed knights to opt out of their duty to fight for their country by paying money to the King. When King John raised the tax massively, and craftily started charging knights not to fight even when there weren't any wars, he was considered to be behaving badly.

Indeed, this low trick was one of the reasons for the signing of the Magna Carta. The Scutage tax died off under Edward III in the 14th century.

Back in the 18th century, curious taxes were introduced with great enthusiasm. There were, for example, special taxes on almanacs, wine, perfume and rock salt.

Here, below, is a selection of a dozen of the oddest taxes which existed in Britain prior to the 20th century. I have, of course, included the chimney tax – which is at the top of my list simply because it appears in the text of this book. The other entries are in no particular order.

A list of daft taxes introduced in the 20th and 21st centuries would, of course, fill several thousand pages and would be enormously boring, probably even for tax collectors:

Chimney tax 1662, repealed 1689

The chimney tax, which was also known as the hearth tax, was introduced by Parliament in 1662 so that money could be raised to pay for King Charles II's lifestyle. After the monarchy had been restored in 1660, the Parliament reckoned that the King needed an annual income of £1,200,000 and a tax was needed to pay for all his necessary extravagances. Parliament decided it would be easier to count the number of chimneys than the number of heads since the former kept still whereas the latter tended to move about a good deal, particularly if they were about to be taxed. When introduced, the tax was set at two shillings a year per fireplace or stove. To begin with, everyone had to pay the tax but amendments were eventually introduced which made the really poor exempt. However, if a house had more than two chimneys, there were no exemptions. The owners of big houses which had lots of chimneys were faced with fairly huge bills. However, the main objection to the tax was not the money involved but the fact that the officials responsible for collecting the taxes had the legal right to enter every property in the country. Large numbers of chimneys were blocked up to try to avoid the tax but if the owners were found out, they had to pay double taxes. The tax didn't last very long. It was repealed by Parliament in 1689 because it was regarded as offensive that homes should be entered and searched by strangers.

Window tax of 1696, repealed in 1851.

This was a property tax on house owners. The size of the tax bill depended upon the number of windows a house possessed. To keep their taxes down, people had windows bricked up and there are many old houses around in Britain which still have bricked up windows. The property tax was a flat rate of two shillings per house, regardless of the number of windows. Houses which had between ten and twenty windows paid an extra four shillings and those which had more than twenty windows paid an extra eight shillings. The window tax was introduced under King William III because there had been much opposition to the idea of an income tax. The people objected to taxes on income because they didn't think the Government had the right to know what they earned – it was considered intrusive and a threat to personal liberty.

Wallpaper tax of 1712, repealed 1836
In 1712, patterned, printed or painted wallpaper was taxed at 1d per square yard. By 1809, the tax had risen to 1 shilling per square yard. Rich people bought plain paper (because there was no tax on plain wallpaper) and hired artists and people who thought they were artists to paint designs and pretty pictures on the plain paper. The result was that rich people avoided the tax completely and only the poorer people paid it. This tax was abolished in 1836.

Brick tax of 1784, repealed 1850
The brick tax was introduced in 1784, during the reign of King George III. The tax was introduced to help pay for the wars in the American Colonies. Bricks were taxed at four shillings per thousand. To get round the tax, brick makers increased the size of their bricks. To squash this crafty move, which enabled builders to put up a wall using no more than a dozen bricks, the Government introduced a maximum size for brick production. The result was that house builders started to avoid the brick tax completely by using more timber in the houses they built. The Government eventually gave up and the brick tax was abolished in 1850.

Glass tax 1746, repealed 1845
The glass tax was introduced in 1746, in the reign of King George II, and existed until it was abolished by Robert Peel's government in 1845. The glass tax, combined with the window tax, meant that houses were built with small and inadequate windows. And since lighting was poor, barely adequate and expensive, the result was that many homes, particularly in towns and cities, were depressingly gloomy. Ireland was exempt from the glass tax for a while and as a result, a number of famous glass factories were set up there.

Hat tax 1784, repealed 1811
The hat tax was introduced in 1784 and lasted until 1811 and was unquestionably sexist since it affected only hats worn by men. The

tax was introduced by the Government of William Pitt the younger, and it was thought that since rich men tended to have more hats than poor men the tax would affect the rich more than the poor. Each new hat had to have a revenue stamp pasted on the lining inside. The amount of the tax depended upon the price of the hat. So, the tax on a hat costing under four shillings was three pence. For expensive hats, costing more than twelve shillings, the tax rose to two shillings. Anyone caught trying to avoid the tax would be fined or hung.

Dice and playing cards tax 1711, repeated 1862

The playing card and dice tax was introduced in 1711 and lasted until 1862. Every pack of cards produced in England had to be stamped by a government official to show that the tax had been paid. Those who tried to cheat the Government (by, for example, producing fake stamps) were hung. Quite a lot of hanging went on in the 18th century which was a good period for rope makers and professional hangmen.

Wig powder tax 1786, repealed 1869

The wig powder tax was introduced in 1786 and repealed in 1869. Unlike other taxes there was no actual duty on the powder itself but anyone who wanted to use hair powder had to buy an annual licence for a guinea. Exemptions included the royal family and their attendants, soldiers and lower ranking army officers and lowly paid clergymen. In the end, the tax pretty well killed off the use of hair powder.

Gin tax 1736, repealed 1743

The gin tax of 1736 was brought in by Act of Parliament in an attempt to curb the consumption of gin. The average citizen in England (including children and the moribund) was at the time drinking 18 pints of gin a year. Even children were drinking the stuff in vast quantities, and gin consumption was blamed for much crime. Gin distillers and sellers had to pay the new tax and small gin shops were driven out of business. However, although the tax reduced the enthusiasm for legally produced gin, the inevitable result was that bootleg gin became popular. Some of the bootleg gin contained turpentine spirit and sulphuric acid and the results were often devastating. Blindness was a common side effect and death not uncommon. The Gin Act was repealed after protestors rioted in London in 1743, but another Gin Act was passed in 1751 which was again designed to control the consumption of gin. The introduction of healthier alternatives such as tea and beer was encouraged but rather a lot of people simply drank the beer and the tea and carried on with the gin as well.

Soap tax 1712, repealed 1835

The soap tax was introduced in 1712 and repealed in 1835 by which time much of the country undoubtedly stank to high heaven. The tax put small soap makers out of business and didn't do much for the cleanliness of the British in that period.

Beard tax 1535, quietly abandoned

A beard tax was introduced in 1535 by Henry VIII (who himself had a beard but presumably didn't tax himself). The tax gradually died out, partly because it was silly but also because it was difficult to collect. ('No, this isn't a beard. I just haven't bothered to shave today.') The tax was, however, reintroduced by Henry VIII's normally sensible daughter, Elizabeth I. Under Elizabeth I, every man with more than two week's growth of beard had to pay the tax. No one seems to know precisely when the beard tax was withdrawn but it seems it was still found difficult to enforce and it probably just fizzled out and was eventually abandoned.

Clock tax 1797, abandoned same year

The clock tax was introduced in 1797 and covered watches as well as clocks. An ordinary watch attracted a tax of two shillings and sixpence. A gold watch was taxed at ten shillings. Clocks costing more than twenty shillings were taxed at five shillings. The inevitable result was that people stopped buying watches and clocks and everyone was late for everything. The tax was, therefore, abandoned after just nine months.

Author's Note

I hope you have enjoyed this book about Bilbury and the people who live in and visit the village. If you did so then I would be very grateful if you would spare a moment to write a short review. A few seconds of your time will mean the world to Patsy (Antoinette) and myself. This is the 13th book in the series entitled 'The Young Country Doctor'.

Thank you

Vernon Coleman